ADULT READING SERIES

Challenger 7

COREA
MURPHY

NEW READERS PRESS
Division of ProLiteracy Worldwide
Syracuse, New York

About the Author

Corea Murphy has worked in the field of education since the early 1960s. In addition to classroom and tutorial teaching, Ms. Murphy has developed language arts curriculum guides for public high schools, conducted curriculum and effectiveness workshops, and established an educational program for residents in a drug rehabilitation facility.

Ms. Murphy became interested in creating a reading series for older students when she began working with adults and adolescents in the early 1970s. The **Challenger Adult Reading Series** is the result of her work with these students.

In a very real sense, the students contributed greatly to the development of this reading series. Their enthusiasm for learning to read and their willingness to work hard provided inspiration, and their many helpful suggestions influenced the content of both the student books and the teacher's manuals.

It is to these students that the **Challenger Adult Reading Series** is dedicated with the hope that others who wish to become good readers will find this reading program both helpful and stimulating.

A special note of gratitude is also extended to Kay Koschnick, Christina Jagger, and Mary Hutchison of New Readers Press for their work and support in guiding this series to completion.

Every effort has been made to locate the heirs of Georgia Douglas Johnson to obtain permission to reprint the poems "Your World" and "The Poet Speaks" used in Lesson 20. If the heirs are located subsequent to publication, they are hereby entitled to due compensation.

ISBN 0-88336-787-4

© 1988
New Readers Press
Division of ProLiteracy Worldwide
1320 Jamesville Ave., Syracuse, New York 13210

Printed in the United States of America

Designed by Chris Steenwerth
Cover by Chris Steenwerth

Cover photo by Royce Bair and Assoc.
The Stock Solution

20 19 18 17 16 15

Table of Contents

Unit 1: Love and Money

7 Introduction

8 Lesson 1
Review of Long and Short Vowels
Definitions (Exercise 1)
Story: The Romance of a Busy Stockbroker
Other Exercises:
2. Understanding the Story
3. What Do You Think?
4. Which Word Does Not Fit?
5. More about the Stock Market

14 Lesson 2
Review of Consonant Blends: Part 1
Definitions (Exercise 1)
Story: The Good Lord Will Provide
Other Exercises:
2. Understanding the Story
3. What Do You Think?
4. Standard English
5. Common Expressions
6. Look It Up

22 Lesson 3
Review of Consonant Blends: Part 2
Definitions (Exercise 1)
Story: Mr. Manning's Money Tree: Part I
Other Exercises:
2. Understanding the Story
3. What Do You Think?
4. Synonyms
5. Standard English
6. Can You Crack the Code?

30 Lesson 4
Review of Consonant Blends
and Digraphs: Part 3
Definitions (Exercise 1)
Story: Mr. Manning's Money Tree: Part II
Other Exercises:
2. Understanding the Story
3. What Do You Think?
4. Words That End in -al
5. Antonyms
6. Look It Up

37 Review: Lessons 1-4
Exercises:
1. Word Review
2. Synonyms and Antonyms
3. Word Families
4. Which Word Does Not Fit?
5. Money
6. A Final Note on Love and Money

Unit 2: Struggle

45 Introduction

46 Lesson 5
Review of Digraphs: Part 4
Definitions (Exercise 1)
Story: All the Years of Her Life
Other Exercises:
2. Understanding the Story
3. What Do You Think?
4. Word Relationships
5. Sounds for ch
6. Standard English

55 Lesson 6
Review of Consonant Blends: Part 5
Definitions (Exercise 1)
Story: Prelude
Other Exercises:
2. Understanding the Story
3. What Do You Think?
4. Synonyms and Antonyms
5. March, 1938
6. Who Was General Pershing?

65 Lesson 7
Review of Consonant Blends: Part 6
Definitions (Exercise 1)
Story: The Test
Other Exercises:
2. Understanding the Story
3. What Do You Think?
4. Word Review
5. Chronological Order
6. Standard English

74 Lesson 8

Review of Vowel Combinations: Part 1
Definitions (Exercise 1)
Story: Charles
Other Exercises:
2. Understanding the Story
3. What Might You Use if You Wanted To...
4. The Suffix -*ly*
5. Spelling
6. Find the Quote

84 Review: Lessons 1-8

Exercises:
1. Word Review
2. Word Review
3. Sound Review
4. Word Families
5. Standard English: A Review
6. A Poet's Thoughts

Unit 3: Courage

93 Introduction

94 Lesson 9

Review of Vowel Combinations: Part 2
Definitions (Exercise 1)
Story: Nobody and the Cyclops
Other Exercises:
2. Understanding the Story
3. More about Odysseus
4. Word Relationships
5. More about Standard Usage
6. Gods and Goddesses

103 Lesson 10

Review of *r*-Controlled Vowels
Definitions (Exercise 1)
Story: The Old Demon: Part I
Other Exercises:
2. Understanding the Story
3. What Do You Think?
4. China
5. Spelling Check

112 Lesson 11

Review of *r*-Controlled Vowel Combinations
Definitions (Exercise 1)
Story: The Old Demon: Part II
Other Exercises:
2. Understanding the Story
3. Word Review
4. Words That Describe
5. Words That *Don't* Describe
6. The Suffix -*ness*

122 Lesson 12

Vowels Followed by the Letters *w* and *l*
Definitions (Exercise 1)
Story: Who Shall Dwell...
Other Exercises:
2. Understanding the Story
3. What Do You Think?
4. Proverbs
5. More about Standard English
6. Word Families

134 Review: Lessons 1-12

Exercises:
1. Word Review
2. Which Word Does Not Fit?
3. A Review of Sounds
4. What Is Often Said When...
5. A Review of Standard Usage
6. On Fear and Courage

Unit 4: Brushes with Death

141 Introduction

142 Lesson 13

The Hard and Soft *g*
Definitions (Exercise 1)
Play: On Golden Pond
Other Exercises:
2. Understanding the Play
3. What Do You Think?
4. Synonyms and Antonyms
5. Tone of Voice
6. Vacations around the World

152 Lesson 14

The Hard and Soft *c*
Definitions (Exercise 1)
Reading: The Execution
Other Exercises:
2. Understanding the Reading
3. Which Word Does Not Fit?
4. Who Might Know Most About...?
5. Look It Up
6. The Mystery Tzar

162 Lesson 15

The Letter *y*
Definitions (Exercise 1)
Story: A Day's Wait
Other Exercises:
2. Understanding the Story
3. Word Relationships
4. Multiple Meanings
5. Working with Measurements
6. Homonyms

172 | **Lesson 16**

The Sound for *ph*
Definitions (Exercise 1)
Story: The Last Leaf
Other Exercises:
2. Understanding the Story
3. What Do You Think?
4. Hyphenated Words
5. The $24 Swindle

182 | **Review: Lessons 1-16**

Exercises:
1. Word Review
2. Word Review
3. Word Sound Review
4. Find the Homonym
5. A Poet's View of Dying

Unit 5: Giving

189 | **Introduction**

190 | **Lesson 17**

Silent Letters
Definitions (Exercise 1)
Folktales: Two Tales of Mortal Foolishness
Other Exercises:
2. Understanding the Folktales
3. Character Descriptions
4. Occupations
5. More about Armenia
6. More about Black Pudding

200 | **Lesson 18**

Double Consonants
Definitions (Exercise 1)
Reading: To Have or to Be
Other Exercises:
2. Understanding the Reading
3. What Do You Think?
4. Word Relationships
5. On Latin and Language
6. State Search

211 | **Lesson 19**

More Work with Two Consonants in the Middle
of Words
Definitions (Exercise 1)
Play: The Woman Who Willed a Miracle: Part I
Other Exercises:
2. Understanding the Play
3. Word Review
4. Synonyms and Antonyms
5. Word Families
6. Using the Dictionary

220 | **Lesson 20**

Four-Letter Words
Definitions (Exercise 1)
Play: The Woman Who Willed a Miracle: Part II
Other Exercises:
2. Understanding the Play
3. Which Word Does Not Fit?
4. Problems
5. A Little Latin
6. On Living and Loving: A Poet's Point of View

230 | **Review: Lessons 1-20**

Exercises:
1. Word Review
2. Who or What Would You Expect to Be...
3. A Little More Latin
4. More Work with Expressions and Proverbs
5. World Capitals
6. Find the Quote

Unit 1
Love and Money

Most of us have heard the saying, "The love of money is the root of all evil." Is there any truth in this saying? In this first unit, we shall see how the desire for money affects the lives of three different groups of characters.

The story for Lesson 1 was written by the famous American short story writer, O. Henry. In "The Romance of a Busy Stockbroker," Harvey Maxwell, the busy stockbroker, finds time in his hectic day for love—or does he?

"The Good Lord Will Provide," the reading for Lesson 2, is a series of letters written between a husband and wife. Like many couples, they have problems with money, and their letters describe their efforts to get ahead of the bills.

"Mr. Manning's Money Tree" is the story for both Lesson 3 and Lesson 4. Henry Manning, the main character in this story, experiences many changes as he begins to think about what is really important in his life.

All the lessons in Book 7 begin with a word chart in which rules you have studied for sounding out words in previous *Challenger* books are reviewed. By completing the definitions that follow each word chart, you will learn words that appear in future stories and word exercises in Book 7.

Lesson 1

Review of Long and Short Vowels

ā	sane	quake	labor	maze	bass		ă	sap	fashion	pasture	pastor	bass
ē	eke	gene	senior	region	impede		ĕ	ebb	yen	zest	temple	pedal
ī	awhile	rival	riot	lilac	finance		ĭ	imp	kindle	quiver	wicked	equip
ō	tote	rove	romance	noble	oval		ŏ	tot	romp	comic	zombie	option
ū	Judy	tulip	rumor	puny	unity		ŭ	muss	juggle	unjust	hub	humdrum

1 **Definitions.** Match the words listed below with the correct definitions.

1. ebb
2. eke
3. hub
4. humdrum
5. imp
6. impede
7. kindle
8. maze
9. option
10. puny
11. rove
12. tot
13. tote
14. yen
15. zombie

ĕ hub 1. a center of activity or interest; the center part of a wheel or fan

ē option 2. a choice; the act of choosing

ă maze 3. a confusing network of walled pathways; any situation in which it is easy to get lost

ē yen 4. a longing for something; also, the basic unit of money in Japan

ŭi zombie 5. a corpse supposedly brought back to a life-like condition

long ā puny tot 6. a small child

ŏ imp 7. a troublesome or extremely playful child

ū humbrum 8. boring; dull; uninteresting

ō impede 9. to block the way

ō kindle 10. to build or fuel (a fire); to ignite

ŏ puny 11. to fall back; a period of fading away

ē tote 12. to haul or lug

ō option eke 13. to make a living, for example, with great effort or strain

rove 14. to roam or wander about

ebb 15. weak; low in strength, size, or importance

Words for Study

secretary	messengers	satisfaction	odor	ordinary
curious	transacted	cancel	dwindled	amazement
presence	precision	mortgages	hurriedly	violin

The Romance of a Busy Stockbroker

by O. Henry

Pitcher, the main clerk in the office of Harvey Maxwell, stockbroker, expressed a look of mild interest and surprise when his employer briskly entered at half-past nine with his young lady secretary. With a snappy "Good morning, Pitcher," Maxwell dashed at his desk as though he were intending to leap over it, and then plunged into the great heaps of letters and messages waiting there for him.

The young lady had been Maxwell's secretary for a year. On this morning she was softly and shyly beautiful. Her eyes were dreamily bright, her expression a happy one, tinted with memories.

Pitcher, still mildly curious, noticed a difference in her ways this morning. Instead of going straight into the next room where her desk was, she stayed awhile in the outer office. Once she moved over by Maxwell's desk, near enough for him to be aware of her presence.

But Maxwell was no longer a man; he had become a machine. The busy New York stockbroker seemed to be moved by buzzing wheels and uncoiling springs.

"Well—what is it? Anything?" asked Maxwell sharply. His opened mail lay like a bank of snow on his crowded desk. His keen gray eyes flashed upon her half impatiently.

"Nothing," answered the secretary, moving away with a little smile.

"Mr. Pitcher," she said to the clerk, "did Mr. Maxwell say anything yesterday about engaging another secretary?"

"He did," answered Pitcher. "I told the agency yesterday afternoon to send over a few applicants this morning. Not a single one has shown up yet."

"I will do the work as usual, then," said the young lady, "until someone comes to fill my place."

Anyone who has not seen a busy Manhattan stockbroker at work may have difficulty understanding just how crowded and busy his day is. And this was Harvey Maxwell's busy day. The ticker began to reel out its coils of tape, the telephone had an attack of continuous buzzing. Men began to crowd into the office and call at him over the railing, happily, sharply, viciously, excitedly. Messengers ran in and out with messages. The clerks in the office jumped about like sailors during a storm. Maxwell shoved his chair against the wall and transacted business after the manner of a toe dancer. He jumped from ticker to telephone, from desk to door with skill and precision.

In the midst of this growing and important stress, the stockbroker became suddenly aware of a blonde woman approaching him.

"Lady from the secretary's agency to see about the position," Pitcher informed him.

"What position?" Maxwell asked with a frown. "Position of secretary," said Pitcher. "You told me yesterday to call them up and have one sent over this morning."

"You are losing your mind, Pitcher," said Maxwell. "Why should I have given you any such instructions? Miss Leslie has given perfect satisfaction during the year she has been here. The place is hers as long as she chooses to keep it. Cancel that order with the agency, Pitcher, and don't bring any more of 'em in here."

The blonde left the office angrily. Pitcher took a moment to remark to the bookkeeper that the "old man" seemed to get more absent-minded and forgetful every day of the world.

The rush and pace of business grew fiercer and faster. On the floor they were pounding half a dozen stocks in which Maxwell's customers were heavy investors. Orders to buy and sell were coming and going as swift as a flight of swallows. Some of his own holdings were in danger, and the man was working like some high-geared, delicate, strong machine—strung to full tension, going at full speed. Stocks and bonds, loans and mortgages, margins and securities—here was a world of finance, and there was no room in it for the human world or the world of nature.

When the lunch hour drew near, there came a slight pause in the uproar.

Maxwell stood by his desk with his hands full of messages and notes, with a pen over his right ear and his hair hanging in disorderly strings over his forehead.

Suddenly, Maxwell stood motionless. He smelled the delicate odor of lilac perfume, and this odor belonged to Miss Leslie. It was her own, and hers only.

The odor brought her into Maxwell's mind, and the world of finance dwindled suddenly to a speck. And she was in the next room—twenty steps away.

"By George, I'll do it now," said Maxwell half aloud. "I'll ask her now. I wonder I didn't do it long ago."

He dashed into the inner office with haste and charged upon the desk of the secretary.

She looked up at him with a smile. A soft pink crept over her cheek, and her eyes were kind and frank. Maxwell leaned one elbow on her desk. He still clutched fluttering papers with both hands and the pen was above his ear.

"Miss Leslie," he began hurriedly, "I have but a moment to spare. I want to say something in that moment. Will you be my wife? I haven't had time to show my love for you in the ordinary way, but I really do love you. Talk quick, please—those fellows are giving my stocks a beating out there."

"Oh, what are you talking about?" exclaimed the young lady. She rose to her feet and gazed upon him, wide-eyed.

"Don't you understand?" said Maxwell impatiently. "I want you to marry me. I love you, Miss Leslie. I wanted to tell you, and I snatched a minute when things had slowed down a bit. They're calling me for the phone now. Tell 'em to wait a minute, Pitcher. Won't you, Miss Leslie?"

The secretary acted very queerly. At first she seemed overcome with amazement. Then tears flowed from her wondering eyes; and then she smiled sunnily through them, and one of her arms slid tenderly about the stockbroker's neck.

"I know now," she said softly. "It's this old business that has driven everything else out of your head for the time. I was frightened at first. Don't you remember, Harvey? We were married last evening at eight o'clock in the Little Church Around the Corner."

Adapted from "The Romance of a Busy Broker" by O. Henry with permission of Airmont Publishing Company, Inc., New York, New York.

2   **Understanding the Story.** Put the letter of the correct answer on the line to the left.

_____ 1. What is unusual about the happenings in the office on this particular morning?

    (a) Maxwell and his secretary arrive together.

    (b) Maxwell is acting like a machine.

    (c) Miss Leslie is wearing perfume.

    (d) Maxwell is in danger of losing money.

_____ 2. O. Henry compares the clerks in the office to sailors jumping about during a storm to indicate _____ .

    (a) how dangerous their occupation is

    (b) how hectic the stockbroker's office is

    (c) how much they respect their employer

    (d) what type of training they have

_____ 3. O. Henry compares Maxwell to a toe dancer to indicate _____ .

    (a) his enjoyment of making money

    (b) his flirting with the blonde

    (c) his gracefulness with Miss Leslie

    (d) his precision while working

_____ 4. When the hectic pace of the office slows down somewhat for the lunch hour, Maxwell _____ .

    (a) chats with Pitcher

    (b) interviews the applicant

    (c) asks Miss Leslie to marry him

    (d) orders lunch

_____ 5. Which of the following does _not_ describe Miss Leslie's reaction to Maxwell's marriage offer?

    (a) outrage   (b) fright   (c) understanding   (d) surprise

_____ 6. Why had Maxwell told Pitcher to find him another secretary the day before?

    (a) He needed more help.

    (b) Miss Leslie had given her notice.

    (c) He planned to marry Miss Leslie.

    (d) He was not pleased with Miss Leslie's work.

_____ 7. Based on this story, which expression best describes the daily thoughts of a broker like Harvey Maxwell?

    (a) All's fair in love and war.

    (b) A bird in the hand is worth two in the bush.

    (c) A stitch in time saves nine.

    (d) Money makes the world go round.

3 **What Do You Think?** Answer the following questions in good sentence form.

1. If the story had continued for a few more lines, how do you think Harvey Maxwell would have responded to Miss Leslie's reminder that she was his wife?

_____

_____

_____

2. If you were Miss Leslie, how would you have responded to Harvey Maxwell's offer of marriage?

_____

_____

_____

3. Do you think it is unusual for people to become so involved in their work that they forget all about the people they love? Be sure to include details to support your answer.

_____

_____

_____

_____

4 **Which Word Does Not Fit?** Choose the word that does not fit with the other words in each row and write it on the line.

1. bass	guitar	banjo	piano	violin	_____
2. drift	roam	romp	rove	wander	_____
3. amusing	creative	humorous	laughable	funny	_____
4. bar	block	dam	foam	impede	_____
5. daisy	fern	lilac	rose	tulip	_____
6. coil	curl	twine	twist	crawl	_____
7. humdrum	occurrence	customary	ordinary	routine	_____
8. cruel	fierce	heartless	vicious	thoughtless	_____
9. flutter	murmur	quiver	shiver	shudder	_____
10. banker	investor	moneylender	messenger	stockbroker	_____

5 **More about the Stock Market.** Use the words listed below to complete these sentences about the stock market.

agents	foreign	ownership	recorded
commission	loss	partner	relays
conditions	network	profit	stockholder

National Archives

First organized in the late 1790s, the New York Stock Exchange on Wall Street is often called the nation's marketplace. The Stock Exchange is a market where member brokers, or _____ , buy and sell stocks and bonds of American and _____ businesses on behalf of the public. The brokers receive a _____ on each transaction they make.

Stock is a right of _____ in a business. The stock is divided into a certain number of shares, and the business issues stockholders one or more stock certificates to show how many shares they hold.

A person who wishes to be a _____ places an order with a brokerage house. The broker gets the price of the stock and _____ the order to the firm's _____ on the floor of the exchange. The transaction, which usually takes only a few minutes, is then _____ on tape and sent to brokerage firms over a nationwide _____ .

Each year, investors trade billions of shares worth hundreds of billions of dollars. The prices change according to business _____ . If the business is doing well, stockholders may be able to sell their stock for a _____ . If it is not, they may have to take a _____ .

Adapted from *The World Book Encyclopedia.* © 1987 World Book, Inc.

Lesson 2

Review of Consonant Blends: Part 1

bl:	blazer	bladder	blemish	blizzard	blockade	blunt	blunder
cl:	clan	clarinet	clergy	cleanliness	clique	nucleus	nuclear
fl:	flank	flimsy	flog	florist	flutter	inflict	reflection
gl:	glacier	glamour	glamorous	glee	glide	glimpse	Gloria
pl:	plaza	plasma	plaid	plod	plush	Pluto	Plymouth
spl:	splat	splay	splice	splendor	split-level		

1 **Definitions.** Match the words listed below with the correct definitions.

blazer
blemish
blunder
blunt
clergy
clique
flog
glacier
glee
nucleus
plasma
Pluto
Plymouth

_____   1. a core; a thing or part forming the center around which other things or parts are gathered

_____   2. a large mass of ice and snow that forms in regions where the rate of snowfall always exceeds the rate at which the snow melts

_____   3. a single-breasted sports jacket in a solid, often bright color or with stripes

_____   4. a small circle of people who tend to be snobbish and exclude others from their company

_____   5. a stupid and serious mistake; a clumsy, foolish act or remark

_____   6. town in southeastern Massachusetts where the Pilgrims from the *Mayflower* landed in 1620

_____   7. any mark that damages the appearance, such as a stain, spot, or scar

_____   8. having a thick, dull edge or end; not sharp or pointed

_____   9. lively joy; merriment

_____   10. men or women who have been given the office of some religious service, such as pastors

_____   11. the fluid part of blood which is used for transfusions

_____   12. the ninth and farthest planet from the sun

_____   13. to beat harshly with a whip or a rod

Words for Study

penitentiary	generous	liable	deputies	acquire
parole	sheriff	Ernie	allowance	behavior
plumb	R.F.D.	bushel	possibility	rheumatism

The Good Lord Will Provide

by Lawrence Treat and Charles M. Plotz

STATE PENITENTIARY

April 3

Dear Judy,

It's been a whole year now a whole long year without you. But I been a real good prisoner staying out of trouble like a cat stays away from water. They all say I'll get my parole next April, plenty of time to put in a crop. So hang on, you and Uncle Ike. The only thing bothering me is I ain't heard from you in so long. Why? What's happening?

Judy, it's not like I done anything wrong. All I did was drive that car. I didn't know they had guns and itchy fingers. I didn't even know them good. They was just a couple of city fellas hanging around a bar. I musta told them I could just about drive a car up the side of a wall and down the other side and if they wanted to see how good I was, why come on out and look. Which they did.

Maybe I was a little stupid but when they allowed they'd pay me right then and there to take them to the bank next day and then on out to the back hills—well all I did was ask how much. And when they told me I plumb near keeled over. Because it was almost as much as we needed for that mortgage payment. I figured money was money and if they was taking a lot of it out of the bank, why wouldn't they be generous? What I didn't know was they didn't have no account there.

So I reckon I was real stupid. But stupid or not I sure was lucky because if I'd stayed with that pair much longer I'da got killed too. But they paid me to get them out of town and up into the hills and after I done that I took off and come straight back to you.

When Ike heard the news on the radio he knowed right off it was me at the wheel of the car. Nobody else could have outdrove and outsmarted the cops and I bet I could have got clear off to Mexico or maybe China if I'da wanted to. And if the planes hadn't spotted me like they did that pair. But I done what I was paid for, and if they took fifty thousand like the papers said or a million I wouldn't know. I was waiting out in the car and all the money I ever seen was what I give you. And like I said, I got it the day before and it wasn't stolen from the bank. Not that bank anyhow.

The sheriff kept asking me where the stolen money was. After all the two bank robbers was dead with no trace of the money and all the sheriff had was me. Just a poor dumb farmer with a knack for handling a car.

But I don't want to worry you with all this. I'm real lonesome for you like I said. So when are you coming up here to visit me? And how are you and how's Ike and the farm?

Your loving husband
Walt

April 10

Dear Walt,

I got your letter and the reason I ain't come to see you is that I just don't have the money for the trip. Besides I got to do all the chores now. Uncle Ike's down with the rhumatiz again. And when Ike's feeling puny he wants me around all the time and all he does is complain and tell me everybody's out to take the skin off me. He even tried to chase George off the place when George come around in his new car to ask me out for a ride. And I sure needed to get away from the farm for awhile.

George was real nice to me too. I told him right out that we was liable to lose the farm unless we got that mortgage installment paid and how could I pay it until I got a crop in? And I said that what with George getting promoted to be vice president of the bank he could maybe do something. He said he'd see what he could manage and that was about as far as we got. Anyway, it was nice getting away from Ike for awhile, specially when George took me to dinner at that new place in town.

Walt, I wish you was a banker too.

> Your loving wife
> Judy

STATE PENITENTIARY

April 15

Dear Judy,

I know it's hard on you with Ike to take care of it's even worse. But the good Lord will provide, Judy, and I know what I'm saying.

About George and the bank holding off— you want to get it writ down. So next time you see him you want to ask him about Ruthie Watkins which I found out about from a guy up here named Ernie. Ernie, his business is selling letters. And like he says, if I got a cow or a bushel of wheat I can sell them, can't I? So why can't he sell letters?

Ernie and me get along fine because the both of us we're innocent men and we shouldn't ought to be here. But as long as we are we talk about things and Ernie happened to mention some letters he got hold of which George writ to this

Ruthie Watkins. So maybe you better mention them to George next time you see him.

> Your loving husband
> Walt

April 22

Dear Walt,

George took me out to dinner again. And like you told me to I just happened to mention Ruthie Watkins and then I said about the mortgage and how it ought to be writ down. And the very next day I got a letter from the bank promising to hold off until autumn but I don't know what good it's going to do. Because Ike got a hold of that white mule stuff and got the idea he ought to go riding in the tractor. You ought to see what's left of that tractor. So how do I make that mortgage payment in the fall with no crop coming in?

I'm tired, Walt. I'm plumb tired. You said the good Lord will provide—but how? How?

> Your loving wife
> Judy

STATE PENITENTIARY

April 28

Dear Judy,

You got to be patient like I said and if you're real patient the Lord *will* provide. Because He come to me in a dream and He said that there was something buried in the south field that would take care of us. So you tell Ike to get over that rhumatiz of his. Tell him I got only a year to go and then I'm going to dig up that something in the south field and after that everything's going to be all right.

> Your loving husband
> Walt

May 4

Dear Walt,

I don't know just how to tell you this but I guess I'll just set it down the way it happened.

You know how Ike hates the law ever since they come around and took you away. So when the sheriff and six deputies showed up the day before yesterday Ike tried to chase them away. He yelled at them and called them all kinds of names and they finally grabbed him and tied him up, so he never did see what they done.

Walt, they went down to that south field and the six of them spent the whole day digging and then they come back the next day and kept on until they dug up just about every inch of that field. And I never did see any six men look so tired and they sure was mad. I asked them lots of questions and one of them—I think he come all the way down from the prison—he allowed as how all your mail gets read. Walter, what did he say that for?

Your loving wife
Judy

STATE PENITENTIARY

May 7

Dear Judy,

Now plant.

Your loving husband
Walt

Adapted from "The Good Lord Will Provide" by Lawrence Treat and Charles M. Plotz.
Adapted with permission of Scott Meredith Literary Agency, New York, New York.

2 **Understanding the Story**. Write the answers to these questions in good sentence form.

1. In his first letter, Walt claims he is "just a dumb farmer." What stupid thing did he do?

_____

_____

2. He also claims he didn't do anything wrong. What reasons does he give to support this claim?

_____

_____

3. Ernie, his fellow inmate, also claims to be innocent. Why is Ernie in jail?

_____

_____

4. Judy has two problems with the farm.

a. One is getting the bank to wait for the mortgage payment until the crop is in. Describe how Ernie helps Walt and Judy with this problem.

_____

_____

_____

_____

b. The second is getting the field ready for planting after Ike ruins the tractor. Describe how Walt solves this problem.

_____

_____

_____

_____

_____

_____

3 **What Do You Think?**

1. Is Walt the stupid farmer he claims to be? Give reasons to support your answer.

_____

_____

_____

2. Why is the story called "The Good Lord Will Provide"?

_____

_____

_____

4 **Standard English.** Walt and Judy use certain words and expressions in their letters which are perfectly all right to use when talking with family and friends. But people generally do not use them when they are in a situation in which they want to make a good impression. In these situations, they adjust the way they say things so that they are speaking what is called *standard English*. They do this so they will sound the same as thousands of other people who are skillful in using language. Study the examples of standard English below and then underline the correct word in the sentences that follow.

1. *Dumb* and *Stupid*

Dumb means not having the power of speech, as in "deaf and dumb." *Stupid* means silly, foolish, or showing a lack of intelligence.

a. Does Walt seem like a poor (dumb, stupid) farmer to you?

b. Not realizing that the servant was (dumb, stupid), Lord Mansfield fired him for refusing to respond to his question.

c. Do you think Ernie was (dumb, stupid) to try to sell the letters?

d. The possibility of losing his farm struck Walt (dumb, stupid) for a while; then he developed a plan.

e. Do you consider these rules about standard English (dumb, stupid)?

2. *Learn* and *Teach*

Learn means to gain knowledge or skill or to acquire a behavior.
Teach means to provide instruction.

a. Many people believe that a penitentiary is strictly interested in punishing prisoners rather than (learning, teaching) them anything useful.

b. Do you believe there is any truth in the old saying, "You can't (learn, teach) an old dog new tricks"?

c. When Andrew asked his aunt why she was taking college courses at her age, she replied, "The older I get, the more I realize I still have a lot to (learn, teach)."

d. The instructor tried to (learn, teach) his students how to spell better.

e. While in prison, Walt didn't (learn, teach) a new trade.

3. *Set* and *Sit*

Set means to put something in a certain place.
Sit means to be seated.

a. The thing Judy disliked most about getting dinner was having to (set, sit) the table.

b. Uncle Ike's rheumatism was so painful that he couldn't do much but (set, sit) around all day.

c. Judy was so exhausted from all her responsibilities on the farm that she wanted an opportunity just to (set, sit) and relax.

d. When Uncle Ike returned from the store, he (set, sit) the groceries on the kitchen counter.

e. Whenever Hiram lost his temper, he always recalled his grandmother's advice: "Never let the sun (set, sit) on an angry heart."

5 **Common Expressions.** Walt's expression, "staying out of trouble like a cat stays away from water," is just one example of the many phrases and words in our everyday speech in which animals are mentioned in order to stress a point. Use the animals listed at the left to complete the following sentences correctly.

bug
bull ✓
butterflies ✓
chicken ✓
chicken ✓
dog ✓
flea
goat
goose ✓
hog ✓
horse ✓
horse ✓
pig's ✓
rat
skunk ✓
tigers ✓

1. Even though horror films gave Fred _____ bumps, he agreed to see *The Revolution of the Zombies* because he didn't want his friends to think he was a _____ .

2. Mr. Adams had always wanted to spend his two-week vacation in a big city, but when his wife pointed out to him that, on their tight budget, they'd have to stay in a _____ bag, he hotly replied, "In a _____ eye!" And that was the end of that idea.

3. Mrs. Carver was such a clothes _____ that she decided to go whole _____ and spend her entire paycheck at Luella's High Fashion Dress Shop.

4. "This isn't an allowance! This is _____ feed!" cried Sonny as he stormed out of the house muttering, "Grownups always try to _____ us poor kids out of our money!"

5. Upon hearing that a new mob was trying to take over his operations on the South Side, Duke said with annoyance, "Those guys don't _____ me. They're nothing but a bunch of paper _____ ."

6. Watching her husband come home from work exhausted and upset for the fourth night in a row, Susan again considered trying to convince him to quit this _____ race and move to the country; but she kept quiet, realizing that she would only be beating a dead _____ .

7. Whenever her daughter-in-law asked her to babysit, Louise would get a bad case of _____ in her stomach because her grandson was like a _____ in a china shop, and she knew by the end of the evening her lovely living room would be in shambles.

8. The foreman's nagging had really gotten Jesse's _____ , so he decided to go out with his friends after work, even though he knew he'd be in the _____ house when he got home.

6 **Look It Up**. Use a dictionary to help you answer the first two questions in this exercise.

1. Judy writes to Walt that she is "plumb tired." What does the word *plumb* mean as Judy uses it in her letter?

_____

2. What does *plumb* mean in the following sentence?
    When Justin *plumbed* the depths of his mind, he finally thought
    of a way to solve his problem.

_____

3. A *plumb line* is used around the home to make sure that things are vertically straight on a wall. For example, if you were hanging wallpaper, you could use a plumb line to be sure the wallpaper was vertically straight before you pasted it. Give another example of some time you might use a plumb line in your home.

_____

_____

Lesson 3

Review of Consonant Blends: Part 2

br:	bravery brief brilliant brilliance brute brutal umbrella
cr:	crayon cradle credit credentials crock crocodile crumble
dr:	drab dragon drama dramatic dribble drowsy drudgery
fr:	frizzy frosty frequent fragrance fragrant frustrate frustration
gr:	grid griddle gruff gracious gravity grief agreeable
pr:	prude prolong profound privilege precious predicament approve

1　**Definitions.** Match the words listed below with the correct definitions.

brilliant
credentials
crocodile
drama
drowsy
drudgery
fragrant
frequent
griddle
gruff
predicament
privilege
prude

_____   1. a letter or certificate that guarantees someone's position, authority, or right to be trusted

_____   2. a flat pan or other flat metal surface used for cooking

_____   3. a large reptile with thick skin and long jaws

_____   4. a person, especially a woman, who is overly concerned with being proper

_____   5. a play

_____   6. a special advantage granted to an individual or a class

_____   7. a troublesome situation

_____   8. boring or unpleasant work

_____   9. sleepy

_____   10. full of light; shining; splendid; excellent

_____   11. having a pleasant odor; sweet-smelling

_____   12. occurring or appearing quite often

_____   13. rough or harsh in manner or speech

Words for Study

cashier	despair	mechanic
thermos	burlap	suburb
intention	compost	patrols
subdivision	erect	disguised
inwardly	mustache	humorist

Mr. Manning's Money Tree: Part I
by Robert Arthur

At exactly noon Henry Manning, a sandy-haired, pleasant young man, closed the grilled window of his cashier's cage in the First National Bank. He picked up his briefcase and hat, let himself out of the cage, and strolled toward the front door of the bank. The briefcase held a thermos bottle and two sandwiches. Everyone knew that on nice days Henry, the promising young assistant cashier, took his lunch to eat in the park.

As Henry went out the door, two men in gray suits at the rear of the bank exchanged nods, and one started after him. Henry spotted him almost at once, and his heart began to beat faster. If they had a detective following him, it meant they were almost ready to arrest him. It also meant that he had no chance to hide the ten thousand dollars which at the moment was safely tucked away inside his innocent-looking thermos bottle.

Since Monday he had known they were on his trail. By now they must be just about certain that it was Henry Manning who had taken twenty thousand from the accounts during the past year. It was amazing, he thought, how a normally honest man could get the stock market fever and plunge in deeper and deeper, hoping at first for the lucky strike that would make him independent, then for the clever guess which would enable him to make up for his losses, then——

Well, the twenty thousand was gone, and he couldn't pay it back. So Henry, hardened by now to taking money that wasn't his, had taken ten thousand more. But with a detective who might arrest him at any moment at his heels, where on earth could he hide it?

As he reached the park, a Lakeside bus was just closing its doors. With a sudden inspiration Henry leaped on as the door slid hissingly shut. Through the window he saw the detective pound up to the bus stop and look helplessly after him. Henry smiled to himself. That was one problem solved.

But the biggest problem still lay ahead. He had no intention of trying to run for it. He'd take his punishment. Who wanted to spend the rest of his life a hunted man? But he did want to be able to count on the money in his briefcase to help him make a new start. How, then, could he possibly hide it where it would stay safe until he had served his sentence and was a free man again?

"Melwood Estates," the driver called presently. "End of the line."

Henry got out. They had stopped at one of the new subdivisions springing up all around the

---

city. A hundred houses, all alike, were ranged up and down the slopes of newly planted lawn. He walked away briskly, as though he lived in one of the houses. But inwardly he felt a deep despair. It was all so naked and empty out here. Where could a man hide anything? Why couldn't he have had one more day? By now the alarm was out for him, but with one more day he could have——

As if stunned, Henry stopped in his tracks. He had reached a corner. Fifty feet away stood a pleasant little Cape Cod house surrounded by naked lawn. Almost beside Henry there was a deep hole in the lawn, and just beyond the hole a handsome spruce, roots wrapped in burlap, waited to be planted.

No one was in sight. Henry took off his hat, mopped his brow, and as if by accident let his hat drop into the hole. When he bent to get it, he slipped the thermos out of his briefcase and swiftly hid it beneath the loose soil and compost in the bottom of the hole.

It was all done in twenty seconds. Henry was standing erect, admiring the tree, when a cheerful, heavyset man with black hair came down the walk carrying a pail of water.

"Just admiring your tree," Henry said, his manner neighborly. "Beautiful spruce."

"Should be," the other chuckled. "They charged me a lot for it because I wanted a big one." He put down the bucket, and Henry stepped forward.

"Let me give you a hand," he said.

Henry stayed until the tree was planted and the soil packed down around it. A pretty young woman with light brown hair came to the door of the little house and watched them. A young couple, not doing too well yet—Henry saw the inexpensive car in the driveway. Mentally he wished them well. As he strolled away, to return to the bank and be arrested, he felt a certain fondness for these strangers who unknowingly had helped him solve his problem.

It was three-and-a-half years before Henry saw the tree again. By then he was heavier, looked older, had a mustache, and had a trade. In the prison garage he had become an expert mechanic.

The tree had changed too. It had grown into a handsome young spruce. And the house had grown also, Henry noted as he strolled by. A two-car garage had been added. The same old car stood in one half of it, but even as he watched, a much more expensive car drove in and the heavyset man Henry remembered got out, looking quite well-to-do. His wife came out to greet him, her brown hair blowing silkily about her ears, a healthy baby in her arms.

Good, Henry thought. They had done well. They'd be able to afford a new tree when he dug this one up and—suddenly confused, he stopped short. It had never occurred to him what a big job it would be to dig up a well-grown young tree. This was a busy suburb now, with regular police patrols, with people coming and going all the time—he could never do it, even at night, without being caught.

Henry gulped and resumed his walking. It looked as if he had outsmarted himself. He'd hidden the money so safely that now even he couldn't get at it.

Finally, he formed a plan. He'd have to get the tree legally. That meant he'd have to buy the house. Of course, he couldn't buy the house now. He had no money, and there was no sign the owner wanted to sell. But he could wait. For ten thousand dollars he could be patient. They were doing well, their family was growing. Sooner or later, they would want a bigger house. By then he'd have some money.

Having made his plans, Henry wasted no time. He dyed his hair and, feeling well disguised, got a job at a nearby garage, the one where Jerome Smith, the man who owned Henry's money tree, was a regular customer.

Continued in the next lesson...

2   **Understanding the Story**. Put the letter of the correct answer on the line to the left.

_____ 1. At the beginning of the story, Henry's fellow employees think _____ .

     (a) he will probably have a successful career in banking

     (b) he will never rise any higher than assistant cashier

     (c) his eating in the park proves he is unfriendly

     (d) his gambling on the stock market will lead to his ruin

_____ 2. Upon spotting the detectives, Henry _____ .

     (a) thinks they are after someone else

     (b) wishes he had not stolen the money

     (c) is shocked that they suspect him of any crime

     (d) knows they have all the evidence they need to make an arrest

_____ 3. When he sees Melwood Estates, Henry is filled with despair because _____ .

     (a) he experiences a keen regret for the wrongs he has done

     (b) he has always wanted to live in a place like this

     (c) subdivisions have always depressed him

     (d) the subdivision offers no hiding place

_____ 4. Henry has no intention of spending the rest of his life running from the law because _____ .

     (a) he doesn't think prison life will be that bad

     (b) he feels he must pay for his crime

     (c) he doesn't want to live as a hunted man

     (d) he is fearful he might be killed

_____ 5. Henry suspects that the couple living in the Cape Cod house is struggling to make ends meet after he notices their _____ .

     (a) automobile   (b) clothing   (c) naked lawn   (d) spruce tree

_____ 6. The owner of the Cape Cod house seems _____ .

     (a) frantic   (b) friendly   (c) distrustful   (d) glum

_____ 7. Upon seeing Jerome Smith's neighborhood the second time, which sight distresses him?

     (a) the child in Mrs. Smith's arms

     (b) the expensive car in the driveway

     (c) the police patrol

     (d) the spruce tree

_____ 8. In what way does Henry's prison experience help him as he forms his future plans?

     (a) He has a new trade.

     (b) He is able to enjoy the Smiths' success.

     (c) He now knows how to disguise himself.

     (d) His moral values have changed completely.

3 **What Do You Think?** Robert Arthur writes, "So Henry, hardened by now to taking money that wasn't his, had taken ten thousand more." Do you think that committing one crime usually leads to committing more crimes? Be sure to include reasons to support your answer.

_____

_____

_____

_____

_____

4 **Synonyms.** A *synonym* is a word that has almost the same meaning as another word. Match each word listed at the left with its synonym.

acquire
comical   _____   1. amusing
effortless
flimsy   _____   2. charm
generous
glamour   _____   3. impose
inflict
mess   _____   4. muss
possibly
recently   _____   5. newly
reflection
unity   _____   6. obtain

                       _____   7. oneness

                       _____   8. perhaps

                       _____   9. easy

                       _____   10. thought

                       _____   11. unselfish

                       _____   12. weak

5 **Standard English.** Study each rule below and then underline the correct word in the sentences which follow it.

1. *Can* and *May*

   Can indicates the knowledge or ability to do something.
   May is used when permission is sought to do something, most often in the form of a question.

   a. "If I (can, may) be so bold," began Andy's advisor cautiously, "I would suggest that, unless you take your homework assignments more seriously, you should forget all about getting a college degree."

   b. Because Karen (can, may) speak five languages, she was chosen to go to Europe.

   c. As the instructor was passing out the tests, one of the seniors asked sweetly, "(Can, May) we abbreviate our answers, or do we have to write them out?"

   d. "You (can, may) go to the movies if you (can, may) finish mowing the lawn before five o'clock," Dennis said to his son.

2. *In* and *Into*

   In is used to indicate that something is already at a place.
   Into is used to indicate that someone or something is moving from the outside to the inside of a place.

   a. "I was (in, into) the cellar selecting the wine for dinner, so you certainly can't suspect me of the murder!" the maid replied scornfully to the detective's first question.

   b. "It figures," Sally sighed, when the telephone started ringing just as she was about to step (in, into) the bathtub.

   c. As he sifted the flour and salt (in, into) the mixing bowl, Bart wondered if he shouldn't have simply followed his sister's suggestion and picked up a birthday cake at Mama's Bakery.

   d. Anthony was (in, into) his closet searching for his all-time favorite sneakers when his mother walked (in, into) his room.

3. *Borrow* and *Lend*

   Borrow means that an individual is on the taking end of a transaction.
   Lend means that an individual is on the giving end of a transaction.

   a. An American humorist wrote, "Let us all be happy and live within our means, even if we have to (borrow, lend) the money to do it."

   b. "I am not in the habit of (borrowing, lending) my clothes," said Alexis to her friend, "but if you really have nothing to wear skiing, you may use my turtleneck if you promise to wash it."

   c. "May I (borrow, lend) your newspaper for a few minutes to kill time?" Mary asked the stranger seated next to her on the bus. "I promise to return it."

   d. Herb grew increasingly annoyed with his boss for (borrowing, lending) money from him just before payday and then giving the staff lectures about how (borrowing, lending) money to fellow workers created nothing but ill feelings in the office.

4. *About* and *Around*

About should be used when size or number is indicated.
Used correctly, *around* indicates direction in a circle around an object.

a. The most recent ice age ended (about, around) 10,000 to 15,000 years ago.

b. Dr. Adams spends most of his time studying the earth's orbit (about, around) the sun.

c. Most glaciers range in thickness from (about, around) 300 to 10,000 feet.

d. After Nancy had lost (about, around) twenty pounds, she was once again able to button her favorite skirt (about, around) her waist.

6 **Can You Crack the Code?** Each group of letters spells the name of a tree, but the names have been concealed by a code in which a new set of letters has been used in place of the normal letters. The code is the same for all the trees. When you have guessed the name of a tree, use those letters to help you figure out the names of the remaining trees. The brief descriptions of these trees may help you solve this puzzle. The first one has been done to get you started.

S P R U C E
1. V A H D Q R   An evergreen tree in the pine family, its wood is widely used for wood pulp by the paper industry. Sometimes the twigs from a young tree are used to make beer.

2. J T G   The male flowers of this tree, which lives from 200 to 400 years, produce pollen which is carried by the wind to female flowers. Once fertilized, a female flower will become an acorn.

3. C T A Z R   Many people in the United States may not know that the leaf of this tree is the national emblem of Canada, but they do know that the delicious golden-brown syrup which comes from the sap of one type of this tree is used on pancakes and waffles.

4. K B H Q F   One type of this tree has a bark that peels in layers. Some Indians used the bark to construct canoes.

5. O B Z Z J O   One of the many trees of this type is native to China. It is described as "weeping" because of its graceful, drooping branches.

6. A B W R   This tree, which ranks as the world's most important source of timber, bears both male and female cones. The female cones are much larger and have woody scales.

7. Q B W W T C J W   The dried bark from this tree is sold in sticks or ground up into a powder which many people enjoy mixing with sugar and sprinkling over buttered toast.

8. H R P O J J P   Growing along the West Coast of the United States, this is among the world's tallest trees. In a forest, these trees grow so close together that they shut out most of the sunlight.

9. Q F R V L W D L   Most of these trees in the U.S. have been killed by blight, but the wood is so lasting that even dead trees are harvested for lumber and pulpwood.

10. X D P T V   Also called the redbud tree, this tree is named after the man who, it is believed, hanged himself from one after betraying Jesus.

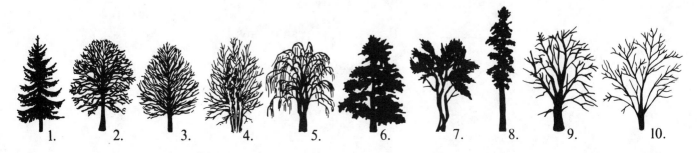

1.   2.   3.   4.   5.   6.   7.   8.   9.   10.

Lesson 4

Review of Consonant Blends and Digraphs: Part 3

scr:	scrawny	scrimp	scrimmage	Scrooge	subscribe	subscription	prescription
shr:	shrew	shrewd	shrewdness	shrinkage	shroud	shrapnel	
spr:	sprayer	spree	sprite	sprightly	sprinkler	sprocket	spry
str:	straddle	stricken	strife	strum	strudel	strategy	strychnine
tr:	tremble	tremendous	trial	triple	trombone	trustworthy	pastry
thr:	thrice	thrive	threesome	throng	throaty	threshold	

1 **Definitions.** Match the words listed below with the correct definitions.

scrawny
Scrooge
shrapnel
shrew
shrewd
shroud
sprite
sprockets
strife
strychnine
threshold
throng

_____

_____

_____

_____

_____

_____

_____

_____

_____

_____

_____

_____

1. a cloth sometimes used to wrap a corpse for burying; something that covers or protects

2. a great number of people gathered together; a crowd

3. a highly poisonous, colorless substance used in small doses to increase the activity of the nervous system

4. a mean, selfish person (from the character of this name in Charles Dickens' *A Christmas Carol*)

5. teeth, as on the rim of a wheel, arranged to fit into the links of a chain

6. a shell filled with an explosive charge and many small metal balls which explodes in the air over the target

7. a small mammal with a long, pointed nose and poor eyesight; this word also refers to a woman who scolds or nags frequently.

8. an elf or pixie; a small or mysterious supernatural being

9. bitter struggle or conflict

10. clever; tricky

11. skinny; thin and bony; lean

12. the entrance or beginning point of something

Words for Study

Constance	divorce	Las Vegas	glint
Mozart	propose	anxious	chum
Jerry	stammered	hurricane	humble
Nevada	casino	topple	gratitude

Mr. Manning's Money Tree: Part II

by Robert Arthur

Henry did his best to become friendly with Jerome Smith, but Smith was gruff, as though his mind was on bigger things. His wife Constance, however, was charming. Henry was on duty when she brought her car in for gas and oil.

"You're new, aren't you?" she asked, her voice musical. Henry nodded.

"Just since last week, Mrs. Smith. Shall I check the radiator and battery?"

"Would you?" Constance Smith sat waiting patiently, the car radio playing.

"Mozart, isn't it?" Henry said.

"Why, yes. You know music?" Constance looked with interest at Henry.

"A bit," Henry said.

It was certainly part of his plan to become friendly with the Smiths so that when they were ready to sell he would be among the first to know. But it wasn't part of his plan to look forward to seeing Constance, to feel somehow gloomy when several days went by and she did not stop in the garage for some service on her car. Nevertheless, it happened. Instead of hoping the Smiths would soon decide to move, Henry began to wish they would stay.

By then Henry was manager of the repair department, and his friendship with Constance, though limited to brief chats while she waited for her car to be fixed or perhaps over a cup of coffee in her kitchen when he went to start the car on a cold morning, was a firm one, important to both of them. They talked about books and music and plays, and Henry knew that Constance enjoyed the talks as much as he did.

One morning Constance called the garage to ask Henry if he could stop in. Her voice sounded upset. She was pale as she led him into the living room.

"Something has happened, Henry," she said, trying to smile, "and I—well, I felt I had to talk about it to a friend."

"I'm glad you think of me as a friend."

"It's a little difficult to say it. You see—" her voice could barely be heard—"Jerry and I haven't been close for a long time. He's away so much and even when he's home...well, anyway, he's in Nevada now. He's starting some business out there. So...he suggests in a letter I got this morning that he might as well stay there and get a divorce."

"A divorce?" Henry stared at her in disbelief.

"I'm going to say yes, of course. Goodness, I certainly don't want a husband who doesn't want *me.*" Her laugh was a little shaky, but it held back the tears.

Now Henry no longer confined himself to business visits, but dropped in at the little house whenever he could. He helped Constance find a job and got the mother of one of his mechanics to become a housekeeper for her son, Peter. He was so concerned with making sure that Constance and Peter were well looked after that it never occurred to him that he could get his money tree until the evening when, after taking Constance to a concert, he found himself proposing to her.

He was in the middle of telling her how much she meant to him when it suddenly struck him that if she married him, the tree was his. And he stopped, wondering in shame whether he really loved her or whether he just wanted to retrieve his hidden money. The possibility rattled him and he stammered, so that Constance laughed softly.

"Henry, are you trying to propose?"

"Yes, I am! I love you! I want you to be my wife, Constance, and Peter to be my son."

She was silent for a long moment, studying his face. "Yes, Henry," she said at last.

So Henry finally became the owner of the money tree. But to him this was unimportant. Now that he had a gracious and loving wife and a handsome son, what need did he have for stolen money?

Still the money proved useful a year later when the owner of the garage decided to retire. Henry didn't have the necessary cash to buy the business. But he knew where the cash was—in his front yard. So he recklessly signed notes. After all, if worse came to worst, he could always pay them off.

There were many nights when Henry strolled in the yard, figuring out how he could keep from digging up the spruce just yet. Somehow, he was unwilling to touch it and, in the end, he managed.

Meanwhile Jerome Smith's photograph appeared frequently in the newspapers. He had become part owner of a big new hotel and gambling casino in Las Vegas and married a stunning showgirl.

Henry and Constance couldn't have cared less. They had a daughter by now, Anne. The children grew from year to year.

Henry bought an auto dealership. Again, there were many anxious nights when he stood beside the tree, thinking this might be the last time he could smell its fragrance. But each time he pulled through somehow.

From then on business boomed. Henry saved for what he knew he must do. At last the day came—just such a sunny day as that one long ago when as a young man he had come out of the bank with stolen money in his briefcase. His hair was graying now, and there were lines of years and living in his face as he entered the bank once more, carrying a briefcase under his arm—the same briefcase.

When he came out, the briefcase was empty. He had returned thirty thousand dollars with interest to date. He went home at peace with the world.

That night he stood beneath his money tree and counted his blessings. The money he had hidden beneath the roots of the tree had done its work. He reached out to stroke the needles of the beautiful spruce.

"You've done a good job, old boy," he said. "You've guarded my stolen fortune even against me. I'll never touch you. You can stand forever."

But one day the following autumn an Atlantic hurricane swung in suddenly from the coast and struck the city. Henry was with Constance in the living room, listening to radio reports of the storm. From the yard there came a creaking and groaning. Henry reached the window just in time to see his proud spruce topple over, leaving a gaping hole.

He felt as if a friend had died. Then he realized he would have to find the long-hidden thermos before anyone else came upon it. Up at dawn the next morning, he scrambled into the hole left by the roots of the spruce.

The rising sun glinted on something bright. He reached in gingerly. It was the silvered core of the thermos—the outer steel covering had rusted away long ago. He eased open the cork with his knife and shook the bottle. Two scraps of paper fell out. Nothing else. Just two scraps of paper. He picked them up.

One was an old newspaper clipping. With a shock he saw it was a picture of himself and the story of his arrest. The other was simply a bit of paper on which was written in Jerome Smith's jagged writing. *I guessed. Thanks, chum.*

A little dazed, Henry went into the house and sat down at the kitchen table. All these years, the money he had counted on hadn't been there! Slowly the shock passed, and it was followed by a feeling of deep and humble gratitude. Life was a curiously complex business. The money he had stolen and buried, but never used, had won him a family, success, contentment. For Jerome Smith it had led to ownership of a big hotel and casino and involvement in the national gambling rackets with illegal interests.

Henry shook his head and picked up the piece of paper on which Smith had written *Thanks, chum.* Beneath it Henry wrote neatly, *You're welcome.* Then he sealed it in an envelope and addressed it. From what he had been reading in the papers lately, he judged that if he simply sent it in care of the Federal Penitentiary at Atlanta, Georgia, it would get to him all right.

2   Understanding the Story.

1. Number these events in the order in which they occur in "Mr. Manning's Money Tree." The first one is done to get you started.

   _____ Constance accepts Henry's marriage proposal.

   _____ Henry helps Constance find a job.

   _____ Henry becomes the manager of the repair department.

   _____ Henry buys an auto dealership.

   _____ Henry returns the money to the bank with interest.

   _____ Henry finds an old newspaper clipping in his thermos.

   _____ Henry writes a letter to Jerome Smith.

   __1___ Jerome Smith leaves a note for Henry.

   _____ Jerome Smith leaves his wife.

   _____ Melwood Estates is struck by a hurricane.

2. In what sense is Henry Manning still a gambler in the second part of "Mr. Manning's Money Tree"?

   _____

   _____

   _____

3. How does Henry's gambling in the second part of the story differ from his gambling in Part I?

_____

_____

_____

_____

4. Cite two examples which show that Henry's attitude regarding the stolen money has changed.

   a. _____

   _____

   b. _____

   _____

3   **What Do You Think?** According to an old saying, "The love of money is the root of all evil." Does Robert Arthur seem to agree with this saying? Be sure to include details from the story to support your answer.

_____

_____

_____

_____

_____

4 **Words That End in -al.** Use the words listed at the left to complete the following sentences.

approval
behavioral
brutal
disposal
intentional
mechanical
personal
proposal
refusal
regional

1. After a _____ four-hour workout at the gym, the heavyweight prizefighter relaxed by soaking in a hot tub and listening to classical tapes.

2. "I don't care whether your being late was _____ or accidental," Peggy shouted at her boyfriend. "The point is I don't like being kept waiting."

3. The safe _____ of nuclear waste is a problem that demands our immediate attention.

4. The cashier's _____ to admit he had given the customer incorrect change led to a highly emotional scene which almost resulted in a fist fight.

5. The teachers' _____ to increase the number of field trips was vetoed by the board of education.

6. Prudes are so judgmental that it seems as if even the saints in heaven couldn't win their _____ .

7. Thomas so enjoyed having a computer at work that he bought one for his _____ use at home.

8. Times were so hard that every farmer in the area attended the monthly _____ meeting to discuss the agricultural problems confronting them.

9. Watching Mr. Jones try to repair his Volkswagen was a comical experience because he had no _____ ability whatsoever.

10. When Mr. Reed finished telling the third grade teacher about his son's actions at home, she replied calmly, "I think if we work together, we can help him overcome his _____ problems."

5 **Antonyms.** An *antonym* is a word whose meaning is opposite to the meaning of another word. Match each word listed at the left with its antonym.

approve
creditor
detect   _____
dwindling
ebb   _____
flustered
glamorous
idleness   _____
impede
ordinary   _____
precious
rumor   _____
shrinkage
unity

_____ 1. assist

_____ 2. composed

_____ 3. debtor

_____ 4. dull

_____ 5. expanding

_____ 6. expansion

_____ 7. fact

_____ 8. flow

_____ 9. labor

_____ 10. overlook

_____ 11. rare

_____ 12. scorn

_____ 13. strife

_____ 14. worthless

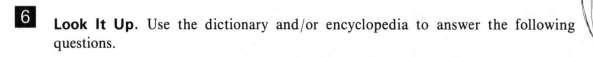

Illustration by Susan Marker

6 **Look It Up.** Use the dictionary and/or encyclopedia to answer the following questions.

1. In order for a storm to be called a hurricane, its winds must be blowing at a certain speed. What is the minimum speed the winds can be blowing in order for a storm to be called a hurricane?

_____

2. Hurricanes begin in the warm regions of which ocean? _____

3. What is a *hurricane lamp*? _____

_____

Review: Lessons 1-4

1 **Word Review.** Use the words listed below to fill in the blanks.

burlap	Dickens	Mozart	rheumatism
casino	finance	parole	rumor
compost	gratitude	plaza	suburb
credit	mortgage	reptile	temple

_____ 1. a building or place devoted to worship; any place or building serving as the center for a special activity or something especially valued

_____ 2. a community on the outskirts of a city

_____ 3. a composer of more than 600 classical works who began composing music at the age of five (1756–1791)

_____ 4. a claim on property, given as security for a loan

_____ 5. a mixture of decaying matter, such as leaves, used to fertilize the soil

_____ 6. a public room or house for entertainment, especially gambling

_____ 7. a public square in a town or city; a paved area for automobiles, such as the widened roadway forming the approach to a group of tollbooths on a highway

_____ 8. a rough woven cloth made of fibers of jute, flax, or hemp, used to make bags

_____ 9. a thankful awareness for a gift or favor

_____ 10. any of several diseased conditions of the muscles, tendons, joints, bones, or nerves which causes discomfort and disability

_____ 11. any of a variety of cold-blooded animals, usually egg-laying, having a covering of scales or horny plates and breathing by means of lungs

_____ 12. gossip; information usually spread by word of mouth which has not been proven true

_____ 13. One of the most popular English writers of all times, this author showed sympathy for the poor and helpless and mocked the selfish, greedy, and cruel in his books. (1812–1870)

_____ 14. the release of a prisoner before his term has ended on condition of continued good behavior

_____ 15. trust; praise; confidence in a buyer's ability to pay money owed at some future time

_____ 16. the use or management of money and other assets

2 **Synonyms and Antonyms.** Choose a synonym to fill in the first blank in each sentence. Choose an antonym to fill in the second blank. Study the example before you begin.

	Synonyms		**Antonyms**	
anxious	nucleus		boastful	inspiring
brilliant	prolong		calm	partner
frequent	puny		despair	✓saintly
glee	rival		drab	seldom
humble	trustworthy		edge	shorten
humdrum	✓wicked		faithless	strong

1. Evil and ___wicked___ are antonyms for ___saintly___ .

2. Extend and _____ are antonyms for _____ .

3. Glowing and _____ are antonyms for _____ .

4. Hub and _____ are antonyms for _____ .

5. Unaffected and _____ are antonyms for _____ .

6. Loyal and _____ are antonyms for _____ .

7. Happiness and _____ are antonyms for _____ .

8. Often and _____ are antonyms for _____ .

9. Challenger and _____ are antonyms for _____ .

10. Boring and _____ are antonyms for _____ .

11. Weak and _____ are antonyms for _____ .

12. Worried and _____ are antonyms for _____ .

3 **Word Families.** Use the words in each set at the left to complete these sentences correctly.

finances
financial
financially

1. After Leslie phoned her father on the East Coast to tell him how proud she was that she had finally gotten the household _____ in order and her budget was _____ faultless, her husband presented her with the latest _____ problem—last month's telephone bill.

unity
disunity
unify

2. Alarmed by the growing _____ in the neighborhood, Ernie urged the parents to _____ their efforts to supervise their children's conduct so that _____ could be restored.

satisfied
satisfactory
satisfaction

3. Although Kenneth was not completely _____ with his current job situation, it gave him a great deal of _____ to know that his supervisor had given him a _____ rating for his job performance.

fashion
fashionable
unfashionable

4. Because Mrs. Miller had been taught that it is not _____ to waste one's time criticizing other women's choices in _____ , she kept to herself her opinions about how _____ the senator's wife had looked at the art museum that morning.

gracious
graciously
graciousness

5. In spite of Mrs. Rich's _____ , Tony decided to refuse _____ her invitation to stay at her home because he was not used to such _____ living.

shrewd
shrewdly
shrewdness

6. In Aesop's fables, the fox is usually a _____ character who _____ convinces others to do exactly as he wants; but sometimes he is outsmarted by his own _____ .

wicked
wickedly
wickedness

7. In *The Wizard of Oz*, the _____ Witch of the West _____ plots Dorothy's destruction, but her _____ results in her own destruction instead.

agreeable
agreeably
disagreeable

8. The Johnsons found the crowded and noisy restaurant so

_____ that they _____ decided

to order a large pizza to go and eat at home where the atmosphere was more

_____ .

instant
instantly
instance

9. As the network newscaster began to report an _____ of

public scandal in their suburb, Mr. Scott _____ rose to

his feet and angrily turned off the set so his family could enjoy their

_____ coffee in peace.

generous
generously
generosity

10. When Mrs. Clark offered all the loose change in her purse to the panhandler

wandering around the busy intersection, he bowed graciously and said, "Your

_____ donation restores my faith, and I know you will

some day be _____ rewarded for your

_____ ."

4 **Which Word Does Not Fit?** Choose the word that does not fit with the other
words in each row and write it on the line.

1. float	glide	plod	sail	skim	_____
2. haul	grasp	lug	tote	pull	_____
3. despair	sorrow	grief	sadness	frustration	_____
4. elf	angel	gnome	pixie	sprite	_____
5. disagree	disjoin	divide	divorce	separate	_____
6. amazing	brisk	lively	spry	sprightly	_____
7. alter	enrich	improve	reform	upgrade	_____
8. Wyoming	Illinois	Nevada	Utah	Colorado	_____
9. delight	zest	passion	spree	enjoyment	_____
10. blizzard	tornado	cyclone	hurricane	earthquake	_____
11. strategy	design	option	plan	blueprint	_____
12. blunt	gruff	abrupt	short	outraged	_____

5 **Money.** Identify the underlined word that is misspelled in each of the following sayings and write it correctly on the line.

_____ 1. Although a dollar bill is only six inchs long, it is used to measure many things.

_____ 2. Striving to live within a budget is almost as hopeless as attemting to find a word that rhymes with "orange."

_____ 3. If you can't pay your debts, at least you can be thankfull you are not one of your creditors.

_____ 4. The way food prices are soaring, being overweight may soon become a sucess symbol.

_____ 5. The buget is a method of being anxious about money before you spend it, instead of afterward.

_____ 6. Whatever assets we possess can often become of double value when we simply share them with a freind.

_____ 7. Everything seems to be under fedral control except the national debt and budget.

_____ 8. Washington, D.C., is the seat of the United States goverment, and the American taxpayer is the pants pocket.

_____ 9. A nickel goes much farther nowadays; it is neccessary to carry it around awhile before you can discover something it will purchase.

_____ 10. A financial fool who excitedly discovers he has money to burn will usualy meet his match.

_____ 11. The reason money is called legal tender is that if you dont have it, it's tough.

_____ 12. The real measure of an individual's welth is how much he would be worth if he lost all his fortune.

Quotations for this exercise are from various Penny Press puzzle magazines and are used by kind permission of the publisher.

A Final Note on Love and Money. Read the poem and then answer the questions which follow.

The Choice
by Dorothy Parker

He'd have given me rolling lands,
　　Houses of marble, and billowing farms,
Pearls, to trickle between my hands,
　　Smoldering rubies, to circle my arms.
You—you'd only a lilting song,
　　Only a melody, happy and high,
You were sudden and swift and strong—
　　Never a thought for another had I.

He'd have given me laces rare,
　　Dresses that glimmered with frosty sheen,
Shining ribbons to wrap my hair,
　　Horses to draw me, as fine as a queen.
You—you'd only to whistle low,
　　Gayly I followed wherever you led.
I took you, and I let him go—
　　Somebody ought to examine my head!

1. The speaker in this poem talks about a choice she was faced with. She had to choose between two men.

   a. The first four lines of each stanza describe what one man could offer her. What did he have to offer?

   _____

   _____

   b. The rest of each stanza describes what the second man had to offer. What did he have to offer?

   _____

   _____

2. Which man does she choose?

   _____

3. Why does she choose this man?

   _____

   _____

4. If she were offered the same choice again, does it seem as if she would make the same decision? Be sure to include reasons to support your answer.

_____

_____

_____

5. If you had to choose between love and money, which would you choose? Be sure to include reasons to explain your answer.

_____

_____

_____

_____

Unit 2
Struggle

It has been suggested by more than one writer that people's characters are formed by their struggles with forces outside themselves. Struggle is the theme of this group of short stories in which the characters find themselves in situations that seem to be too much for them to handle. What are their struggles and how do they cope with them?

In "All the Years of Her Life," the story for Lesson 5, three characters struggle to deal with their reactions to stealing.

"Prelude," the story for Lesson 6, is set in New York City just before the United States enters World War II. The family in this story struggles to cope with prejudice.

Prejudice is also the cause of tension in "The Test," the story for Lesson 7. In this story the author encourages us to ask: Is there more than one way to fail a test?

We often tend to think that struggles are something that teenagers and grownups have to face—something that children know nothing about. In "Charles," the story for Lesson 8, the author sees things differently, however, as she describes one child's response to being sent off to kindergarten.

Lesson 5

Review of Digraphs: Part 4

sh:	shadow	shanty	shawl	shepherd	shield	shiftless	shun
ch:	chute	machinist	chandelier	chauffeur	chiffon	Cheyenne	Charlotte
ch:	charity	Chile	chili	chickadee	merchant	spinach	parched
ch:	chord	chorus	choir	chemistry	characteristic	orchestra	orchid
th:	filth	filthy	panther	thermometer	thoroughfare	theory	ether
th:	thy	thyself	thine	thou	bothersome	fatherly	motherly

1 **Definitions.** Match the words listed below with the correct definitions.

chandelier
characteristic
chauffeur
chemistry
Chile
chute
merchant
orchid
parched
shawl
shanty
shiftless
shun
theory
thoroughfare

_____ 1. a piece of cloth worn by women as a covering for the head, neck, and shoulders

_____ 2. a feature, trait, or quality

_____ 3. a main road or public highway

_____ 4. a person employed to drive a private car

_____ 5. a person whose occupation is the wholesale buying and retail selling of goods for profit

_____ 6. a branched fixture usually hung from the ceiling that holds light bulbs or candles

_____ 7. a plant found chiefly in hot climates and often having brightly colored flowers

_____ 8. a republic of western South America

_____ 9. a shack; a roughly built or ramshackle cabin

_____ 10. an idea that explains the causes for something

_____ 11. an inclined passage or channel down which things may pass; a waterfall or rapid

_____ 12. lazy; showing a lack of energy or goals

_____ 13. the study of the structure, characteristics, and reactions of a substance or matter

_____ 14. thirsty or very dry

_____ 15. to avoid a person, group, or thing

Alfred	alert	earnestness
blustered	swaggering	clasped
indignation	contempt	grimly
eh	wavered	decency
familiar	embarrassed	assured

All the Years of Her Life

by Morley Callaghan

They were closing the drugstore, and Alfred Higgins, who had just taken off his white jacket, was putting on his coat and getting ready to go home. The little gray-haired man, Sam Carr, who owned the drugstore, was bending down behind the cash register, and when Alfred Higgins passed him, he looked up and said softly, "Just a moment, Alfred."

The soft, confident, quiet way in which Sam Carr spoke made Alfred start to button his coat nervously. He felt sure his face was white. Sam Carr usually said, "Good night," without looking up. In the six months he had been working in the drugstore Alfred had never heard his employer speak softly like that. His heart began to beat so loud it was hard for him to get his breath. "What is it, Mr. Carr?" he asked.

"Maybe you'd be good enough to take a few things out of your pocket and leave them here before you go," Sam Carr said.

"What things? What are you talking about?"

"You've got a compact and a lipstick and at least two tubes of toothpaste in your pocket, Alfred."

"What do you mean? Do you think I'm crazy?" Alfred blustered. His face got red and he knew he looked fierce with indignation. But Sam Carr only nodded his head. Then Alfred grew very frightened and he didn't know what to say. Slowly he raised his hand and dipped it into his pocket. With his eyes never meeting Sam Carr's eyes, he took out a blue compact, two tubes of toothpaste, and a lipstick, and he laid them one by one on the counter.

"Petty thieving, eh, Alfred?" Sam Carr said. "And maybe you'd be good enough to tell me how long this has been going on."

"This is the first time I ever took anything."

"So now you think you'll tell me a lie, eh? What kind of a sap do I look like, huh? I tell you you've been doing this pretty steady," Sam Carr said.

Ever since Alfred had left school he had been getting into trouble wherever he worked. He lived at home with his mother and his father, who was a printer. His two older brothers were married and his sister had got married last year. It would have been all right for his parents now if Alfred had only been able to keep a job.

While Sam Carr smiled, Alfred began to feel that familiar terror growing in him that had been in him every time he had got into such trouble.

"I liked you," Sam Carr was saying. "I liked you and would have trusted you, and now look what I got to do." While Alfred watched with his alert, frightened blue eyes, Sam Carr drummed with fingers on the counter. "I don't like to call a cop in point blank," he was saying as he looked very worried. "You're a fool, and maybe I should call your father and tell him you're a fool. Maybe I should let them know I'm going to have you locked up."

"My father's not at home. He's a printer. He works nights," Alfred said.

"Who's at home?"

"My mother, I guess."

"Then we'll see what she says." Sam Carr went to the phone and dialed the number. Alfred was not so much ashamed, but there was that deep fright growing in him, and he blurted out rudely, "Just a minute. You don't need to tell her." He wanted to sound like a swaggering, big guy who could look after himself, yet the old, childish hope was in him, the longing that someone at home would come and help him.

"Yeah, that's right, he's in trouble," Mr. Carr was saying. "You'd better come down in a hurry." And when he was finished, Mr. Carr went over to the door and looked out at the street and said, "I'll keep my eye out for a cop."

Alfred knew how his mother would come rushing in. She would rush in with her eyes blazing, or maybe she would be crying, and she would push him away when he tried to talk to her, and make him feel her dreadful contempt. Yet he longed that she might come before Mr. Carr saw the cop on the beat passing the door.

While they waited—and it seemed a long time—they did not speak, and when at last they heard someone tapping on the closed door, Mr. Carr, turning the latch, said crisply, "Come in, Mrs. Higgins." He looked hard-faced and stern.

Mrs. Higgins must have been going to bed when he telephoned, for her hair was tucked in loosely under her hat, and her hand at her throat held her light coat tightly across her chest so her dress would not show. She came in, large and plump, with a little smile on her friendly face. Most of the store lights had been turned out and at first she did not see Alfred, who was standing in the shadow at the end of the counter. Yet as soon as she saw him she did not look as Alfred thought she would look.

She smiled, and her blue eyes never wavered. With a calmness and dignity that made them forget that her clothes seemed to have been thrown on her, she put out her hand to Mr. Carr and said politely, "I'm Mrs. Higgins, I'm Alfred's mother."

Mr. Carr was a bit embarrassed by her lack of terror and her simple manner, and he hardly knew what to say to her, so she asked, "Is Alfred in trouble?"

"He is. He's been taking things from the store. I caught him red-handed. Little things like compacts and toothpaste and lipsticks. Stuff he can sell easily," the owner said.

When Sam Carr had finished, she said, "Is it so, Alfred?"

"Yes."

"Why have you been doing it?"

"I been spending money, I guess."

"On what?"

"Going around with the guys, I guess," Alfred said.

Mrs. Higgins put out her hand and touched Sam Carr's arm with an understanding gentleness and said, "If you would only listen to me before doing anything." Her simple earnestness made her shy. Then she said with a kind of patient dignity, "What did you intend to do, Mr. Carr?"

"I was going to get a cop. That's what I ought to do."

"Yes, I suppose so. It's not for me to say, because he's my son. Yet I sometimes think a little good advice is the best thing for a boy when he's at a certain period in his life," she said.

Alfred couldn't understand his mother's quiet manner. If they had been at home and someone had suggested he was going to be arrested, he knew she would be in a rage and would cry out against him. Yet now she was standing there with that gentle pleading smile on her face, saying, "I wonder if you don't think it would be better just to let him come home with me. He looks a big fellow, doesn't he? It takes some of them a long time to get any sense," and they both stared at Alfred, who shifted away with a bit of light shining for a moment on his thin face and the tiny pimples over his cheekbone.

But even while he was turning away uneasily Alfred was realizing that Mr. Carr had become aware that his mother was really a fine woman. He knew that Sam Carr was puzzled by his mother, as if he had expected her to come in and plead with him tearfully, and instead he was being made to feel a bit ashamed by her vast understanding.

"Of course, I don't want to be harsh," Mr. Carr was saying. "I'll tell you what I'll do. I'll just fire him and let it go at that. How's that?" and he bowed low to Mrs. Higgins in deep respect.

There was such warmth and gratitude in the way she said, "I'll never forget your kindness," that Mr. Carr began to feel warm and friendly himself.

"Sorry we had to meet this way," he said. "But I'm glad I got in touch with you. Just wanted to do the right thing, that's all," he said.

"It's better to meet like this than never, isn't it?" she said. Suddenly they clasped hands as if they liked each other, as if they had known each other a long time. "Good night, sir," she said.

The mother and son walked along the street together, and the mother was taking a long, firm stride as she looked ahead with her stern face full of worry. Alfred was afraid to speak to her, so he only looked ahead too. He began to wonder what she was thinking of as she stared ahead so grimly. She seemed to have forgotten that he walked beside her.

Finally he said in his old blustering way, "Thank God it turned out like that. I certainly won't get in a jam like that again."

"Be quiet. Don't speak to me. You've disgraced me again and again," she said bitterly.

"That's the last time. That's all I'm saying."

"Have the decency to be quiet," she snapped. They kept on their way, looking straight ahead.

When they were at home and his mother took off her coat, Alfred saw that she was really only half-dressed, and she made him feel afraid again when she said, without even looking at him, "You're a bad lot. God forgive you. It's one thing after another and always has been. Why do you stand there stupidly? Go to bed, why don't you?"

When he was going, she said, "I'm going to make myself a cup of tea. Mind, now, not a word about tonight to your father."

While Alfred was undressing in his bedroom, he heard his mother moving around the kitchen. As he listened there was no shame in him, just wonder and a kind of respect of her strength and calmness. He could still see Sam Carr nodding his head encouragingly to her; he could hear her talking simply and earnestly. "She certainly was smooth," he thought. "Gee, I'd like to tell her she sounded swell."

He got up and went along to the kitchen, and when he was at the door he saw his mother pouring herself a cup of tea. He watched and didn't move.

Her face, as she sat there, was a frightened, broken face utterly unlike the face of the woman who had been so assured a little while ago in the drugstore. When she reached out and lifted the kettle to pour hot water in her cup, her hand trembled and the water splashed on the stove. Leaning back in the chair, she sighed and lifted the cup, swallowing the hot tea eagerly. Her hand holding the cup still trembled, and she looked very old.

It seemed to Alfred that this was the way it had been every time he had been in trouble before, that this trembling had really been in her as she hurried out half-dressed to the drugstore. He understood why she had sat alone in the kitchen the night his young sister had kept repeating stubbornly that she was getting married. Now he felt all that his mother had been thinking of as they walked along the street together a little while ago. He watched his mother, and he never spoke, but at that moment his youth seemed to be over. He knew all the years of her life by the way her hand trembled as she raised the cup to her lips. It seemed to him that this was the first time he had ever looked upon his mother.

Adapted and used by permission of Don Congdon Associates, Inc. Copyright © 1934 by Morley Callaghan; renewed 1962 by Morley Callaghan

2   **Understanding the Story.** The three characters in "All the Years of Her Life" experience many feelings and reactions as they deal with the fact that Alfred has been caught stealing. State a reason for each feeling or reaction listed below. Study the example before you begin.

Sam Carr

angry: _He has caught Alfred, whom he trusted, stealing from him._

puzzled: _____

_____

softhearted: _____

_____

Alfred Higgins

blustering: _____

_____

frightened: _____

_____

astonished: _____

_____

Mrs. Higgins

polite: _____

_____

angry: _____

_____

trembling: _____

_____

3   **What Do You Think?** Answer the following questions in complete sentence form. Be sure to use examples to support your answers.

1. What do you think Morley Callaghan meant when he wrote, "It seemed to him that this was the first time he had ever looked upon his mother"?

_____

_____

_____

_____

2. In light of what happens in the story, do you think Alfred will change his behavior?

_____

_____

_____

_____

3. What feelings do you experience when you find yourself in a situation in which there is some kind of pressure?

_____

_____

_____

_____

4   **Word Relationships.** Complete each statement by writing out the best answer.

1. Shepherd is to flock as _____ .
   (a) clotheshorse is to shopping   (c) inventor is to laboratory
   (b) cowboy is to herd   (d) merchant is to goods

2. Chile is to South America as _____ .
   (a) China is to Europe   (c) Iowa is to Midwest
   (b) Egypt is to Africa   (d) Paris is to France

3. Theory is to idea as _____ .
   (a) quiz is to assignment   (c) flag is to emblem
   (b) organization is to details   (d) strategy is to method

4. Container is to crock as _____ .
   (a) fixture is to chandelier   (c) odor is to skunk
   (b) fun is to drudgery   (d) thermos is to coffee

5. Carol is to Christmas as _____ .
   (a) chord is to composer   (c) hymn is to church
   (b) conductor is to orchestra   (d) melody is to choir

6. Cheyenne is to Wyoming as _____ .
   (a) Atlantic City is to New York   (c) Cleveland is to Pennsylvania
   (b) Baltimore is to New Jersey   (d) Memphis is to Tennessee

7. Ruler is to inches as _____ .
   (a) cup is to pint   (c) speedometer is to gasoline
   (b) scale is to pressure   (d) thermometer is to temperature

8. Millimeter is to measurement as _____ .
   (a) ether is to pill   (c) sermon is to clergyman
   (b) oval is to shape   (d) snobbishness is to clique

9. Glee is to gloom as _____ .
   (a) approval is to assurance   (c) silliness is to gravity
   (b) generosity is to charity   (d) strife is to disunity

10. Troublesome is to effortless as _____ .
    (a) bothersome is to convenient   (c) wholesome is to healthy
    (b) threesome is to trio   (d) worrisome is to anxious

5 **Sounds for *ch*.** Classify each word listed below according to its sound for *ch*.

ache	chapel	Cherokee	choir	machinery	mustache
chalk	chef	Chicago	echo	mechanical	scorch
champagne	chemical	chief	lynch	Michigan	strychnine

*ch*ina	*ch*andelier	*ch*aracter
1. _____	1. _____	1. _____
2. _____	2. _____	2. _____
3. _____	3. _____	3. _____
4. _____	4. _____	4. _____
5. _____	5. _____	5. _____
6. _____	6. _____	6. _____

6 **Standard English.** Study each rule below and then underline the correct word in the sentences which follow it.

1. *All ready* **and** *Already*

All ready means just what the two words indicate—all prepared.
Already means previously.

a. Ralph was (all ready, already) for his first performance when he suddenly realized in horror that he had left his clarinet on the bus.

b. Gloria's husband pleaded with her to work hard for a promotion, but she was (all ready, already) so frustrated that she decided to forget the whole idea.

c. Justin's blunder had (all ready, already) cost the firm thousands of dollars, and he worked overtime for several weeks, hoping that it would not also cost him his livelihood.

d. Charlotte was (all ready, already) to serve the chili when she realized that she had forgotten to buy any crackers to go with it.

2. *Beside* **and** *Besides*

Beside means at the side of.
Besides means in addition.

a. (Beside, Besides) being the best shooter on the basketball team, John was also a good sport.

b. "How do you expect me to enjoy this juicy steak," roared Mr. Polk at the startled waiter, "when you place the bill right (beside, besides) my dinner plate!"

c. (Beside, Besides) the mortgage and insurance payments, Wendy figured the bank loan would also have to cover the expense of her son's shoulder operation.

d. Judy placed the vase containing the single, fragrant rose her boyfriend had given her (beside, besides) his picture.

3. *Affect* **and** *Effect*

Affect most commonly means to influence.
Effect usually means a result.

a. Jerry hoped that the accident he had had two years ago would not (affect, effect) his chances of becoming Mr. Snow's chauffeur.

b. Sir Isaac Newton's writings about the law of gravity had a great (affect, effect) on scientists both in his own time and in future generations.

c. Defining work as honest toil rather than unjust drudgery can have a positive (affect, effect) on the way we view our jobs.

d. The new tax laws did not (affect, effect) Steven's giving money to charities he considered worthwhile.

Lesson 6

Review of Consonant Blends: Part 5

sl:	slab slacken slender slink sliver slogan slugfest
sm:	smattering smashup smug smidgen smithereens
sn:	sniffle snicker snug snuggle sneer snoop
sk:	skeleton skimpy skirmish tusk husk husky whiskers
sch:	schedule scholar scholarly scholarship
sc:	scan Scandinavia landscape scurry scope microscope telescope
sc:	scent scenery scenic scissors descend descendant

1   **Definitions.** Match the words listed below with the correct definitions.

descend
descendant
microscope
scan
Scandinavia
scholarship
scurry
skirmish
slacken
slogan
smithereens
snicker
telescope

_____ 1. a minor incident in a war

_____ 2. a catch phrase used to advertise a product

_____ 3. a gift of money or other aid given by a foundation, etc., to help a student continue his studies

_____ 4. a person or animal descended from another

_____ 5. a region in northern Europe which includes Norway, Sweden, Denmark, and sometimes Finland and Iceland

_____ 6. a word used in informal speech to describe fragments or splintered pieces; bits

_____ 7. an instrument that enlarges the images of objects too small to be seen by the naked eye

_____ 8. an instrument used to observe distant objects

_____ 9. to become less active or intense; to reduce the tension or relax

_____ 10. to laugh in a sly and impolite way at someone

_____ 11. to look at something in a broad or searching way

_____ 12. to move from a higher to a lower place; to slope, extend, or incline downward

_____ 13. to run hastily; to scamper

Words for Study

prelude	Silverstein	hoodlums	merely
Sylvia	respectable	instructive	Austria
Harry	communist	demonstrated	it'll
sergeant	edition	squat	prejudiced

Prelude

by Albert Halper

I was coming home from school, carrying my books by a strap, when I passed the poolroom and saw the big guys hanging around.

"Hey, Ike, how's your good-looking sister?" they called, but I didn't turn around. The guys are eighteen or nineteen and haven't ever had a job in their life. "What they need is work," my father is always saying when they bother him too much. "They're not bad; they get that way because there's nothing to do," and he tries to explain the meanness of their ways. But I can't see it like my father. I hate those fellas and I hope every one of them dies under a truck. Every time I come home from school past Lake Street they jab me, and every time my sister Sylvia comes along they say things. So when one of them calls, "Hey, Ike, how's your sister?" I don't answer. Besides, Ike isn't my name anyway. It's Harry.

I passed along the sidewalk, keeping close to the curb. Someone threw half an apple but it went over my head. When I went a little farther, someone threw a stone. It hit me in the back of the leg and stung me but it didn't hurt much. I kept a little toward the middle of the sidewalk because I saw a woman coming along the other way, and I knew they wouldn't throw.

I came up to the newsstand and put my school books inside. "Well, Pa," I said, "you can go to Florida now." So my Pa went to "Florida," which was a chair near the radiator that Nick lets him use in his restaurant. He has to use Nick's place because our own flat is too far away, about a quarter-mile off.

The first ten minutes after coming home from school and taking care of the newsstand always excite me. I like everything about selling papers for my father. The fresh air gets me and I like to talk to customers and see the rush when people are let out from work. The only thing I don't like is those guys from the poolroom. But since my father went to the police station to complain, they don't come around so often. The desk sergeant there said, "Don't worry, Mr. Silverstein, we'll take care of it. You're a respectable citizen and taxpayer and you're entitled to protection." And the next day they sent over a patrolman who stood around almost two hours.

Well, all this happened three or four weeks ago and so far the gang has let us alone. They stopped pulling my sixteen-year-old sister by her sweater and when they pass the stand going home to supper all they give us is dirty looks. During the last three or four days, however, they passed by and kinda muttered, calling my father a communist banker and me and my sister Reds. My father says they really don't mean it; it's the hard times and bad feelings, and they got to put the blame on somebody, so they put the blame on us. It's certain speeches on the radio and the pieces in some of the papers, my father told us. "Something is happening to some of the people and we got to watch our step," he says.

I am standing there when my father comes out from Nick's looking like he liked the warm air in Nick's place. His cheeks look rosy, but they look that way from high blood pressure and not from good health. "Well, Colonel," he says smiling, "I am back on the job." My old man starts to stamp around in a little while and, though he says nothing, I know he's got pains in his legs again.

Then I see my sister coming from high school carrying her briefcase. She's a girl with a hot temper, and when she thinks she's right, you can't tell her a thing. When she comes by the pool hall, two guys come out and say something to her, but she just holds herself tight and goes right on past them both.

My old man went into Nick's once more for some "sunshine," and me and Sylvia got busy making sales to the men from the furniture factory which, lately, had been checking out early. Sylvia is a fast worker, faster than me, and we took care of the rush all right. Then we stood waiting for the next rush from the cocoa factory up the block to start.

Our old man returned from Nick's just as the *Times* truck, which was a little late, roared up and dropped the evening edition, which we were waiting for. Sylvia had to go home and make supper. "I'll be back in an hour," she told me. "Then Pa can go home and rest a bit and me and you can take care of the stand."

I said, "All right."

Then the guys from the poolroom began passing the stand on their way home to supper after a day of just killing time. One or two of them said something mean to us, but my old man and me didn't answer. "If you don't answer hoodlums," my father once told me, "sometimes they let you alone."

But then it started. In a flash I realized it was all planned out. My father looked kind of worried but stood quiet. There were about eight or nine of them, all big boys around eighteen or nineteen, and for the first time I got scared.

Finally one of them smiled and said, "Well, this physical fitness magazine you got here is mighty instructive, but don't you think we ought to have some of the exercises demonstrated?"

So another fella pointed to some of the pictures in the magazine and wanted me to squat on the sidewalk and do the first exercise. I wouldn't do it. My father put his hand on the fella's arm and said, "Please, please." But the guy pushed my father's hand away.

"We're interested in your son, not you. Go on, squat."

"I won't," I told him.

"Go on," he said. "Do the first exercise so that the boys can learn how to keep fit."

"I won't," I said.

"Go on," he said. "Do it. Do it if you know what's good for you."

Before I knew it, someone got behind me and tripped me so that I fell on one knee. Then another of them pushed me, trying to make me squat. I shoved someone, and then someone hit me. While they had me down on the sidewalk, Sylvia came running up the street. When she saw what was happening, she began kicking them and yelling and trying to make them let me up. But they didn't pay any attention to her, merely pushing her away.

"Please," my Pa kept saying. "Please let him up; he didn't hurt you. I don't want to have to call the police —"

Then Sylvia turned to the small crowd that had gathered and yelled, "Why don't you help us? What are you standing there for?" But none of them moved. Then Sylvia began to scream: "Listen, why don't you help us? Why don't you make them stop picking on us? We're human beings the same as you!"

But the people just stood there afraid to do a thing. Then while a few guys held me, about five others went for the stand, turning it over and mussing and stamping on all the newspapers they could find. Sylvia started to scratch them, so they hit her, then I broke away to help her, and then they started socking me too. My father tried to reach me, but three guys kept him away. Four guys got me down and started kicking me and all the time my father was begging them to let me up and Sylvia was screaming at the people to help. And while I was down, my face was squeezed against some papers on the sidewalk, telling about how people were fleeing Austria to escape Hitler's approaching army.

Then someone yelled, "The cops!" and they got off me right away. Nick had looked out the window and had called the station, and the guys let me up and beat it away fast.

But when the cops came, it was too late; the stand was a wreck. Newspapers and magazines were all over the sidewalk.

Then the cops came through the crowd and began asking questions right and left. In the end they wanted to take us to the station to enter a complaint, but Sylvia wouldn't go. She looked at the crowd watching and she said, "What's the use? All those people standing around and none of them would help!" They were standing all the way to the second post and when the cops asked for witnesses none of them except one woman offered to give them names. Then Sylvia looked at Pa and me and saw our faces and turned to the crowd and began to scream: "In another few years, you wait! Some of you are working people and they'll be marching through the streets and going after you too! They pick on us Jews because we're weak and haven't got any country; but after they get us down, they'll go after you! And it'll be your fault; you're all cowards, you're afraid to fight back!"

"Listen," one of the cops told my sister, "are you coming to the station or not? We can't hang around here all evening."

Then Sylvia broke down. "Oh, leave us alone," she told them and began wailing her heart out. "What good would it do?"

The cops started telling people to break it up and move on. Nick came out and took my father by the arm into the lunchroom for a drink of hot tea. As the crowd began to dwindle, it started to snow. The woman who had offered to give the names and I were down on our hands and knees, trying to save some of the magazines. There was no use going after the newspapers, which were smeared up, torn, and dirty from the gang's feet. But I thought I could save a few, so I picked a couple of them up.

"Oh, leave them be," Sylvia wept. "Leave them be."

2   **Understanding the Story.** Put the letter of the best answer on the line to the left.

_____ 1. Mr. Silverstein *says* that the basic cause of the tension between the gang and his family is that the gang members ____ .

(a) are prejudiced against Jewish people
(b) are unemployed
(c) have not been raised properly
(d) suffer from poor educational opportunities

_____ 2. The *real* reason the poolroom gang doesn't like the Silversteins is because the Silversteins are ____ .

(a) bankers   (b) Communists   (c) Jewish   (d) prejudiced

_____ 3. The word that best describes Harry's attitude toward the gang is ____ .

(a) amusement   (b) fear   (c) hatred   (d) indifference

_____ 4. As it is used in the story, *Florida* is a symbol of ____ .

(a) escape   (b) retirement   (c) vacation   (d) warmth

_____ 5. Sylvia's resentment is directed mostly at ____ .

(a) Adolf Hitler
(b) the gathered crowd
(c) the policemen
(d) the poolroom gang

_____ 6. The word that best describes the policemen's attitude toward Sylvia is ____ .

(a) concern   (b) contempt   (c) duty   (d) indifference

_____ 7. Who demonstrates the least concern for the Silverstein family?

(a) Nick
(b) the policemen who arrive at the newsstand
(c) the woman who offers to give names
(d) the other people in the crowd who saw the incident

_____ 8. The word that best describes Sylvia's mood at the end of the story is ____ .

(a) despair   (b) indifference   (c) scorn   (d) terror

_____ 9. A main theme presented in this story is that ____ .

(a) people's fear of becoming involved is a major part of the problem of prejudice
(b) people who are unemployed are troublemakers
(c) prejudice is so widespread that nothing can really be done about it
(d) the American people generally agreed with Hitler's treatment of the Jews

_____ 10. This story takes place just before the United States entered ____ .

(a) the Civil War
(b) the Spanish-American War
(c) World War I
(d) World War II

3 **What Do You Think?** Answer these questions in good sentence form. Be sure to include reasons to support your answers.

1. If you had been one of the crowd watching this situation, what do you think your response would have been?

_____

_____

_____

_____

2. *Prelude* means "an event or action that introduces and comes before a more important one." Using details from the story to support your answer, why do you think Halper has entitled his work "Prelude"?

_____

_____

_____

_____

_____

3. How is the pressure which the Silverstein family experiences different from the pressure in the Higgins family in "All the Years of Her Life"?

_____

_____

_____

_____

_____

4 **Synonyms and Antonyms.** If the pair of words is similar in meaning, write *synonyms* on the line to the left. If the pair is opposite in meaning, write *antonyms*.

_____ 1. accidental——intentional

_____ 2. brute——sissy

_____ 3. characteristic——trait

_____ 4. descendant——offspring

_____ 5. expansion——contraction

_____ 6. filthy——spotless

_____ 7. furious——outraged

_____ 8. parched——thirsty

_____ 9. scamper——scurry

_____ 10. scenic——unsightly

_____ 11. shiftless——hardworking

_____ 12. smidgen——smattering

_____ 13. smug——ashamed

_____ 14. snicker——sneer

_____ 15. snoop——pry

_____ 16. utterly——totally

5 | **March, 1938.** In "Prelude" Halper mentioned that Germany invaded Austria. This happened in March of 1938. The items below are based on the March 1, 1938, edition of the *New York Times*. Although the facts, opinions, and ads might be different from what you would find in a current newspaper, the spelling should be the same. Identify the underlined word in each set that is spelled incorrectly and write its correct spelling on the line.

_____ 1. Raging winter weather returned to this city on a <u>fierce</u> gale that <u>caused</u> <u>widespread</u> damage yesterday as <u>furious</u> March weather came in like a lion a day ahead of <u>scedule</u>.

_____ 2. All <u>German</u> officers ever in <u>service</u> before, during, or after the World War <u>learned</u> by a decree <u>issued</u> today that they might be drafted at any time. The decree is <u>planely</u> the result of the great need for officers to train the new troops.

_____ 3. Back upon the Bench after a two weeks' <u>absence</u> the <u>Justices</u> of the Supreme Court were thought to have set a record for speed when today they handed down nineteen <u>formal</u> <u>decisions</u> in a little less <u>then</u> half an hour.

_____ 4. Albert Warner, motion picture producer, reported to police today the theft of <u>jewlry</u> he valued at $90,000 from his winter home. <u>Detective</u> <u>Chief</u> Earl D. Carpenter said the <u>thief</u> gained <u>entrance</u> through a second-floor window by using an icepick and walked past Mr. and Mrs. Warner's bed as they slept.

_____ 5. <u>Transfer</u> of a part of an eye of a dead man in what was described by the attending <u>physician</u> as the first <u>operation</u> of its kind in the United States partly restored the <u>eyesight</u> of an 84-year-old <u>preist</u>.

_____ 6. Big Charley Ruffing and Lefty Gomez signed Yankee <u>contracts</u> today. Manager McCarthy made no <u>referance</u> to terms in his <u>announcement</u>. It is <u>believed</u>, however, that each will <u>receive</u> about $18,500 for the season.

_____ 7. Since the very <u>begining</u> Howard has worked hard to <u>tailor</u> clothes as fine as humanly <u>possible</u>. When you step out to buy your new clothes, <u>remember</u> that <u>style</u> is important. Suits, topcoats, and tuxedos—all $22.50 with ten weeks to pay.

_____ 8. The <u>assistant</u> director of public <u>welfare</u> said that the <u>Republican</u> party had lost the <u>Negro</u> and labor vote because it failed to support legislation <u>helpfull</u> to the masses.

_____ 9. Churches will hold special services <u>tomorrow</u> to <u>celebrate</u> Ash <u>Wendsday</u>, and there will be special services daily in many of the churches <u>throughout</u> the <u>forty</u> days of Lent.

_____ 10. MILES AHEAD - This smart new chophouse. <u>Youll</u> agree when you dine at Longchamps Broilings Bar. <u>Select</u> your own steak, <u>hamburger</u>, chops, chicken, or lobster from the larder and watch it broil to your <u>exact</u> taste. A FLAVOR <u>SENSATION</u>! Oversize steak broiled to order—$1.75.

_____ 11. To think is the crying need of our nation and in the opinion of us women it seems <u>increasingly</u> <u>evident</u> that all men have gone either haywire or numb in the <u>passed</u> few years. It is my firm <u>belief</u> that once enough women get really thinking, organized action will <u>surely</u> follow, and the results will make history.

_____ 12. The following <u>telegram</u> was sent yesterday to General Pershing by a <u>comittee</u> representing twelve <u>veterans'</u> organizations: "We pray for your speedy <u>recovery</u>. To us you are the greatest American <u>commander</u>."

Question: How much do you think a copy of the daily edition of the *New York Times* cost in 1938? _____

6 **Who Was General Pershing?** Use an encyclopedia, dictionary, or other reference book to help you answer the following questions.

Library of Congress

1. What was General Pershing's full name? _____

2. What were the dates of his life? _____

3. In what wars did he fight? _____

4. During what years did World War I take place? _____

5. What was General Pershing's nickname? _____

Lesson 7

Review of Consonant Blends: Part 6

sp:	spatula spectator spectacles spiritual wasp wisp
st:	stable stampede stereo stocky sturdy teamster quest
squ:	squatter squiggle squire squadron squabble
sw:	swab swan swap Swedish swine swoop
tw:	twelfth tweak twerp twilight twiddle twinkle
dw:	dwarf dwell dwelling Dwight
wh:	whew whimper whinny whisk whirlwind
chr:	chromium chromosome Christine chronological

1 **Definitions.** Match the words listed below with the correct definitions.

chromium
chronological
quest
spatula
squabble
squadron
squatter
swab
swine
teamster
tweak
whisk

_____ 1. a group of aircraft or naval vessels

_____ 2. a hard, grayish white element used in the production of stainless steel, etc.

_____ 3. a petty argument; to engage in a minor quarrel

_____ 4. a wad of absorbent cotton on the end of a stick used for cleansing or applying medicine

_____ 5. a tool with a broad, flat blade used to mix, spread, or lift food

_____ 6. a truck driver; a person who drives a team

_____ 7. arranged in order of time of occurrence

_____ 8. pigs or hogs; a greedy or cruel person

_____ 9. one who settles on land without legal claim

_____ 10. the act of seeking something; a search

_____ 11. to brush with a quick, light sweeping motion

_____ 12. to pinch, pluck, or twist sharply; a sharp, twisting pinch

Words for Study

Marian	boulevard	marvelous	astonished
Ericson	competent	official	proceed
unaccented	registration	insignia	neutral
profile	dreary	bewildered	random

The Test
by Angelica Gibbs

On the afternoon Marian took her second driver's test, Mrs. Ericson went with her. "It's probably better to have someone a little older with you," Mrs. Ericson said as Marian slipped into the driver's seat beside her. "Perhaps the last time your Cousin Bill made you nervous, talking too much on the way."

"Yes, Ma'am," Marian said in her soft unaccented voice. "They probably do like it better if a white person shows up with you."

"Oh, I don't think it's *that*," Mrs. Ericson began, but quickly stopped after a glance at the girl's set profile. Marian drove the car slowly through the shady suburban streets. It was one of the first hot days in June, and when they reached the boulevard they found it crowded with cars headed for the beaches.

"Do you want me to drive?" Mrs. Ericson asked. "I'll be glad to if you're feeling jumpy." Marian shook her head. Mrs. Ericson watched her dark, competent hands and wondered for the thousandth time how the house had ever managed to get along without her, or how she had lived through those earlier years when her household had been run by a series of untidy white girls who had considered housework beneath them and the care of children an added insult. "You drive beautifully, Marian," she said. "Now, don't think of the last time. Anybody would slide on a steep hill on a wet day like that."

"It takes four mistakes to flunk you," Marian said. "I don't remember doing all the things the inspector marked down on my blank."

"People say that they only want you to slip them a little something," Mrs. Ericson said doubtfully.

"*No*," Marian said. "That would only make it worse, Mrs. Ericson, I know."

The car turned right, at a traffic signal, into a side road and slid up to the curb at the rear of a short line of parked cars. The inspectors had not arrived yet.

"You have the papers?" Mrs. Ericson asked. Marian took them out of her bag: her learner's permit, the car registration, and her birth certificate. They settled down to the dreary business of waiting.

"It will be marvelous to have someone dependable to drive the children to school every day," Mrs. Ericson said.

Marian looked up from the list of driving requirements she had been studying. "It'll make things simpler at the house, won't it?" she said.

"Oh, Marian," Mrs. Ericson exclaimed, "if I could only pay you half of what you're worth!"

"Now, Mrs. Ericson," Marian said firmly. They looked at each other and smiled with affection.

Two cars with official insignia on their doors stopped across the street. The inspectors leaped out, very brisk and military in their neat uniforms. Marian's hands tightened on the wheel. "There's the one who flunked me last time," she whispered, pointing to a stocky, self-important man who had begun to shout directions at the driver at the head of the line. "Oh, Mrs. Ericson."

"Now, Marian," Mrs. Ericson said. They smiled at each other again, rather weakly.

The inspector who finally reached their car was not the stocky one but a friendly, middle-aged man who grinned broadly as he thumbed over their papers. Mrs. Ericson started to get out of the car. "Don't you want to come along?" the inspector asked. "Mandy and I don't mind company."

Mrs. Ericson was bewildered for a moment. "No," she said, and stepped to the curb. "I might make Marian self-conscious. She's a fine driver, Inspector."

"Sure thing," the inspector said, winking at Mrs. Ericson. He slid into the seat beside Marian. "Turn right at the corner, Mandy-Lou."

From the curb, Mrs. Ericson watched the car move smoothly up the street.

The inspector jotted notes in a small black book. "Age?" he inquired presently, as they drove along.

"Twenty-seven."

He looked at Marian out of the corner of his eye. "Old enough to have quite a flock of pickaninnies, eh?"

Marian did not answer.

"Left at this corner," the inspector said, "and park between that truck and the green car."

The two cars were very close together, but Marian squeezed in between them without too much difficulty. "Driven before, Mandy-Lou?" the inspector asked.

"Yes, sir. I had a license for three years in Pennsylvania."

"Why do you want to drive a car?"

"My employer needs me to take her children to and from school."

"Sure you don't really want to sneak out nights to meet some young blood?" the inspector asked. He laughed as Marian shook her head.

"Let's see you take a left at the corner and then turn around in the middle of the next block," the inspector said. He began to whistle "Swanee River." "Make you homesick?" he asked.

Marian put out her hand, swung around neatly in the street, and headed back in the direction from which they had come. "No," she said. "I was born in Scranton, Pennsylvania."

The inspector acted astonished. "You-all ain't Southern?" he said. "Well, dog my cats if I didn't think you-all came from down yondah."

"No, sir," Marian said.

"Turn onto Main Street and let's see how you-all does in heavier traffic."

They followed a line of cars along Main Street for several blocks until they came in sight of a concrete bridge which arched high over the railroad tracks.

"Read that sign at the end of the bridge," the inspector said.

" 'Proceed with caution. Dangerous in slippery weather,' " Marian said.

"You-all sho' can read fine," the inspector exclaimed. "Where d'you learn to do that, Mandy?"

"I got my college degree last year," Marian said. Her voice was not quite steady.

As the car crept up the slope of the bridge the inspector burst out laughing. He laughed so hard he could scarcely give his next direction. "Stop here," he said wiping his eyes, "then start 'er up again. Mandy got her degree, did she? Dog my cats!"

Marian pulled up beside the curb. She put the car in neutral, pulled on the emergency, waited a moment, and then put the car into gear again. Her face was set. As she released the brake her foot slipped off the clutch pedal and the engine stalled.

"Now, Mistress Mandy," the inspector said, "remember your degree."

"*Damn* you!" Marian cried. She started the car with a jerk.

The inspector lost his jolly attitude in an instant. "Return to the starting place, please," he said, and made four very black crosses at random in the squares on Marian's application blank.

Mrs. Ericson was waiting at the curb where they had left her. As Marian stopped the car, the inspector jumped out and brushed past her, his face purple. "What happened?" Mrs. Ericson asked, looking after him with alarm.

Marian stared down at the wheel and her lip trembled.

"Oh, Marian, *again*?" Mrs. Ericson said.

Marian nodded. "In a sort of different way," she said, and slid over to the right-hand side of the car.

2   Understanding the Story. Answer the following questions in good sentence form.

1. At what point did you realize that the theme of this story deals with prejudice?

_____

_____

2. Why do you think Marian rejects Mrs. Ericson's suggestion that she bribe the inspector?

_____

_____

3. At what point in the story do you first realize that the inspector who rides with Marian is prejudiced?

_____

_____

4. Cite three ways in which the inspector goads Marian into losing her self-control.

   a. _____

   b. _____

   c. _____

5. At what point does Marian's self-control begin to crack?

_____

_____

6. Based on what happens in the story, do you think Marian had any chance of passing the driver's test? Be sure to use evidence from the story to support your answer.

_____

_____

_____

7. To what extent is Mrs. Ericson aware of what Marian is going through? Cite evidence from the story to support your answer.

_____

_____

8. Could Mrs. Ericson have been of more assistance? If so, how? If not, why not?

_____

_____

9. The driver's test is not the only test that Marian fails. Describe at least one other test she fails.

_____

_____

_____

3　What Do You Think?

1. What advice would you give Marian regarding her next attempt to pass the driver's test?

_____

_____

_____

2. Do you think this story was written recently or a number of years ago? Be sure to support your answer with sound reasons.

_____

_____

_____

_____

4 **Word Review.** In the blanks at the right, write the word that is the best example of the first word or phrase in each line.

1. **fixture:** landscape chandelier shroud stereo _____

2. **continent:** Africa Central America Iceland Scandinavia _____

3. **dwelling:** casino subdivision ramshackle house _____

4. **woodwind:** bass flute trombone trumpet _____

5. **vine:** beech ivy spruce willow _____

6. **country:** Peru Europe Plymouth Scranton _____

7. **covering:** core stone nucleus husk _____

8. **employee:** creditor debtor machinist squire _____

9. **star:** meteor Milky Way Pluto sun _____

10. **author:** Dickens Braille Edison Mozart _____

11. **pastry:** brownie gingersnap pizza strudel _____

12. **organ:** spleen vein chromosome skeleton _____

13. **mammal:** crocodile robin panther wasp _____

14. **fruit:** eggplant soybean spinach banana _____

15. **absorbent material:** shield spatula sponge umbrella _____

5 **Chronological Order.** If necessary, use an almanac or other reference book to help you put the following in chronological order.

American Presidents

James Garfield
Herbert Hoover
Andrew Jackson
Thomas Jefferson
John F. Kennedy
Abraham Lincoln

1. _____

2. _____

3. _____

4. _____

5. _____

6. _____

American Holidays

Columbus Day
Fourth of July
Good Friday
Labor Day
Memorial Day
Veterans Day

1. _____

2. _____

3. _____

4. _____

5. _____

6. _____

6 **Standard English.** Study the suggestions below for using standard English. Then correct the mistakes in the sentences at the end of the exercise by crossing out and/or adding words as necessary.

1. **Use *off*, not *off of*.**

   Right: John fell off the ladder.
   Wrong: John fell off of the ladder.

2. **Use *different from*, not *different than*.**

   Right: A movie director is different from a movie producer.
   Wrong: A movie director is different than a movie producer.

3. **Use *since* or *because* rather than *being that*.**

   Right: Since Helen was tired, she went to bed.
   Wrong: Being that Helen was tired, she went to bed.

4. **Use *this* or *that*.** *This here* and *that there* are not considered standard English.

   Right: Roger does not like to shop in that supermarket.
   Wrong: Roger does not like to shop in that there supermarket.

5. **Use *all right*.** *Alright* is not a word.

   Right: The change of plans was not all right with Adam.
   Wrong: The change of plans was not alright with Adam.

6. **Use *any* and *ever* with *scarcely* and *hardly*.** Do not use *no* or *never*.
   Scarcely and *hardly* are negative words even though they don't begin with *n*.

   Right: The Chapmans hardly ever went out for dinner.
   Wrong: The Chapmans hardly never went out for dinner.

1. Scarcely no Americans had heard of the Suwannee River until Stephen Foster made it famous in his song, "Old Folks at Home," which he composed in the mid-1800s.

2. Stephen Foster spelled it *Swanee*, which is different than its correct spelling, *Suwannee*.

3. Stephen Foster was a Northerner and probably had hardly no knowledge of the Suwanee River.

4. The Suwannee River is important being that it helps to drain the Okefenokee Swamp, a vast swamp in southern Georgia.

5. This here word *Okefenokee* comes from an Indian word meaning "trembling earth," which refers to the quivering of the small bushes and weeds that float on water.

6. The Okefenokee was once a favorite hunting ground of local Indians who lived off of the animals that inhabited the swamp.

7. Today the swamp is a safe home for animals being that the United States government has set much of it aside as a wildlife preserve.

8. Those who want to conserve our natural resources do not believe it is alright to let people develop the Okefenokee.

Lesson 8

Review of Vowel Combinations: Part 1

ai:	aide aimless maintain maim Haiti acquaint
au:	auction auditorium Australia precaution sauna
ea:	beacon cleaver eavesdrop queasy New Zealand
ea:	homestead steadfast treasury treachery treacherous
ee:	wee heed peeve feeble beetle referee
oa:	moat bloat petticoat goalie coax loam
oe:	doe foe woe hoe hoe-down mistletoe
oi:	oink sirloin loiter poinsettia thyroid

1   **Definitions.** Match the words listed below with the correct definitions.

bloat
cleaver
foe
heed
hoe-down
loiter
maim
moat
peeve
queasy
thyroid
treacherous
woe

_____ 1. a gland located in front and on either side of the windpipe

_____ 2. a heavy, axlike knife or hatchet used by butchers

_____ 3. a loud and noisy dance, especially a square dance

_____ 4. a personal enemy; an enemy in war

_____ 5. a wide, deep ditch, usually filled with water, surrounding towns, fortresses, or castles in the Middle Ages as a protection against attack

_____ 6. an annoyance; to annoy or make resentful

_____ 7. deep sorrow; grief

_____ 8. not to be trusted; dangerous; disloyal

_____ 9. to cause to swell up or inflate, as with liquid or gas

_____ 10. to disfigure or disable; to deprive a person of the use of a limb

_____ 11. to loaf; to stand idly about; to linger aimlessly

_____ 12. to pay attention to; to listen and consider

_____ 13. uneasy; troubled; sickening

Words for Study

Laurie	era	unsettling	determine	primly
kindergarten	nursery	grammar	haggard	occasional
renounced	casual	PTA	apologized	lapses

Charles
by Shirley Jackson

The day my son Laurie started kindergarten he renounced overalls with bibs and began wearing blue jeans with a belt. I watched him go off the first morning with the older girl next door, seeing clearly that an era of my life was ended. My sweet-voiced nursery-school tot was replaced by a long-trousered, swaggering character who forgot to stop at the corner and wave good-bye to me.

He came home the same way, the front door slamming open, his hat on the floor, and the voice suddenly become rough-sounding shouting, "Isn't anybody *here*?"

At lunch he spoke rudely to his father, spilled his baby sister's milk, and remarked that his teacher said we were not to take the name of the Lord in vain.

"How *was* school today?" I asked, striving to sound casual.

"All right," he said.

"Did you learn anything?" his father asked.

Laurie regarded his father coldly. "I didn't learn nothing," he said.

"Anything," I said. "Didn't learn anything."

"The teacher spanked a boy, though," Laurie said. "For being fresh," he added with his mouth full.

"What did he do?" I asked. "Who was it?"

Laurie thought. "It was Charles," he said. "He was fresh. The teacher spanked him and made him stand in a corner. He was awfully fresh."

"What did he do?" I asked again, but Laurie slid off his chair, took a cookie, and left, while his father was still saying, "See here, young man."

The next day Laurie remarked at lunch, as soon as he sat down, "Well, Charles was bad again today." He grinned broadly and said, "Today Charles hit the teacher."

"Good heavens," I said, mindful of the Lord's name. "I suppose he got spanked again?"

"He sure did," Laurie said. "Look up," he said to his father.

"What?" his father said, looking up.

"Look down," Laurie said. "Look at my thumb. Gee, you're dumb." He began to laugh insanely.

"Why did Charles hit the teacher?" I asked quickly.

"Because she tried to make him color with red crayons," Laurie said. "Charles wanted to color with green crayons so he hit the teacher and she spanked him and said nobody play with Charles but everybody did."

The third day—it was Wednesday of the first week—Charles bounced a seesaw on the head of a little girl and made her bleed, and the teacher made him stay inside all during recess. Thursday Charles had to stand in a corner during story time because he kept pounding his feet on the floor. Friday Charles was deprived of blackboard privileges because he threw chalk.

On Saturday I remarked to my husband, "Do you think kindergarten is too unsettling for Laurie? All this toughness and bad grammar, and this Charles boy sounds like such a bad influence."

"It'll be all right," my husband said. "Bound to be people like Charles in the world. Might as well meet them now as later."

On Monday Laurie came home late, full of news. "Charles," he shouted as he came up the hill. I was waiting anxiously on the front steps. "Charles," Laurie yelled all the way up the hill, "Charles was bad again."

"Come right in," I said as soon as he came close enough. "Lunch is waiting."

"You know what Charles did?" he demanded, following me through the door. "Charles yelled so in school they sent a boy in from first grade to tell the teacher she had to make Charles keep quiet, and so Charles had to stay after school. And so all the children stayed to watch him."

"What did he do?" I asked.

"He just sat there," Laurie said, climbing into his chair at the table. "Hi, Pop, y'old dust mop."

"Charles had to stay after school today," I told my husband. "Everybody stayed with him."

"What does this Charles look like?" my husband asked Laurie. "What's his other name."

"He's bigger than me," Laurie said. "And he doesn't have any rubbers and he doesn't ever wear a jacket."

Monday night was the first Parent-Teachers meeting, and only the fact that the baby had a cold kept me from going. I was dying to meet Charles's mother. On Tuesday Laurie remarked suddenly, "Our teacher had a friend come to see her today."

"Charles's mother?" my husband and I asked at the same time.

"Naaah," Laurie said scornfully. "It was a man who came and made us do exercises. We had to touch our toes. Look." He climbed down from his chair and squatted down and touched his toes. "Like this," he said. "Charles didn't even *do* exercises."

"That's fine," I said heartily. "Didn't Charles want to do the exercises?"

"Naaah," Laurie said. "Charles was so fresh to the teacher's friend he wasn't *let* do exercises."

"What are they going to do about Charles, do you suppose?" Laurie's father asked him.

Laurie shrugged. "Throw him out of school, I guess," he said.

By the third week of kindergarten, Charles was an institution in our family. The baby was being a Charles when she cried all afternoon; Laurie did a Charles when he filled his wagon full of mud and pulled it through the kitchen. Even my husband, when he caught his elbow in the telephone cord and pulled the telephone, ashtray, and a bowl of flowers off the table, said, "Looks like Charles."

During the third and fourth weeks it looked like Charles had reformed. Laurie reported grimly at lunch on Thursday of the third week, "Charles was so good today the teacher gave him an apple."

"What?" I said.

"He gave the crayons around and he picked up the books afterward and the teacher said he was her helper."

"What happened?" I asked in disbelief.

"He was her helper, that's all," Laurie said, and shrugged.

For over a week Charles was the teacher's helper. Each day he handed things out and he picked things up. No one had to stay after school.

"The PTA meeting's next week," I told my husband one evening. "I'm going to find Charles's mother there."

"Ask her what happened to Charles," my husband said. "I'd like to know."

"I'd like to know myself," I said.

On Friday that week things were back to normal. "You know what Charles did today?" Laurie demanded at the lunch table. "He told a little girl to say a word and she said it and the teacher washed her mouth out with soap and Charles laughed."

"What word?" his father asked unwisely, and Laurie said, "I'll have to whisper it to you, it's so bad." He got down off his chair and went around to his father. His father bent his head down and Laurie whispered joyfully. His father's eyes widened.

"Did Charles tell the little girl to say *that*?" he asked.

"She said it *twice*," Laurie said. "Charles told her to say it *twice*."

"What happened to Charles?" my husband asked.

"Nothing," Laurie said. "He was passing out the crayons."

My husband came to the door with me that Monday evening as I set out for the PTA meeting.

"Invite her over for a cup of tea after the meeting," he said. "I want to get a look at her."

"If only she's there," I said prayerfully.

"She'll be there," my husband said. "I don't see how they could hold a PTA meeting without Charles's mother."

At the meeting I sat restlessly, scanning each face, trying to determine which one hid the secret of Charles. None of them looked to me haggard enough. No one stood up in the meeting and apologized for the way her son had been acting. No one mentioned Charles.

After the meeting I identified and sought out Laurie's kindergarten teacher. She had a plate with a cup of tea and a piece of chocolate cake. I had a plate with a cup of tea and a piece of marshmallow cake. We approached each other cautiously and smiled.

"I've been so anxious to meet you," I said. "I'm Laurie's mother."

"We're all so interested in Laurie," she said.

"Well, he certainly likes kindergarten," I said. "He talks about it all the time."

"We had a little trouble adjusting, the first week or so," she said primly, "but now he's a fine little helper. With occasional lapses, of course."

"Laurie usually adjusts very quickly," I said. "I suppose this time it's Charles's influence."

"Charles?"

"Yes," I said laughing, "you must have your hands full in that kindergarten, with Charles."

"Charles?" she said. "We don't have any Charles in the kindergarten."

2 Understanding the Story. Answer the following questions in good sentence form.

1. Cite three clues Jackson gives you which indicate that Laurie—not Charles—is the problem in the kindergarten class.

   a. _____

   _____

   b. _____

   _____

   c. _____

   _____

2. What is the attitude of Laurie's mother toward Charles's mother?

   _____

   _____

3. Does Laurie's mother seem like the type of mother who thinks her child can do no wrong? Be sure to include details from the story to support your answer.

   _____

   _____

   _____

4. Experts in child behavior find that children often create imaginary people as a way of protecting themselves from pressure. Explain how this finding relates to the story "Charles."

   _____

   _____

   _____

   _____

3 **What Might You Use if You Wanted To...** Match each task on the right with the item you could use to complete it.

burlap
cleaver
compost
explosives
grid
griddle
microscope
plasma
sauna
scissors
scraper
slogan
spectacles
stereo
telescope

_____ 1. blast a mountainside

_____ 2. cut out items for a scrapbook

_____ 3. cut the carcass of a swine into pieces

_____ 4. listen to classical music

_____ 5. examine bacteria

_____ 6. fertilize your garden

_____ 7. locate a point on a map

_____ 8. manufacture bags for agricultural products

_____ 9. observe Mars

_____ 10. perform a transfusion

_____ 11. prepare to repaint the front porch

_____ 12. read the fine print on a mortgage

_____ 13. catch consumers' attention

_____ 14. ease the tensions of a stressful day

_____ 15. treat yourself to a pancake breakfast

4 **The Suffix -ly.** Use both words in each set to complete these sentences.

evident
evidently

1. After a lengthy cross-examination, it was _____ to the foreman of

the jury that the witness was _____ lying in order to protect

the defendant.

responsible
responsibly

2. As the cleaning woman _____ finished the last chore on the list

her employer had left with her, she hoped she would not be held

_____ for the expensive china vase she had accidentally dropped.

probable
probably

3. Convinced that it was highly _____ he would win the election by

a landslide, the Republican candidate dismissed the polls that had predicted he

would _____ be badly defeated.

furious
furiously

4. Dennis _____ devoured the last of the lemon chiffon pie, knowing

full well that he would be _____ with himself the next morning

for having broken his strict diet.

spiritual
spiritually

5. Even among those who usually sneered at _____ people, the local

pastor was highly respected for being so _____ concerned with

the welfare of everyone he encountered.

indignant
indignantly

6. "How can you sit there and say I'm being _____," said Alfred

_____ to his secretary, "when you know perfectly well I never lose

my temper at the office!"

earnest
earnestly

7. "If you make an _____ attempt to explain your financial

predicament to the creditors, I'm sure they will try to work out another payment

plan with you," Johnny _____ told his brother.

physical
physically

8. None of her friends could understand how Betsy could be so

_____ fit when it was a well-known fact that she shunned all

_____ exercise as if it were the plague.

casual
casually

9. The _____ conversations among the players in the locker room

came to an immediate halt when the coach _____ announced that

he intended to resign his position right after the game.

smug
smugly

10. With a _____ look on his face, the imp sprawled out on the couch

to watch the late movie, _____ ignoring the screams from the

babysitter whom he had locked in the hall closet.

5 **Spelling.** Change the *y* to *i* before adding *-ly* to these words. Study the example before you begin.

1. shaky   _Shakily_   7. stocky   _____

2. hungry   _____   8. naughty   _____

3. bossy   _____   9. nasty   _____

4. fancy   _____   10. hasty   _____

5. thrifty _____   11. ordinary _____

6. sturdy   _____   12. extraordinary _____

6 **Find the Quote.** The first kindergarten was opened by Friedrich Frobel in Germany in 1837. Can you find this quote by the founder, which describes what he thought kindergarten should be?

A. Each of the fourteen descriptions defines or gives a clue for a certain word. Write that word on the lines to the left of each description.

B. Put the letters of those words in the blanks on the next page. The quote, when all the blanks are filled in, will be Frobel's description of kindergarten.

C. The first one has been done for you. Study it before you begin.

F O O T N O T E
84 31 46 13 4 40 74 53

1. a note placed at the bottom of a page of a book

― ― ― ―
64 56 3 68

2. the residence of the old woman who had so many children that she didn't know what to do

― ― ― ― ― ― ― ―
20 89 60 43 71 7 38 78

3. an explosive used to blast mines, foundations, etc.

― ― ― ― ― ― ― ― ―
75 27 33 57 83 17 25 51 42

4. invented in 1876 by Alexander Graham Bell

― ― ― ― ― ―
36 82 66 9 62 48

5. a common glass container for liquids

― ― ― ― ―
1 70 29 30 89

6. how poison ivy makes you feel

― ― ― ― ― ― ― ―
76 11 86   65 14 18 85 35

7. the fraction that represents how much of our lives we spend sleeping

― ― ― ― ― ― ―
28 16 5 32 6 80 54

8. a vehicle that helps tots get around fast

― ― ― ― ― ― ― ― ―
44 1 24 39 10 21 26 50 58

9. a person who discards his trash carelessly in public areas

― ― ―
77 37 2

10. a slang synonym for *failure* or *flop*

― ― ―   ― ― ― ― ― ― ―
23 63 47   15 73 58 19 69 8 52

11. the northeastern United States (2 words)

― ― ― ― ― ― ―
12 72 84 45 43 55 87

12. an antonym for *inflate*

$\overline{61}$ $\overline{7}$ $\overline{71}$ $\overline{59}$ $\overline{66}$ $\overline{69}$ $\overline{41}$ $\overline{81}$ $\overline{22}$

13. what passengers at the bus station study to see when their bus leaves

$\overline{26}$ $\overline{76}$ $\overline{50}$ $\overline{88}$ $\overline{34}$ $\overline{79}$ $\overline{43}$ $\overline{67}$ $\overline{49}$

14. a broad city street, often tree-lined and landscaped

Quote:

$\overline{1}$ $\quad$ $\overline{2}$ $\overline{3}$ $\quad$ $\overset{N}{\overline{4}}$ $\overline{5}$ $\overline{6}$ $\quad$ $\overline{7}$ $\overline{8}$ $\overline{9}$ $\overline{10}$ $\overline{11}$ $\overline{12}$ $\quad$ $\overset{T}{\overline{13}}$ $\overline{14}$ $\overline{15}$ $\quad$ $\overline{16}$ $\overline{17}$ $\overline{18}$ $\overline{19}$ $\overline{20}$ $\overline{21}$ $\overline{22}$ $\overline{23}$

$\overline{24}$ $\overline{25}$ $\quad$ $\overline{26}$ $\overline{27}$ $\quad$ $\overline{28}$ $\overline{29}$ $\overline{30}$ $\overset{O}{\overline{31}}$ $\overline{32}$ $\overline{33}$ $\overline{34}$ $\overline{35}$ ' $\quad$ $\overline{36}$ $\overline{37}$ $\overline{38}$ $\quad$ $\overline{39}$ $\overset{O}{\overline{40}}$ $\quad$ $\overline{41}$ $\overline{42}$

$\overline{43}$ $\overline{44}$ $\overline{45}$ $\overset{O}{\overline{46}}$ $\overline{47}$ $\overline{48}$ $\overline{49}$ $\quad$ $\overline{50}$ $\overline{51}$ $\overline{52}$ $\overset{E}{\overline{53}}$ $\overline{54}$ $\quad$ $\overline{55}$ $\overline{56}$ $\overline{57}$ $\quad$ $\overline{58}$ $\overline{59}$ $\overline{60}$ $\overline{61}$ $\overline{62}$ $\overline{63}$ $\overline{64}$ $\overline{65}$

$\overline{66}$ $\overline{67}$ $\overline{68}$ $\overline{69}$ $\overline{70}$ $\overline{71}$ $\overline{72}$ $\overline{73}$ $\overset{T}{\overline{74}}$ $\quad$ $\overline{75}$ $\overline{76}$ $\quad$ $\overline{77}$ $\overline{78}$ $\overline{79}$ $\overline{80}$ $\overline{81}$ $\overline{82}$ $\overline{83}$ $\quad$ $\overset{F}{\overline{84}}$ $\overline{85}$ $\overline{86}$ $\overline{87}$ $\overline{88}$ $\overline{89}$.

Review: Lessons 1-8

1   **Word Review.** Use the words listed below to fill in the blanks.

charity	fragment	memorial	pigment	schedule
decree	Iceland	New Zealand	prejudice	scope
dignity	lapse	nursery	republic	stampede

_____ 1. a minor slip or failure

_____ 2. a negative judgment or opinion formed beforehand or without knowledge or examination of the facts

_____ 3. a part broken off or detached from the whole; something incomplete

_____ 4. a place where plants are grown for sale, transplanting, or experiments; a room or area set apart for children

_____ 5. a program of upcoming events or appointments; a student's program of classes

_____ 6. a sudden headlong rush of startled animals, especially cattle or horses, or of a crowd of people

_____ 7. an island country which is a member of the Commonwealth of Nations and is located about 1,200 miles southeast of Australia

_____ 8. an island republic located in the North Atlantic

_____ 9. an order having the force of law

_____ 10. a government that does not have a king or queen

_____ 11. any substance or matter used as coloring

_____ 12. something, such as a monument or a holiday, designed or established to serve as a remembrance of a person or event

_____ 13. the area covered by a given activity or subject; the range of one's thoughts or actions

_____ 14. the presence of poise and self-respect in a person to a degree that inspires respect from others

_____ 15. the provision of help or relief to the poor

2 **Word Review.** Put the letter of the best answer on the line to the left.

_____ 1. Which animal's scent is its defense?

     (a) skunk   (b) gerbil   (c) beaver   (d) squirrel

_____ 2. Which of the following do you see least often during the Christmas season?

     (a) holly   (b) mistletoe   (c) orchids   (d) poinsettias

_____ 3. Which prices usually offer the consumer the best deal?

     (a) advertised   (b) inflated   (c) retail   (d) wholesale

_____ 4. Whose favorite pastime is eavesdropping?

     (a) sniper   (b) snoop   (c) snob   (d) snip

_____ 5. What would you purchase if you wanted to swab the deck of your boat?

     (a) broom   (b) dishwasher   (c) hoe   (d) mop

_____ 6. A candidate's interests are usually _____ .

     (a) cultural   (b) political   (c) religious   (d) social

_____ 7. If you had trouble breathing because you had a bad cold, you would probably _____ .

     (a) sniffle   (b) murmur   (c) howl   (d) whimper

_____ 8. What kind of meals might a person on a diet eat?

     (a) hasty   (b) ordinary   (c) skimpy   (d) uninteresting

_____ 9. Which people do not live in Scandinavia?

     (a) Danes   (b) Norwegians   (c) Russians   (d) Swedes

_____ 10. Drinking more orange juice than usual when you feel a cold coming on is an example of a _____ .

     (a) precaution   (b) schedule   (c) symptom   (d) theory

_____ 11. If the sight of blood makes you feel queasy, you are probably a(n) _____ person.

     (a) cowardly   (b) dizzy   (c) squeamish   (d) unhealthy

_____ 12. When two friends who have been arguing decide to "bury the _____ ," they have declared a truce.

     (a) cleaver   (b) hatchet   (c) machine gun   (d) muzzle

_____ 13. An official car usually bears a(n) _____ .

     (a) aide   (b) deputy   (c) microphone   (d) insignia

_____ 14. The country that is traditionally neutral in world affairs is _____ .

     (a) Switzerland   (b) Russia   (c) Greece   (d) United States

3 **Sound Review.** On the line to the right, write the word in which the underlined sound is different from the other words.

1. _e_qual   recip_e_   r_e_gional   s_e_nator   th_e_ater   _____

2. d_ai_ly   f_ai_thful   pl_ai_d   unafr_ai_d   w_ai_tress   _____

3. an_ch_or   _ch_rome   dis_ch_arge   me_ch_anically   te_ch_nicolor   _____

4. _th_icken   _th_orough   _th_yroid   _th_yself   _Th_anksgiving   _____

5. di_sc_   _sc_andal   _sc_ience   _sc_our   _sc_ulpture   _____

6. _ch_apter   _ch_andelier   _ch_auffeur   _Ch_eyenne   para_ch_ute   _____

7. br_oa_dcast   c_oa_ster   g_oa_d   _oa_tmeal   p_oa_ch   _____

8. _au_dience   _au_thorize   h_au_nted   l_au_ghter   n_au_ghtily   _____

4 **Word Families.** Use the words in each set at the left to complete these sentences.

apologize
apology
apologetic

1. While offering his _____ for his absence, Albert was

so _____ that his boss, who had been thinking of

firing him on the spot, experienced a change of heart and said kindly, "It's

all right; there's no need to _____ ."

disloyal
disloyally
disloyalty

2. Astonished that Charlotte suspected him of behaving

_____ , Dwight said, "If _____

means simply disagreeing with you, then probably every person you've

ever known has been _____ at one time or another."

competent
incompetent
competence

3. If you tell a person he's _____ often enough, even the

most _____ person will suffer a decline in his

_____ .

official
officially
unofficial

4. Firmly but politely, the _____ explained to the press

that the accident report was still _____ , but that he

would tell them everything as soon as the information was

_____ released.

acquaint
unacquainted
acquaintance

5. _____ with the new equipment that had been ordered

for the shop, Earl was so eager to _____ himself with

its operation that he rushed up to the special instructor as soon as she

arrived as if she were a long lost _____ .

observed
observer
observations

6. Gene was highly regarded as an _____ of human

nature because he limited his written _____ to what he

actually _____ .

residence
resident
residential

7. When asked to state his place of _____ , the hobo

cheerfully replied, "You might say my _____ quarters

are everywhere; for, I, sir, am a _____ of the entire

universe."

familiar
unfamiliar
familiarity

8. When her English professor asked if she was _____

with the old saying, "_____ breeds contempt,"

Christine responded, "No, and I'm glad I'm _____ with

it because it's the most negative expression I've ever heard."

respect
respectful
respectable
disrespect

9. Mrs. Sands always seemed _____ to the caseworkers at

the welfare department; but, inwardly, she felt no

_____ toward those who treated her with

_____ even if others claimed they were highly

_____ employees.

determine
determined
undetermined
determination

10. The _____ look in the chief investigator's eye told

everyone that he would continue trying to _____ who

had murdered wealthy Aunt Sylvia. But the guilty chauffeur was filled

with _____ that no new evidence would come to light,

and the cause of her death remained _____ .

5 **Standard English: A Review.** Each of the following sentences has four underlined sections. Choose the number of the section that is incorrect. Then circle that number in the answer row. If there are no incorrect sections, circle number 5.

1 2 3 4 5   1. <u>About</u> fifteen minutes before bedtime every evening, Johnny would come <u>in</u> the den
                  ₁   ₂

and plead, "<u>May</u> I please have just five cookies before I brush my teeth <u>since</u> I've been
            ₃   ₄

such a good boy all day?"

1 2 3 4 5   2. "For me, being single is <u>hardly any</u> <u>different from</u> being married," responded the movie
                                        ₁   ₂

star in answer to the interviewer's question, "and <u>being that</u> I've been both many times,
                                                     ₃

I don't think I'm far <u>off</u> the mark."
                       ₄

1 2 3 4 5   3. Having <u>all ready</u> called the police, Jerry decided to sit in his car parked <u>beside</u> the
                       ₁   ₂

hardware store—no matter how <u>stupid</u> he looked—until the police told him that
                              ₃

everything in the store was <u>all right.</u>
                             ₄

1 2 3 4 5   4. Mr. Madison tried to <u>teach</u> his children that <u>borrowing</u> their friends' possessions was a
                                    ₁   ₂

bad habit, but his words of wisdom had <u>scarcely any</u> <u>affect</u> on them.
                                        ₃   ₄

1 2 3 4 5   5. When the woman at the employment agency sat down <u>beside</u> Mr. Weaver to tell him
                                                                ₁

that he had <u>scarcely any</u> mistakes on his test, he was so <u>affected</u> that he looked at her
             ₂   ₃

as if he had been struck <u>dumb.</u>
                          ₄

1 2 3 4 5   6. "You may think you're healthy," cried Mrs. Jefferson to her husband in alarm, "but I

think <u>this here</u> jogging <u>around</u> the block could cause another heart attack, and I
      ₁   ₂

<u>can hardly</u> <u>sit</u> in peace until you consult our physician."
 ₃   ₄

6 **A Poet's Thoughts.** Study this poem by English poet Christina Rossetti (1830-1894) and then answer the questions which follow in complete sentence form.

Uphill
by Christina Rossetti

Does the road wind uphill all the way?
    Yes, to the very end.
Will the day's journey take the whole long day?
    From morn to night, my friend.

But is there for the night a resting-place?
    A roof for when the slow dark hours begin.
May not the darkness hide it from my face?
    You cannot miss that inn.

Shall I meet other wayfarers at night?
    Those who have gone before.
Then must I knock, or call when just in sight?
    They will not keep you standing at that door.

Shall I find comfort, travel-sore and weak?
    Of labor you shall find the sum.
Will there be beds for me and all who seek?
    Yes, beds for all who come.

1. Does Rossetti seem to think that pressures and problems are common or uncommon in life? Cite evidence from the poem to support your answer.

_____

_____

_____

_____

2. Rossetti says the difficulties that one confronts in life continue until night. But she probably is using night to represent something else. What do you think night represents?

_____

_____

Reprinted from *The Norton Anthology of Poetry*, edited by Arthur M. Eastman, et als. Copyright © 1983, 1975, 1970 by W. W. Norton & Company, Inc.

3. According to Rossetti, there will be an inn and beds waiting at the end of the journey. What do you think the inn and the beds represent?

_____

_____

4. There are two speakers in this poem. One speaker asks the questions in the odd lines in the poem. The other speaker answers them in the even lines in the poem.

   a. What kind of person do you think is asking the questions?

   _____

   _____

   b. Who do you think is giving the answers?

   _____

   _____

Unit 3
Courage

The dictionary defines courage as "the quality of mind or spirit that enables one to face danger with confidence." This group of stories features characters who display great courage in life-or-death situations.

"Nobody and the Cyclops," the story for Lesson 9, is taken from a famous Greek tale called *The Odyssey*. In this particular adventure, the hero Odysseus must outsmart a one-eyed giant who wants to destroy him and all his men.

China provides the setting for "The Old Demon," the story for Lessons 10 and 11. In this story, the main character is the oldest woman in a Chinese village. She makes a courageous decision when death and destruction threaten not only her family but also her very way of life.

Lesson 12 features the story "Who Shall Dwell..." As in "The Old Demon," a war is going on, and the main characters are forced to make some courageous decisions.

Lesson 9

Review of Vowel Combinations: Part 2

ei:	perceive	deceive	conceive	conceited	seize
ei:	freighter	reindeer	reign	neigh	beige
ie:	achieve	hygiene	grievance	wield	siege
oo:	hoop	zoom	voodoo	kangaroo	raccoon typhoon
ou:	oust	vouch	douse	spouse	arouse scoundrel
ou:	coupon	roulette	rouge	souvenir	bayou
ue:	pursue	subdue	residue	revenue	virtue
ui:	bruiser	pursuit	recruit	nuisance	

1 **Definitions.** Match the words listed below with the correct definitions.

grievance
hygiene
oust
reign
residue
revenue
siege
spouse
typhoon
virtue
vouch

_____ 1. a complaint based on an actual or supposed circumstance

_____ 2. a strong hurricane occurring in the western Pacific or China Sea

_____ 3. goodness; the quality of moral excellence

_____ 4. one's marriage partner; a husband or wife

_____ 5. the exercise of power by a king or queen

_____ 6. the income of a government from money set aside for the payment of public expenses

_____ 7. the remainder of something after removal of a part

_____ 8. the science of health and the prevention of disease

_____ 9. the surrounding and blockading of a town or fortress by an army bent on capturing it

_____ 10. to force out; to remove from a position

_____ 11. to serve as a guarantee; to furnish supporting evidence

Words for Study

Cyclops	Poseidon	savagely	horrible
Odysseus	heave	sword	grieving
Ithaca	folly	dismal	motive
Athena	companions	olive	revenge

Nobody and the Cyclops

The ships of Odysseus went on merrily, and the men thought that they would soon come to rocky Ithaca where their homes were. But the goddess Athena was angry with Odysseus, and she asked Poseidon, the lord of the sea, to send a great storm and scatter his ships. So the wind arose, and the waters of the sea began to heave and swell, and the sky was black with clouds and rain.

Many days and nights the storm raged fiercely; and when it was over, Odysseus could see only four or five of all the ships which had sailed with him from Troy. The ships were drenched with the waves which had broken over them, and the men were wet and cold and tired; and they were glad indeed when they saw an island far away. So they sat down on the benches and took the great oars and rowed the ships toward the shore.

When they had landed, Odysseus said that he would take some of his men and go to see who lived on the island. So they set out, and at last they came to the mouth of a great cave, where many sheep and goats were penned up in large folds; but they could see no one in the cave or anywhere near it. They waited a long while, but no one came. So they lit a fire and made themselves merry as they ate the cheese and drank the milk which was stored up round the sides of the cave.

Presently they heard a great noise of heavy feet stamping on the ground, and they were so frightened that they ran inside the cave and crouched down at the end of it. Nearer and nearer came the Cyclops, and his tread almost made the earth shake.

At last in he came, with many dry logs of wood on his back; and in came all the sheep, which he milked every evening; but the rams and the goats stayed outside. But if Odysseus and his men were afraid when they saw the Cyclops come in, they were much more afraid when he took up a great stone, which was almost as big as the mouth of the cave, and set it up against it for a door.

Then the men whispered to Odysseus, "Did we not beg and pray you not to come into the cave? And now how are we to get out again?" But they were shut in now, and there was no use in thinking of their folly for coming in.

So there they lay, crouching in the corner of the cave and trembling with fear lest the Cyclops should see them. But the Cyclops went on milking all the sheep, and then he put the milk into the bowls round the sides of the cave, and lit the fire to cook his meal. As the flames shot up from the burning wood to the roof of the cave, it showed him the forms of Odysseus and his companions where they lay huddled together in the corner; and he cried out to them with a loud voice, "Who are you that dare to come into my cave?"

Then Odysseus said, "We are not come to do you harm. We are Greeks who have been fighting

Adaptation of "Nobody and Polyphemus" from *A Harvest of World Folk Tales* edited by Milton Rugoff. Copyright 1949 by The Viking Press, Inc., renewed © 1977 by The Viking Press, Inc., and Milton Rugoff. Reprinted by permission of Viking Penguin, Inc.

at Troy, and we are on our way home to Ithaca."

The Cyclops frowned savagely, "I know nothing of Troy"; and he seized two of the men, and broke their heads against the stones, and cooked them for dinner. After that he fell fast asleep, and Odysseus thought how easy it would be to plunge a sword into his breast. He was just going to do it when he thought of the great stone which the Cyclops had placed at the mouth of the cave; and he knew that if the Cyclops were killed, no one else could move away the stone, and so they would all die shut up in that dismal place.

The next morning the Cyclops arose and milked all the sheep again. When he had done this, he went to the end of the cave and took up two more men and killed and ate them. Then he took down the great stone from the mouth of the cave and drove all the cattle out to graze. As soon as the cattle were gone out, the Cyclops took up the huge stone again as easily as if it had been a little pebble and put it up against the mouth of the cave; and there were Odysseus and his friends shut up again as fast as ever.

Then Odysseus began to think more and more how they were to get away, for if they stayed

there they would all soon be killed. At last, he saw a club which was the size of a whole trunk of an olive tree. Odysseus cut off a bit from the end, as much as a man could carry, and told the men to cut it to a very sharp point. When they had done this, he hardened it in the fire, and then hid it away till the Cyclops should come home.

By and by, when the sun was sinking down, they heard the terrible tramp of his feet. Later, after the Cyclops had milked the sheep and the goats and killed two more men for supper, Odysseus went toward him with a bottle full of wine.

The Cyclops drank the wine greedily and said, "Tell me your name, for I should like to do you a kindness for giving me this wine."

Then Odysseus said, "O Cyclops, my name is Nobody."

And the Cyclops said, "Very well, I shall eat up Nobody last of all." Then he was so stupid with all he had been eating and drinking that he could say no more, but fell fast asleep.

Odysseus cried to his friends, "Now is the time. We will punish this Cyclops for all that he has done." He took the piece of olive tree and put it into the fire till it almost burst into a flame. Then he and two of his men went and stood over the Cyclops and pushed the burning wood into his one great eye as hard and as far down as they could. It was a terrible sight to see.

Cyclops roared out for help to his friends who lived on the hills round about. His roar was as deep and loud as the roar of twenty lions. His friends, when they heard him shouting so loud, went to the cave and stood outside the great stone. "Why have you waked us up in the middle of the night with all this noise?" they asked.

And the Cyclops said, "Nobody, my friends, is killing me by craft and force."

When the others heard this they were angry and said, "Well, then, if nobody is killing you, why do you roar so?" And they walked off to their beds and left the Cyclops to make as much noise as he pleased.

The Cyclops got up at last, moaning and groaning with the dreadful pain, and groped his way to the door. Then he took down the great stone and sat with arms stretched out wide, saying to himself, "Now I shall be sure to catch them, for no one can get out without passing me."

But Odysseus was too clever for him. For he went quietly and fastened the great rams of the Cyclops together with long bands of willow. He tied them together by threes, and under the stomach of the middle one he tied one of his men, until he had fastened them all up safely. Then he went and caught hold of the largest ram of all, and clung on with his hands to the thick wool underneath his stomach. And so they waited in great fright, lest after all the giant might catch and kill them.

At last the pale light of the morning came into the eastern sky, and very soon the sheep and the goats began to go out of the cave. The Cyclops passed his hands over the backs of all the sheep as they passed by, but he did not feel the willow bands, because their wool was long and thick, and he never thought that anyone would be tied up underneath their stomachs.

Last of all came the great ram to which Odysseus was clinging. When the Cyclops passed his hand over his back, he stroked him gently and said, "Is there something the matter with you, too, as there is your master? You were always the first to go out of the cave, and now today for the first time you are the last. I am sure that horrible Nobody is at the bottom of all this. Ah, old ram, perhaps it is that you are sorry for your master, whose eye Nobody has put out! I wish you could speak like a man and tell me where he is. If I could catch him, I would take care that he never got away again, and then I should have some comfort for all the evil which Nobody has done to me." So he sent the ram on.

And when he had gone a little way from the cave, Odysseus got up from under the ram and went and untied all his friends who were very glad to be free once more. But they could not help grieving when they thought of the men whom the Cyclops had killed. Odysseus told them to make haste and drive as many of the sheep and goats as they could to the ships.

So they drove them down to the shore and hurried them into the ships and began to row away. Soon, they would have been out of the reach of the Cyclops if Odysseus could only have held his tongue. But he was so angry himself that he thought he would like to make the Cyclops also still more angry, so he shouted to him, "If anyone asks you how you lost your eye, remember, O Cyclops, to say that you were made blind by Odysseus who lives in Ithaca."

Terrible indeed was the fury of the Cyclops when he heard this, and he took up a great rock and hurled it high into the air with all his might. It fell just behind the ship of Odysseus: up rose the water and drenched Odysseus and all his people and almost sank the ship under the sea. Though the Cyclops hurled more rocks after them, they now fell far behind the fast-moving ship and did the men no harm. But even when they had rowed a long way, they could still see the Cyclops standing on the high cliffs and shaking his hands at them in rage and pain. But no one came to help him for all his shouting, because he had told his friends that Nobody was doing him harm.

2 **Understanding the Story.** Put the letter of the correct answer on the line to the left.

_____ 1. Odysseus and his men have come to the island of the Cyclops because _____ .

(a) Athena, angry with Odysseus, is having him punished
(b) they want to see the Cyclops
(c) they are in search of fresh supplies
(d) they are exhausted from the war and need to rest

_____ 2. Upon seeing the island, Odysseus and his men feel _____ .

(a) curious   (b) disappointed   (c) grateful   (d) uncertain

_____ 3. The men begin to feel frightened when the Cyclops _____ .

(a) approaches the cave
(b) breaks a few of their heads
(c) declares he has never heard of Troy
(d) rolls a stone against the door of the cave

_____ 4. Which description does not apply to the Cyclops?

(a) flesh-eater   (b) shepherd   (c) god   (d) giant

_____ 5. _Folly_ in the sentence "... and there was no use in thinking of their folly..." means _____ .

(a) competent behavior
(b) cowardly behavior
(c) disgraceful behavior
(d) foolish behavior

_____ 6. The fact that Odysseus tells the Cyclops that his name is Nobody indicates that Odysseus is _____ .

(a) absent-minded   (b) sly   (c) indignant   (d) frustrated

_____ 7. To escape the danger into which he has put his men, Odysseus depends on his _____ .

(a) knowledge   (b) strength   (c) weapons   (d) wits

_____ 8. When Odysseus is in the cave, he does not kill the Cyclops because _____ .

(a) he has no opportunity to do so
(b) he is a peace-loving man
(c) it would be folly to do so
(d) the Cyclops is too strong for him.

_____ 9. As Odysseus and his men escape the Cyclops, Odysseus's motive for shouting to him is _____ .

(a) revenge   (b) arrogance   (c) protection   (d) determination.

3 **More about Odysseus.** Use the words listed below to complete these paragraphs about Odysseus correctly.

character	Homer's	myth	portrayed	scholars
hero	journeying	ninth	probably	shrewd
Homer	however	noble	recounts	twelfth

Odysseus is the _____ of a long Greek poem called the *Odyssey*. The word *odyssey* means an adventurous and long wandering. Although it is not known for certain, _____ believe that the *Odyssey* was written by _____ , a blind Greek poet who lived in the _____ century B.C.

The *Odyssey* _____ the adventures of Odysseus and his men who are _____ home to Ithaca after having fought in the Trojan War. Although the *Odyssey* is a _____ , there actually was a Trojan War, which was _____ fought near the beginning of the _____ century B.C.

In _____ work, Odysseus is _____ as a crafty and _____ leader, but he is also generous and _____ in his dealings with others. In the works of later writers, _____ , Odysseus is basically a very cruel _____ .

4 **Word Relationships.** On the line to the left, write the letter of the phrase that best completes each statement.

_____ 1. Whale is to mammal as ____ .

    (a) bug is to insect   (c) skeleton is to human being
    (b) cobra is to reptile   (d) wings are to bird

_____ 2. Sailor is to navy as ____ .

    (a) colonel is to rank   (c) soldier is to army
    (b) informer is to treason   (d) troop is to combat

_____ 3. Humble is to conceited as ____ .

    (a) stable is to unsteady   (c) aroused is to alert
    (b) probable is to likely   (d) subdued is·to rapid

_____ 4. Kindle is to douse as ____ .

    (a) devour is to fast   (c) parole is to pardon
    (b) loiter is to trespass   (d) scrimp is to save

_____ 5. Honesty is to virtue as ____ .

    (a) goal is to achievement   (c) hygiene is to health
    (b) truth is to lie   (d) smoking is to vice

_____ 6. Recruit is to untried as ____ .

    (a) conversation is to undisturbed
    (b) miracle is to unexplainable
    (c) predicament is to unexpected
    (d) rheumatism is to uncommon

_____ 7. Erect is to upright as ____ .

    (a) apologetic is to guilty   (c) parched is to dry
    (b) haggard is to stubborn   (d) slender is to slippery

_____ 8. Offense is to defense as ____ .

    (a) contradict is to agree   (c) siege is to blockade
    (b) moat is to castle   (d) tackle is to quarterback

_____ 9. Reign is to rain as ____ .

    (a) kingdom is to weather   (c) dough is to doe
    (b) king is to forecaster   (d) rule is to downpour

_____ 10. Yen is to Japan as ____ .

    (a) dollar is to England   (c) pound is to Canada
    (b) peso is to New Mexico   (d) rouble is to Russia

5 **More about Standard Usage.** Study each rule below and then underline the correct word in the sentences which follow it.

1. *All together* **and** *Altogether*

All together means just what the two words indicate—all the persons in a group.
Altogether means completely or entirely.

a. Gene felt (all together, altogether) bewildered when Mrs. Bacchus chose him to chair the safety committee at the plant.

b. The students were making (all together, altogether) too much noise, so the teacher told them to discuss their answers more quietly.

c. The family was (all together, altogether) when Donald announced that he intended to marry Wendy in the spring.

d. The first thing the foreman told his crew when they were (all together, altogether) was that they were (all together, altogether) wrong in thinking that he did not respect their skills.

2. *Last* **and** *Latest*

Last means final.
Latest means the most recent in a series.

a. Jenny, a great fan of "As the World Squirms," didn't learn of the leading lady's (last, latest) scheme until she returned from her trip to Austria.

b. Television stations sometimes break into the regular programs to bring viewers the (last, latest) news.

c. The scatterbrain promised himself that this was the (last, latest) time he would act without thinking.

d. "You may call these slacks the (last, latest) fashion," the woman said to the clerk, "but I call them the (last, latest) straw. I wouldn't wear them to do my gardening."

3. *Between* **and** *Among*

Between is used when only two persons or things are involved.
Among is used when more than two persons or things are involved.

a. Whenever the Monroe twins had to share a dessert (between, among) them, one did the cutting and the other got to choose the piece he wanted.

b. Only two students (between, among) the five hundred in the class failed to graduate.

c. The manager had a tough time deciding (between, among) the applicants for the job because many of them seemed able to handle the work.

d. When the first student walked into the classroom, the English professor said, "Just (between, among) us, (between, among) all the lectures I give in this course, today's is my favorite."

4. *Proceed* and *Precede*

Proceed means to go on.
Precede means to come before.

a. John Quincy Adams (proceeded, preceded) Andrew Jackson as president of the United States.

b. After Gloria finished practicing her clarinet, she (proceeded, preceded) to do her homework.

c. In a restaurant, the salad course generally (proceeds, precedes) the main course.

d. Dick (proceeded, preceded) Jane into the lobby of the movie theater and then (proceeded, preceded) to comment on how ill-mannered people were acting as they waited for the next show to begin.

6 **Gods and Goddesses.** Many gods and goddesses in Greek mythology held similar positions in Roman mythology. Use an encyclopedia or dictionary to help you complete the chart below. The first one is done for you to get you started.

Greek Name	Roman Name	Position Held
1. Poseidon	Neptune	god of the sea
2. Hades	_____	_____
3. Athena	_____	_____
4. Hermes	_____	_____
5. Aphrodite	_____	_____
6. Ares	_____	_____

Lesson 10

Review of *r*-Controlled Vowels

ar:	ark	Arkansas	article	bargain	sardine	narcotic
ar:	Gary	vary	various	wary	comparison	apparent
are:	beware	carefree	Delaware	threadbare		
er:	hermit	verdict	persuade	Mercury	proverb	eternal
ere:	mere	sincere	severe	sphere	hemisphere	
ir:	irk	irksome	virgin	Virginia	circuit	
or:	adore	corridor	torture	Oregon	fortunate	
ur:	lurk	furnace	Saturn	urban	rural	

1 **Definitions**. Match the words listed below with the correct definitions.

hermit
irksome
lurk
Mercury
narcotic
proverb
rural
Saturn
threadbare
urban
vary
wary

_____ 1. a person who, withdrawn from society, lives alone

_____ 2. a saying expressing a well-known truth or fact

_____ 3. any drug that dulls the senses and with prolonged use can become an addiction

_____ 4. causing annoyance or bother; boring

_____ 5. characteristic of the city or city life

_____ 6. related to the country as opposed to the city

_____ 7. on one's guard; cautious; watchful

_____ 8. shabby; wearing old, shabby clothing

_____ 9. the sixth planet from the sun and the second-largest. It has nine satellites and is encircled by a system of rings composed of many small, solid bodies.

_____ 10. the smallest planet and the one nearest the sun

_____ 11. to lie in wait, as in ambush; to sneak or slink

_____ 12. to make or cause changes in characteristics

Words for Study

demon	purgatory	populated
Wang	coaxingly	suitable
bamboo	severely	Buddhism
eaves	hesitated	traditional
Buddhist	bandits	India

The Old Demon: Part I

by Pearl S. Buck

Old Mrs. Wang knew, of course, that there was a war. Everybody had known for a long time that there was war going on and that Japanese were killing Chinese. But still it was not real and no more than hearsay since none of the Wangs had been killed. The Village of Three Mile Wangs on the flat banks of the Yellow River, which was old Mrs. Wang's clan village, had never even seen a Japanese. This was how they came to be talking about Japanese at all.

It was evening and early summer, and after her supper Mrs. Wang had climbed the dike steps, as she did every day, to see how high the river had risen. She was much more afraid of the river than of the Japanese. She knew what the river would do. And one by one the villagers had followed her up the dike, and now they stood staring down at the spiteful yellow water, curling along like a lot of snakes, and biting at the high dike banks.

"I never saw it as high as this so early," Mrs. Wang said. She sat down on a bamboo stool that her grandson, Little Pig, had brought for her and spat into the water.

"It's worse than the Japanese, this old devil of a river," Little Pig said recklessly.

"Fool!" Mrs. Wang said quickly. "The river god will hear you. Talk about something else."

So they had gone on talking about the Japanese...How, for instance, asked Wang, the baker, who was old Mrs. Wang's nephew twice removed, would they know the Japanese when they saw them?

Mrs. Wang at this point said positively, "You'll know them. I once saw a foreigner. He was taller than the eaves of my house and he had mud-colored hair and eyes the color of a fish's eyes. Anyone who does not look like us—that is a Japanese."

Everybody listened to her since she was the oldest woman in the village and whatever she said settled something.

Then Little Pig spoke up, "You can't see them, Grandmother. They hide up in the sky in airplanes."

Mrs. Wang did not answer immediately. Once she would have said positively, "I shall not believe in an airplane until I see it." But so many things had been true which she had not believed.

"I don't believe in the Japanese," she said flatly.

They laughed at her a little, but no one spoke. Someone lit her pipe—it was Little Pig's wife, who was her favorite—and she smoked it.

"Sing, Little Pig!" someone called.

So Little Pig began to sing an old song, and old Mrs. Wang listened and forgot the Japanese. The evening was beautiful; the sky so clear and still that the willows overhanging the dike were reflected even in the muddy water. Everything was at peace.

Year in and year out she had spent the summer evenings like this on the dike. The first time she was seventeen and a bride, and her husband had shouted to her to come out of the house and up the dike, and she had come, blushing and twisting her hands together, to hide among the women while the men roared at her and made jokes about her. All the same, they had liked her.

"A pretty piece of meat in your bowl," they had said to her husband.

He, poor man, had been drowned in a flood when he was still young. And it had taken her years to get him prayed out of Buddhist purgatory. Finally she had grown tired of it, what with the child and the land all on her back, and so when the priest said coaxingly, "Another ten pieces of silver and he'll be out entirely," she asked, "What's he got in there yet?"

"Only his right hand," the priest said, encouraging her.

Well, then her patience broke. Ten dollars! It would feed them for the winter. Besides, she had had to hire labor for her share of repairing the dike, too, so there would be no more floods.

"If it's only one hand, he can pull himself out," she said firmly.

She often wondered if he had, poor silly fellow. As like as not, she had often thought gloomily in the night, he was still lying there, waiting for her to do something about it. That was the sort of man he was. Well, some day, perhaps, when Little Pig's wife had had the first baby safely and she had a little extra, she might go back to finish him out of purgatory. There was no real hurry, though...

"Grandmother, you must go in," Little Pig's soft voice said. "There is a mist rising from the river now that the sun is gone."

"Yes, I suppose I must," old Mrs. Wang agreed. She gazed at the river a moment. That river—it was full of good and evil together. It would water the fields when it was curbed and checked, but then if an inch were allowed, it crashed through like a roaring dragon. That was how her husband had been swept away—careless, he was, about his bit of the dike. He was always going to mend it, always going to pile more earth on top of it, and then in a night the river rose and broke through. He had run out of the house, and she had climbed on the roof with the child and had saved herself and it while he was drowned. Well, they had pushed the river back again behind its dikes, and it had stayed there this time.

Little Pig suddenly stopped singing.

"The moon is coming up!" he cried. "That's not good. Airplanes come out on moonlight nights."

"Where do you learn all this about airplanes?" old Mrs. Wang exclaimed. "It is tiresome to me," she added, so severely that no one spoke. In this silence, leaning upon the arm of Little Pig's wife, she descended slowly the earthen steps which led down into the village, using her long pipe in the other hand as a walking stick. Behind her the villagers came down, one by one, to bed. No one moved before she did, but none stayed long after her.

And in her own bed at last, she fell peacefully asleep. She had lain awake a little while thinking about the Japanese and wondering why they wanted to fight. Only very crude persons wanted wars.

So she was not in the least prepared for Little Pig's wife screaming at her that the Japanese had come. She sat up in bed muttering, "The tea bowls—the tea—"

"Grandmother, there's no time!" Little Pig's wife screamed. "They're here—they're here!"

"Where?" old Mrs. Wang cried, now awake.
"In the sky!" Little Pig's wife wailed.

They had all run out at that, into the clear early dawn, and gazed up. There, like wild geese flying in autumn, were great birdlike shapes.

"But what are they?" old Mrs. Wang cried.

And then, like a silver egg dropping, something drifted straight down and fell at the far end of the village in a field. A fountain of earth flew up, and they all ran to see it. There was a hole thirty feet across, as big as a pond. They were so astonished they could not speak, and then, before anyone could say anything, another and another egg began to fall and everybody was running, running...

Everybody, that is, but Mrs. Wang. When Little Pig's wife seized her hand to drag her along, old Mrs. Wang pulled away and sat down against the bank of the dike.

"I can't run," she remarked. "I haven't run in seventy years, since before my feet were bound. You go on. Where's Little Pig?" She looked around. Little Pig was already gone. "Like his grandfather," she remarked, "always the first to run."

But Little Pig's wife would not leave her, not, that is, until old Mrs. Wang reminded her that it was her duty.

"If Little Pig is dead," she said, "then it is necessary that his son be born alive." And when the girl still hesitated, she struck at her gently with her pipe. "Go on—go on," she exclaimed.

So unwillingly, because now they could scarcely hear each other speak for the roar of the dipping planes, Little Pig's wife went on with the others.

By now, although only a few minutes had passed, the village was in ruins and the straw roofs and wooden beams were blazing. Everybody was gone. As they passed they had shrieked at old Mrs. Wang to come on, and she had called back pleasantly:

"I'm coming—I'm coming!"

But she did not go. She sat quite alone watching now what was an extraordinary sight.

For soon other planes came, from where she did not know, but they attacked the first ones. When this was over, she thought, she would go back into the village and see if anything was left. Here and there a wall stood, supporting a roof. She could not see her own house from here. But she was not unused to war. Once bandits had looted their village, and houses had been burned then, too. Well, now it had happened again. Burning houses one could see often, but not this darting silvery shining battle in the air. She understood none of it—not what those things were, nor how they stayed up in the sky. She simply sat, growing hungry, and watching.

Continued in the next lesson...

Adapted from "The Old Demon" by Pearl S. Buck. Reprinted by permission of Harold Ober Associates, Incorporated. Copyright 1939 by Pearl S. Buck. Copyright renewed 1966 by Pearl S. Buck.

2 **Understanding the Story.** Write the letter of the correct answer on the line to the left.

_____ 1. The war is not a reality to the villagers at the beginning of the story because _____ .

(a) Buddhists are a peace-loving people
(b) it has not yet affected their lives
(c) Mrs. Wang is not concerned about it
(d) they have never experienced war

_____ 2. The villagers listen to Old Mrs. Wang because she is the _____ in the village.

(a) most forceful woman   (c) oldest woman
(b) most talkative woman   (d) best educated woman

_____ 3. Old Mrs. Wang _____ .

(a) has seen a Japanese
(b) knows what the Japanese look like
(c) has seen a foreigner
(d) has never seen a foreigner

_____ 4. Mrs. Wang's husband had died _____ .

(a) during a flood   (c) in a previous war
(b) during a raid by bandits (d) of natural causes

_____ 5. Mrs. Wang had decided not to pay for the removal of her husband's hand from purgatory because she _____ .

(a) did not have the money
(b) felt she had fulfilled her responsibility to her husband
(c) was angered by the priest's greediness
(d) had more pressing need for the money

_____ 6. Pearl Buck compares the falling bombs to _____ .

(a) eggs   (c) silver
(b) a fountain   (d) the dike

_____ 7. Little Pig's wife finally runs off with the others because _____ .

(a) she grows impatient with her grandmother-in-law's stubbornness
(b) she desires to be with her husband
(c) she is reminded of her duty to bear a child
(d) she is fearful of what will happen if she remains behind

_____ 8. Mrs. Wang compares her grandson to her husband in that both men _____ .

(a) died in disasters
(b) thought they knew everything
(c) were excellent providers
(d) were the first to run

_____ 9. Mrs. Wang has no understanding of _____ .

(a) bandits   (c) burning people's homes
(b) bombing   (d) looting

_____ 10. The "old demon" is _____ .

(a) death   (c) the Japanese
(b) the airplanes (d) the Yellow River

3　**What Do You Think?** Answer these questions in good sentence form. Be sure to include details from the story or personal reasons to support your answers.

1. Do you think the villagers would have acted differently if they had been better informed about the war?

_____

_____

_____

_____

2. As the war becomes an even sharper reality to Old Mrs. Wang in Part II of "The Old Demon," how do you think she will react?

_____

_____

_____

_____

4　**China.** Use the words listed at the left to complete these statements about China.

agriculture
exceeded
major
populated
suitable
vast

1. A _____ country located in eastern Asia, China is _____ in land area only by Russia and Canada. In terms of people, China is the most _____ country in the world. The people live mainly in the eastern third of the country. Most of China's _____ cities are in this region, and nearly all the land is _____ for China's chief occupation—_____ .

current
official
ordinary
previous
society
tradition

2. In _____ times, the clothing people wore indicated their position in Chinese _____ . It was a _____ among scholars, for example, to wear long, blue gowns. In _____ times, however, it is difficult to tell from a person's clothing whether he is an _____ worker or a government _____ .

fair
formal
former
ideal
legal
units

3. In _____ times, the _____ for Chinese families was "five generations under one roof;" and, until 1949, some Chinese lived in large family _____ . Relationships within the family have become far less _____ and more _____ . A father, for example, no longer has the _____ right to kill his children if they disobey him.

alphabet
characters
China
Chinese
foreigners
frequently

4. The _____ call their country Chung-Kuo, which means Middle Country. _____ was the name given to the country by _____ . One of the world's oldest languages, Chinese has no _____ . Instead, the language consists of about 50,000 _____ . A person who knows about 5,000 of the most _____ used characters can read a Chinese newspaper with little difficulty.

appealed
discouraged
standards
strife
traditional
worshipped

5. Although religion is _____ by the present government, it has played an important role in the _____ life of the Chinese people. Buddhism, which reached China from India before A.D. 100, taught not only strict moral _____ but also the ideas of rebirth and life after death. Chinese Buddhists _____ many gods and _____ to them for help during times of _____ .

Adapted from *The World Book Encyclopedia.* © 1987 World Book, Inc.

5   **Spelling Check.** Eleven countries border China. Solve this spelling puzzle to discover one of these countries.

- Use each syllable in the box only once. The number next to the clue tells you how many syllables are in the answer.

- When you have finished, the first letter of each answer, reading down, should spell the name of a capital city and the country in central Asia in which it is located.

- Study the example before you begin.

a	a	a	al	ance	ar	as	bam	boo	ca	der	dro	er	feb	gar
hear	ith	√knap	laun	lip	low	mat	men	mint	naut	net	nep	new
phe	pos	ru	√sack	say	spear	tak	ton	tro	tro	tu	tune	un	y

K n a p s a c k   1. a case or bag worn on the back, especially on a hike or march (2)

— — — — — — — — —   2. a regular sum of money given to a child, often in return for chores (3)

— — — — — —   3. a grass, the hollow, woody stem of which is used in crafts, etc. (2)

— — — — — — — — —   4. the person who makes arrangements for the dead and assists at funerals (4)

— — — — — — — — — —   5. where you might go if you don't own a washing machine (3)

— — — — — — — — — —   6. a mark used when forming contractions and the possessive case (4)

— — — — — — — —   7. the month of Valentine's Day (4)

— — — — — —   8. the birthstone for January (2)

— — — — — — —   9. information heard from another (2)

— — — — — — — — —   10. a person trained for space flights (3)

_ _ _ _ _ _ _   11. the eighth planet from the sun (2)

_ _ _ _ _ _ _   12. an island of Greece that was the home of Odysseus and his
                         men (3)

_ _ _ _ _ _ _ _ _   13. a popular flavor of chewing gum (2)

_ _ _ _ _   14. a bright flower that is native to Asia and widely grown in
                     Holland (2)

_ _ _ _   15. a word said at the end of a prayer (2)

_ _ _ _ _ _   16. an English scholar who proposed the law of gravity (2)

Capital: _ _ _ _ _

Country: _ _ _ _ _ _ _ _ _ _ _

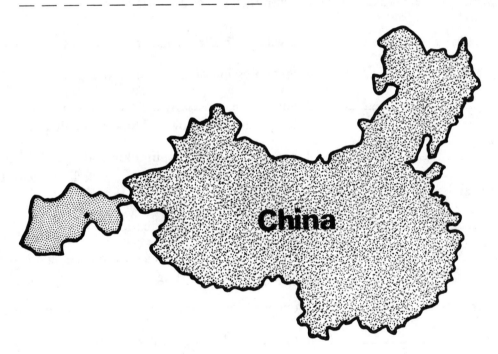

Lesson 11 _____

Review of *r*-Controlled Vowel Combinations

air:	fair-haired	millionaire	lair	prairie	impair
ear:	shears	endear	endearment	weary	bleary
ear:	earthy	yearn	hearse	rehearse	rehearsal
eer:	veer	leer	eerie	peerless	pioneer auctioneer
oar:	boar	coarse	coarsely	hoarse	hoarsely
our:	journal	courtesy	nourish	flourish	adjourn
our:	mourn	mournful	resource	courtship	gourd outpouring
our:	tour	tourist	tournament	tourniquet	gourmet

1 **Definitions.** Match the words listed below with the correct definitions.

bleary
boar
eerie
endearment
gourd
gourmet
impair
lair
peerless
tourniquet
veer
weary
yearn

_____ 1. a wild pig having dense, dark bristles

_____ 2. an expression of affection; a loving word

_____ 3. any device, especially a cloth, used to stop temporarily the flow of blood through a large artery

_____ 4. a vine related to the pumpkin and squash; a drinking vessel or utensil made from the shell of one of these fruits

_____ 5. blurred or dimmed by tears

_____ 6. mysterious; inspiring fear without being openly threatening; unsettling

_____ 7. one who knows about and enjoys fine food and drink

_____ 8. the den or dwelling of a wild animal

_____ 9. tired

_____ 10. to have a strong or deep desire

_____ 11. to injure; to lessen in strength or value

_____ 12. to turn aside from a course, direction, or purpose; to shift or swerve

_____ 13. without equal; unmatched

Words for Study

doubtless	plaster	distinctly	sluice
inert	unbearably	horizon	enfolded
Southerner	crumpled	wavered	deliberate

The Old Demon: Part II

by Pearl S. Buck

"I'd like to see one close," she said aloud. And at that moment, as though in answer, one of them pointed suddenly downward, and, wheeling and twisting as though it were wounded, it fell head down in a field which Little Pig had plowed only yesterday for soybeans. And in an instant the sky was empty again, and there was only this wounded thing on the ground and herself.

She hoisted herself carefully from the earth. At her age she need be afraid of nothing. She could, she decided, go and see what it was. So, leaning on her bamboo pipe, she made her way slowly across the fields. Behind her in the sudden stillness two or three village dogs appeared and followed, creeping close to her in terror. When they drew near to the fallen plane, they barked furiously. Then she hit them with her pipe.

"Be quiet," she scolded, "there's already been noise enough to split my ears."

She tapped the airplane. "Metal," she told the dogs. "Silver, doubtless," she added. Melted up, it would make them all rich.

She walked around it, examining it closely. What made it fly? It seemed dead. Nothing moved or made a sound within it. Then, coming to the side to which it tipped, she saw a young man in it, slumped into a heap in a little seat. The dogs growled, but she struck at them again and they fell back.

"Are you dead?" she inquired politely.

The young man moved a little at her voice, but did not speak. She drew nearer and peered into the hole in which he sat. His side was bleeding.

"Wounded!" she exclaimed. She took his wrist. It was warm, but inert, and when she let it go, it dropped against the side of the hole. She stared at him. He had black hair and a dark skin like a Chinese and still he did not look like a Chinese.

"He must be a Southerner," she thought. "You had better come out. I'll put some herb plaster on your side," she said.

The young man muttered something.

"What did you say?" she asked. But he did not say it again.

"I am still quite strong," she decided. So she reached in and seized him about the waist and pulled him out slowly, panting a good deal. Fortunately, he was rather a little fellow and very light. When she had him on the ground, he seemed to find his feet; and he stood shakily and clung to her, and she held him up.

"Now if you can walk to my house," she said, "I'll see if it is there."

Her house was quite gone. She found the place easily enough. This was where it should be, opposite the water gate into the dike.

So she went back to the young man. He was lying as she had left him, propped against the dike, panting and very pale. He was trying to tell her something, but she could understand nothing.

"You must be from the South, sir," she said. It was easy to see that he had education. He looked very clever. "You would be better with food," she went on. "And so would I," she added. She was beginning to feel unbearably hungry.

It occurred to her that in Wang the baker's shop there might be some bread.

The baker's shop was, like everything else, in ruins. No one was there. At first she saw nothing but the mass of crumpled earthen walls. But then she remembered that the oven was just inside the door. There might be some steamed bread. She worked her arm delicately and carefully in. It took quite a long time, but even so clouds of lime and dust almost choked her. Nevertheless she was right. She squeezed her hand under the cover and felt the firm smooth skin of the big steamed bread rolls, and one by one she drew out four.

"It's hard to kill an old thing like me," she remarked cheerfully to no one, and she began to eat one of the rolls as she walked back. If she had a bit of garlic and a bowl of tea—but one couldn't have everything in these times.

It was at this moment that she heard voices. When she came in sight of the soldier, she saw surrounding him a crowd of other soldiers, who had apparently come from nowhere. They were staring down at the wounded soldier, whose eyes were now closed.

"Where did you get this Japanese?" they shouted at her.

"What Japanese?" she asked, coming to them.

"This one!" they shouted.

"Is he Japanese?" she cried in the greatest astonishment. "But he looks like us—"

"Give me that bread!" another shouted.

"Take it," she said, "all except this one for him." She began to dislike these men. But then, she had always disliked soldiers.

"I wish you would go away," she said. "What are you doing here? Our village has always been peaceful."

"It certainly looks very peaceful now," one of the men said grinning, "as peaceful as a grave.

Do you know who did that, Old Mother? The Japanese!"

"I suppose so," she agreed. Then she asked, "Why? That's what I don't understand."

"Why? because they want our land, that's why!"

"Our land!" she repeated. "Why, they can't have our land!"

"Never!" they shouted. But all this time while they were talking and chewing the bread they had divided among themselves, they were watching the eastern horizon.

"They'll be coming, those little black dwarfs," they were saying. "We'd best go on."

A Japanese, was he? Old Mrs. Wang, left alone with this inert figure, looked at him cautiously.

"Eat," she said very loudly and distinctly. "Bread!"

But there was no answer. Evidently he was dead. He must have died while she was getting the bread out of the oven. There was nothing to do then but to finish the bread herself. And when that was done, she wondered if she ought not to follow after Little Pig and his wife. The sun was mounting and it was growing hot. If she were going, she had better go. But first she would climb the dike and see what the direction was.

So she climbed the dike slowly, getting very hot. There was a slight breeze on top of the dike and it felt good. She was shocked to see the river very near the top of the dike. Why, it had risen in the last hour!

"You old demon!" she said severely. Let the river god hear it if he liked. He was evil, that he was—so to threaten flood when there had been all this other trouble.

Just as she was about to climb down and start out, she saw something on the eastern horizon. It was at first only an immense cloud of dust. But, as she stared at it, very quickly it became a lot of black dots and shining spots. Then she saw what it was. It was a lot of men—an army. Instantly she knew what army.

"That's the Japanese," she thought. Yes, above them were the buzzing silver planes. They circled about, seeming to search for someone. It occurred to her that on the dike she could easily be seen. So she climbed hastily down.

It was when she was about halfway down that she thought of the water gate. This old river—it had been a curse to them since time began. Why should it not make up a little now for all the wickedness it had done? It was plotting wickedness again, trying to steal over its banks. Well, why not? She wavered a moment.

She knew perfectly how to open the water gate. Any child knew how to open the sluice for crops. But she knew how to swing open the whole gate. The question was, could she open it quickly enough to get out of the way.

"I'm only one old woman," she muttered. She hesitated a second more. Well, it would be a pity not to see what sort of a baby Little Pig's wife would have, but one could not see everything. She had seen a great deal in this life. There was an end to what one could see, anyway.

She glanced again to the east. There were the Japanese coming across the plain. They were a long clear line of black, dotted with thousands of glittering points. If she opened this gate, the water would roar toward them, rushing into the plains, rolling into a wide lake, drowning them, maybe. Certainly they could not keep on marching nearer and nearer to her and to Little Pig and his wife who were waiting for her. Well, Little Pig and his wife—they would wonder about her—but they would never dream of this. It would make a good story—she would have enjoyed telling it.

She turned to the gate. Well, some people fought with airplanes and some with guns, but you could fight with a river, too, if it were a wicked one like this one. She wrenched out a huge wooden pin. When she wrenched one more pin, the rest would give way themselves. She began pulling at it, and felt it slip a little from its hole.

"I might be able to get myself out of purgatory with this," she thought, "and maybe they'll let me have that old man of mine, too. What's a hand of his to all this? Then we'll—"

The pin slipped away suddenly, and the gate burst flat against her and knocked her breath away. She had only time to gasp to the river:

"Come on, you old demon!"

Then she felt it seize her and lift her up to the sky. It was beneath her and around her. It rolled her joyfully here and there, and then, holding her close and enfolded, it went rushing against the enemy.

Adapted from "The Old Demon" by Pearl S. Buck. Reprinted by permission of Harold Ober Associates, Incorporated. Copyright 1939 by Pearl S. Buck. Copyright renewed 1966 by Pearl S. Buck.

Understanding the Story. Put the letter of the best answer on the line to the left.

_____ 1. Mrs. Wang is not afraid to approach the airplane because _____ .

    (a) she feels she has nothing to lose by doing so
    (b) she knows the pilot is either wounded or dead
    (c) she wants to learn why China and Japan are at war
    (d) she wants to see what a Japanese pilot looks like

_____ 2. At first, Mrs. Wang believes the wounded man is _____ .

    (a) a Southerner   (b) treacherous   (c) Japanese   (d) a Chinese soldier

_____ 3. Mrs. Wang decides to fight the Japanese when she is told they _____ .

    (a) are winning the war
    (b) show no mercy toward people like herself
    (c) want the land
    (d) want to kill Little Pig, his wife, and her

_____ 4. Mrs. Wang climbs the dike to see _____ .

    (a) how close the Japanese army is
    (b) if more airplanes are approaching
    (c) in what direction she should walk
    (d) in what direction the Chinese soldiers have gone

_____ 5. In the sentence, "...a long line of black, dotted with thousands of glittering points," the "glittering points" are _____ .

    (a) airplanes   (b) rifles   (c) sunbeams   (d) tanks

_____ 6. In the sentence, "Any child knew how to open the sluice..." a _sluice_ is a _____ .

    (a) dam   (b) floodgate   (c) lock   (d) pin

_____ 7. Which statement indicates that Mrs. Wang knows she will probably die when she opens the main water gate?

    (a) "...could she open it quickly enough to get out of the way?"
    (b) "It would make a good story—she would have enjoyed telling it."
    (c) "What's a hand of his to all this?"
    (d) "...you could fight with a river, too..."

_____ 8. Which word does _not_ describe Mrs. Wang's character?

    (a) bold   (b) caring   (c) strong   (d) stupid

_____ 9. The ending of the story gives the impression that Mrs. Wang's effort to stop the Japanese is _____ .

    (a) foolish   (b) hopeful   (c) in vain   (d) successful

_____ 10. In this story, Pearl Buck probably did _not_ intend to _____ .

    (a) convince the reader of the benefits of warfare
    (b) describe the reactions of one character to war
    (c) explain the customs of the Chinese during this period of history
    (d) present information about life in China during World War II.

3   **Word Review.** Fill in the blanks in each sentence with the best pair of words. Study the example before you begin.

1. Graham had a(n) _____eerie_____ feeling that his boss's avoiding him in the workers'

   lounge was a(n) _____omen_____ that he was about to be ousted from his position in order

   to make room for a younger employee.

   (a) constant — omission   (c) eerie — omen
   (b) earthy — establishment   (d) mere — persuasion

2. "I don't know why we're _____ over whether to buy sirloin steak or shrimp for

   dinner when we really don't have the _____ for either," exclaimed Virginia.

   (a) wavering — resources   (c) contending — fondness
   (b) bickering — profit   (d) yearning — patience

3. A _____ home is referred to as a _____ .

   (a) boar's — cave   (c) swan's — stable
   (b) crocodile's — sty   (d) lion's — lair

4. The king found it _____ that his public duties demanded so much of his time that

   he had little opportunity to pursue the _____ of his sweetheart.

   (a) sickening — courthouse   (c) irksome — courtship
   (b) evident — courtrooms   (d) disagreeable — courtyards

5. Kirk had always wanted to photograph _____ , so he purchased an airline ticket

   to _____ .

   (a) Buddhists — Central America   (c) the Chinese — Kabul
   (b) Pearl Harbor — Hawaii   (d) the Okefenokee — Delaware

6. In writing her report on state capitals for history class, Jackie discovered that

   _____ was not the capital of _____ .

   (a) Salt Lake City — Utah   (c) New York City — New York
   (b) Atlanta — Georgia   (d) Columbia — South Carolina

7. Many students think that the _____ were a(n) _____ group of

   people because they are often pictured with dark clothes and grim expressions.

   (a) forty-niners — coarse   (c) frontiersmen — reckless
   (b) Founding Fathers — earthy   (d) Pilgrims — dull

8. Howard thought he had spoken _____ to the woman standing ahead of him in the line, but the _____ of her response made him wish he had kept quiet.

(a) courteously — bluntness
(b) encouragingly — drowsiness
(c) jokingly — graciousness
(d) mysteriously — feebleness

9. After having _____ a perfect swan dive, Glen _____ his hidden tension by furiously biting his fingernails as he awaited the judges' decision.

(a) achieved — bemoaned
(b) attempted — repressed
(c) completed — betrayed
(d) created — subdued

10. Kate found the working conditions at the plant _____ , but she felt _____ because of the limited opportunities for advancement.

(a) agreeable — frustrated
(b) convenient — unsuitable
(c) fulfilling — privileged
(d) specialized — unskilled

11. A(n) _____ may be _____ with people who are not reserved in their behavior.

(a) actress — unintentional
(b) hostess — unbearable
(c) housewife — uncertain
(d) prude — displeased

12. At half time, Coach McCormick tried to _____ confidence in his players by reminding them how _____ they had played the last time the two teams met, but the final score revealed that his effort was fruitless.

(a) incite — responsibly
(b) inflict — smugly
(c) insert — generously
(d) instill — boldly

4   **Words That Describe.** Use the words listed below to complete the sentences. Use each word only once.

beige	eerie	romantic	sincere
classified	feeble	scarlet	steadfast
dismal	hoarse	severe	treacherous

1. A harsh scolding is _____ .

2. Secret government papers are _____ .

3. An icy road is _____ .

4. A dreary winter day is _____ .

5. A male cardinal is _____ .

6. A honeymoon is _____ .

7. A lame excuse is _____ .

8. A loyal companion is _____ .

9. A haunted house is _____ .

10. A light brown suit is _____ .

11. An exhausted auctioneer is _____ .

12. An earnest apology is _____ .

5 **Words That *Don't* Describe.** Use the words listed below to complete the sentences. Use each word only once.

apparent	forgiving	hasty	persistent
deafening	frizzy	heartfelt	savage
distinct	generous	nourishing	unintentional

1. Perfectly straight hair is not _____.

2. A deliberate action is not _____.

3. A gentle lamb is not _____.

4. A hidden motive is not _____.

5. A phony compliment is not _____.

6. A quitter is not _____.

7. A slowpoke is not _____.

8. A tightwad is not _____.

9. An act of revenge is not _____.

10. Junk food is not _____.

11. Slurred speech is not _____.

12. The sound of one hand clapping is not _____.

6   **The Suffix -ness.** Use the words listed below to complete these sentences.

bluntness	earnestness	idleness	skimpiness
casualness	feebleness	queasiness	sturdiness
cleanliness	godliness	scornfulness	suddenness
drowsiness	graciousness	scrawniness	thriftiness

1. Paul knew from the _____ with which his girlfriend stormed out of the living

    room that the _____ of his remarks had hurt her deeply.

2. As _____ overcame Grandfather and he began to snore softly in his favorite

    armchair, Christina was saddened to see that his _____ was increasing daily and

    he would soon require almost constant care.

3. From the _____ of the meals his wife had been serving lately, Emory could tell

    that she was on another one of her _____ campaigns and was probably squirreling

    away money like crazy.

4. Although Mr. and Mrs. Kelly were impressed with the _____ of the service in the

    charming little French restaurant, their stomachs filled with _____ as they warily

    watched the waiter approach with a platter of sizzling snails swimming in garlic butter.

5. The _____ of the teenagers who hung out at the game room all hours of the day

    and night prompted much sneering and _____ from the town's older residents who

    spent all their spare time hanging out at the coffee shop next door.

6. Even her aides didn't fully realize the _____ with which Mrs. Alexander pursued

    the Republican nomination because she delivered her speeches with such _____

    that no one took her campaign seriously.

7. When Mrs. Porter compared the _____ of her neighbor's sick child with the

    _____ of her own healthy baby, she realized how much she had to be grateful for.

8. In an effort to cheer up her sister-in-law, who resented the fact that most of her day seemed to be

    spent mopping and sweeping and scouring and scrubbing, Carol said, "Now just remember, dear,

    '_____ is next to _____'."

Lesson 12

Vowels Followed by the Letters *w* and *l*

aw: awe awkward brawl tomahawk	
ew: dew pew steward stewardess	
ow: fowl scow browse trowel	
ow: widow widower bellow tow stowaway	

al: halter alternate	**ol:** jolt mole voltage bolster
al: valve balance Alps	**ol:** trolley polish volume solitaire
el: elevator relish delicatessen cello	**ul:** bulldozer pull-up full-fledged
il: jilt kilt mildew villain	**ul:** pulpy pulpit culprit cultivate

1   **Definitions.** Match the words listed below with the correct definitions.

bolster
brawl
culprit
fowl
jilt
jolt
kilt
pew
pulpit
scow
stowaway
widow
widower

_____ 1. a pleated skirt reaching to the knees, especially the skirt worn sometimes by men of the Scottish Highlands

_____ 2. a large, flat-bottomed boat with square ends, used for carrying coal, garbage, etc., and often towed by a tug

_____ 3. a long narrow pillow or cushion

_____ 4. a man who outlives the woman to whom he was married

_____ 5. a noisy fight or quarrel

_____ 6. a person accused of a crime, or a person who is guilty of a crime

_____ 7. a person who hides aboard a ship, airplane, etc., to get free passage or hide from port officials

_____ 8. a platform from which a clergyman preaches in church

_____ 9. a woman who outlives the man to whom she was married

_____ 10. any bird used as food or hunted as game

_____ 11. a bench with a back found in churches

_____ 12. to bump into; to shake or knock about; to jiggle

_____ 13. to deceive or cast aside a lover

Words for Study

interrupted	cannibal	eternity	physicists
missiles	Noah	retaliation	Truman
garments	agony	obligation	endorsed
atomic	jabbering	atom	prophesied

Who Shall Dwell...

by H. C. Neal

It came on a Sunday afternoon and that was good, because if it had happened on a weekday the father would have been at work and the children at school. The mother would have been home alone, leaving the whole family separated with hardly any hope at all. They had prayed that it would never come, but suddenly here it was.

The father, a slender, young-old man, slightly stooped from years of work, was resting on the couch and half-listening to a program of waltz music on the radio. Mother was in the kitchen preparing a chicken for dinner. The younger boy and girl were in the bedroom drawing pictures of familiar barnyard animals. The older boy was in the shed out back, cleaning some harnesses.

Suddenly the waltz program was interrupted by an announcer with a political message. The father rose, tapped the ash from his pipe, and walked lazily into the kitchen.

"How about joining me in a little glass of iced tea?" he asked, patting his wife fondly.

"If you don't think it would be too crowded," she replied, smiling easily at their old joke.

He grinned and reached into the cupboard for the glasses.

Suddenly the radio message was cut off. A moment of humming silence. Then, in a voice of barely controlled excitement, the announcer almost shouted:

"Bomb alert! Bomb alert! Attention! Attention! A number of missiles has just been launched across the sea, heading this way. Attention! They are expected to strike within the next sixteen minutes. Sixteen minutes! This is a real alert! Take cover! Take cover! Keep your radios on for further instructions."

"Oh, no!" the father gasped, dropping the glasses. "Oh, no!" His handsome face was the color of ashes, puzzled, as though he knew beyond the shadow of a doubt that this was real—but still could not quite believe it.

"Get the children," the woman screamed. Then she dashed to the door to call the older boy. Standing in the middle of the kitchen floor, her husband stared at her a brief moment, seeing the fear in her pretty face. But he saw something else, too, something other than fear. Pride. And a hatred for all people who would either make or launch a nuclear weapon.

He turned then, and ran to the bedroom. "Let's go!" he ordered. "Shelter drill!" In spite of his attempt to sound calm and make it seem like just another of the many rehearsals they'd had, his voice and manner made the children jump into instant action. They leaped from the bed without a word and dashed for the door.

He hurried them through the kitchen and sent them scrambling to the shelter. As he returned to the bedroom for outer garments, the older boy came running in.

"This is the hot one, Son," said his father quickly. "The real one." He and the boy stared at each other a long moment. Both knew what must be done. Each knew that the other would do more than his share. Yet they wondered still at the frightening fact that it must be done at all.

"How much time have we got, Dad?"

"Not long," the father replied, glancing at his watch. "Maybe twelve minutes, maybe fourteen."

The boy disappeared into the front room, going after the flashlight and battery radio. The father stepped to the closet and slid the door open. He picked up the flat metal box containing their important papers. Then he took down his wife's coat and his own hunting jacket. Draping the clothing over his arm, he picked up the metal box and the big family Bible from the table near the bed. Everything else they would need had been stored in the shelter the past several months. He heard his wife approaching and turned as she entered the room.

"Ready, dear?" she asked.

"Yes, we're ready now," he replied. "Have the kids gone in?"

"They're all down," she answered. Then she added with a faint touch of wonder, "I still can't believe it's real."

"We've got to believe it," he said, looking her steadily in the eye. "We can't afford not to."

Outside, the day was crisp and clear. A wonderful early fall day, he thought. Just right for boating on the river, fishing, or bird shooting. Who was the writer who had said about atomic weapons, "Would any well-brought-up cannibal toss one into a village of women and children?" He looked at his watch again. Twelve minutes, more or less, remained.

Inside the shelter, he blocked the door with its double-strength iron bar. He looked around to see if his family was in order and all right. His wife was checking the food supplies. The older boy was helping her. The small children had

already put their first fright behind them and were drawing pictures again.

Now it began. The waiting.

They knew, he and his wife, that others would come soon. People would come begging and crying to be taken in now that the time was here, now that the missiles had come screaming toward them, stabbing through the sky on wings of shining steel.

They had argued about this when the shelter was being built. It was her idea to share the shelter. "We can't call ourselves religious people if we don't," she stated. "That isn't what God teaches."

"No," he replied firmly. "I can't buy that." Then he thought for a moment, while he searched for the words to make her understand the truth that burned deep within his soul. "It is my family I must save, no one more. Our friends are like the people of Noah's time. He warned them of the coming flood. He told them about God's command. But he was laughed at, just as we have been laughed at for building our shelter. No." Here his voice took on a new tone, sad and sure at the same time. "It is meant that if they don't prepare, they die. I see no need for further argument."

And so, his wife had gone along with his wishes.

Now, with seven minutes left, the first knock rang at the shelter, "Let us in! For Pete's sake, man, let us in!"

"No!" shouted the father. "There is only room for us. Go! Take shelter in your homes. You may yet be saved."

Again came the pounding. Louder. More urgent.

"You let us in or we'll break down the door!"

The seconds ticked away. Four minutes left.

His wife stared at the door, lost in her own thoughts. She moaned slightly. "Steady girl," he said evenly. The children, having stopped their game at the first shouting, looked at him with fear and wonder. He glanced at his watch, ran his hands through his hair, and said nothing.

Three minutes left.

At that moment came a woman's loud voice from outside. It stabbed through him in a tender spot, a place the men could never have touched with their loud demands. "If you won't let me in," she cried, "at least take my baby, my little girl."

He was shocked by her plea. What must I do? he asked himself in agony. What man on earth could refuse a child the chance to live?

At that point, his wife rose sobbing. Before he could move to stop her, she let down the bar of the door and dashed outside. Instantly, a three-year-old girl was thrust into the shelter. He rushed to put the bar on the door again, then stared at the frightened little newcomer in quiet anger. He hated her, not for herself but because she was there in his wife's place. He knew he could not turn her out.

He tried to think. The voices outside grew louder. He looked at the faces of his own children a long moment. There were two minutes left, and he had made his decision. He wondered now that he had even thought of any other choice.

"Son," he said to the older boy, "you take care of them." It was as simple as that.

Unlatching the door, he thrust it open and stepped out. The crowd moved toward him like a wave. Blocking the door with his body, he snatched up the two children nearest him and shoved them into the shelter. "Bar that door!" he shouted to his son. "And don't open it for at least a week!"

Hearing the bar drop into place, he turned and glanced around at the faces in the crowd. Some of the people were still jabbering, still filled with panic. Others were quiet now, expecting the worst but no longer afraid.

Stepping to his wife's side, he took her hand. He spoke in a warm, low tone. "They will be all right," he said. "The boy will lead them." He grinned with understanding and added, "We should be together, you and I."

She smiled silently through her tears and squeezed his hand, exchanging with him in one brief motion a lifetime and more of love.

Then struck the first bomb, blinding them, burning them, blasting them into eternity. Streaking across the top of the world, across the extreme northern tip of Greenland, then flaming through the chilled Arctic skies, it had passed over Moscow, over Voronezh, and on over Krasny to explode high above their city of Shakhty.

The bird had been nineteen minutes in flight, launched from a bomb-blasted, burned-over missile pit on the coast of California. America's retaliation to the enemy attack continued for several more hours.

Adapted from *Who Shall Dwell...* by H. C. Neal, with permission of Scott Meredith Literary Agency, New York, New York.

2   **Understanding the Story.** Answer the following questions in good sentence form.

1. Cite three details which show that the family in "Who Shall Dwell..." is a happy one.

   a. _____

   b. _____

   c. _____

2. What are the mother's thoughts about the bomb shelter?

   _____

   _____

   _____

3. Why does the father disagree with the mother?

   _____

   _____

   _____

4. What causes the father to change his mind about "who should dwell"?

   _____

   _____

   _____

   _____

3 **What Do You Think?** Be sure to include reasons to support your point of view.

1. Who do you think shows more courage in the story—the father or the mother?

_____

_____

_____

2. Why do you think none of the characters in the story were given names?

_____

_____

_____

3. Why do you think Neal waits until the closing paragraphs to disclose the setting of this story?

_____

_____

_____

4. Does this story have less or more of an impact on you when you learn where the action takes place?

_____

_____

_____

5. Why do you think Neal mentions that the attack is "America's retaliation"? Does this affect your reaction to the story?

_____

_____

_____

4 **Proverbs.** A proverb is a short saying that expresses a well-known truth or fact. Choose the best meaning for the following proverbs and write its letter on the line to the left.

_____ 1. "You can't teach an old dog new tricks" means about the same as:

    (a) Be kind to animals.

    (b) Learn from nature.

    (c) Lightning never strikes twice in the same place.

    (d) People become set in their ways.

    (e) Time does not stand still.

_____ 2. "All is not gold that glitters" means about the same as:

    (a) Beware of false appearances.

    (b) Chase a rainbow, catch a cold.

    (c) Gold is where you find it.

    (d) Out of the frying pan, into the fire.

    (e) Waste not, want not.

_____ 3. "People who live in glass houses shouldn't throw stones" means about the same as:

    (a) Do unto others as you would have them do unto you.

    (b) People who have faults shouldn't criticize others.

    (c) If you live a stone's throw away, don't throw stones.

    (d) Soft heart, hard head.

    (e) Your mirror never lies.

_____ 4. "Don't look a gift horse in the mouth" means about the same as:

    (a) As the pony trots, the horse gallops.

    (b) Beware of Greeks bearing gifts.

    (c) Don't be too critical of a gift.

    (d) If you get a horse for a gift, feed it.

    (e) One man's horse is another man's headache.

_____ 5. "Don't judge a book by its cover" means about the same as:

    (a) Appearances can be deceiving.

    (b) Beware of strangers.

    (c) Books make the best friends.

    (d) Don't judge others unless you want to be judged yourself.

    (e) The early bird gets the worm.

_____ 6. "Too many cooks spoil the broth" means about the same as:

    (a) All roads lead to Rome.

    (b) It doesn't pay to work too hard.

    (c) The more people in charge, the less gets done.

    (d) There's safety in numbers.

    (e) Two is company; three's a crowd.

_____ 7. "Hitch your wagon to a star" means about the same as:

(a) A good cart needs a good horse.
(b) It's good to have great goals.
(c) If you live in the space age, ride a missile.
(d) Great haste wears out horseshoes.
(e) Wish upon a star for good luck.

_____ 8. "A stitch in time saves nine" means about the same as:

(a) Cheap clothes have a short life.
(b) Opportunity only knocks once.
(c) Sewing is an important skill.
(d) Take care of small problems before they become large.
(e) Waste not, want not.

_____ 9. "When in Rome, do as the Romans do" means about the same as:

(a) Do unto others as you would have them do unto you.
(b) Italian laws are strict.
(c) Make love, not war.
(d) Adjust to your surroundings.
(e) Traveling is educational.

_____ 10. "A bird in the hand is worth two in the bush" means about the same as:

(a) Birds require man's protection.
(b) Most hunters are greedy.
(c) Don't risk what you have to go after something you want.
(d) Respect nature's creatures.
(e) This exercise is for the birds.

5   **More about Standard English.** Study the following rules and then correct the mistakes in the sentences at the end of the exercise by crossing out and/or adding words as necessary.

1. Use *have*, not *of*, after *could, should, would,* and *might*.

    Right: I could have worked longer.
                   She should have gone to bed earlier.
                   It would have been better to save our money.
                   He might have enjoyed this movie.

    Wrong: I could of worked longer.
                   She should of gone to bed earlier.
                   It would of been better to save our money.
                   He might of enjoyed this movie.

2. Use *doesn't*, not *don't*, after *he, she,* and *it*.

    Right: He doesn't want to stay home.
                   She doesn't like raw rhubarb.
                   It doesn't matter to me when we leave.

    Wrong: He don't want to stay home.
                   She don't like raw rhubarb.
                   It don't matter to me when we leave.

3. Use *ought*, not *had ought*. *Ought* alone expresses duty or obligation without the need for any other word.

    Right: We ought to call home.

    Wrong: We had ought to call home.

4. Use *the reason ... is that*, not *the reason ... is because*.

    Right: The reason I didn't go to the party was that I was sick.

    Wrong: The reason I didn't go to the party was because I was sick.

5. Don't use *a* or *an* after the expressions *a kind of* or *the kind of* and *a sort of* or *the sort of*.

    Right: This is the kind of party I enjoy.
                   Charles is the sort of friend everyone would like.

    Wrong: This is the kind of a party I enjoy.
                   Charles is the sort of a friend everyone would like.

1. One reason the early Greeks couldn't go much further with their theory of atoms was because the microscope had not yet been invented.

2. It don't seem possible, but an atom is actually more than a million times smaller than the thickness of a human hair.

3. Thoughts of developing an atom bomb surfaced in the late 1890s, and if the U.S. government had not provided the money, research that was carried on during the following years might of come to a halt.

4. Some people think the United States had ought to be blamed for the current nuclear arms race, because it was the United States that dropped the first atomic bombs on two Japanese cities in 1945.

5. Alarmed by the treacherous power of their creation, some of the physicists responsible for making the atomic bomb tried to convince President Truman that if the United States were to use it in the war against Japan, it had ought to send a message of warning first.

6. The reason President Truman fully endorsed the atomic bomb was because he was certain it would not only save many lives, but also bring the war to a rapid end.

7. One of the photographers aboard the plane that dropped the first atomic bomb reported seeing a sort of a purple, mushroom-shaped cloud coming toward them.

8. The pilot of this plane served as a kind of a prophet when he prophesied that the world would never be the same again.

---

6 **Word Families.** Use the words in each set at the left to complete these sentences correctly.

rehearsed
unrehearsed
rehearsal

1. At the talent show, the _____ skits turned out to be far more

entertaining than those the performers had _____ repeatedly

during the eight-hour _____ on Saturday.

achieved
achievements
unachieved

2. Thor believed he had not _____ as much as he might have in

life because he spent more time bemoaning his _____ goals

than he did striving for new _____ .

nourishing
nourishment
unnourishing

3. The three glazed doughnuts Francis gobbled down each morning during his coffee

break were _____ as far as the nutrition books were

concerned. But as far as he was concerned, they were _____ to

his spirits, and that was the only kind of _____ he wanted.

mourning
mournful
mournfully

4. Hearing a _____ song on the radio that brought back

memories of her youth, Martha began to weep _____ ,

_____ the passing of those days which were gone forever.

apparent
unapparent
apparently

5. "If it is _____ to you that this home is falling apart while

you're off with your friends," shrieked the shrew shrilly at her husband, "then it's

_____ to me that you've lost your mind and

_____ need a psychiatrist!"

courtesy
courteous
courteously

6. Even though she feared her stomach would burst, Mrs. Court was so eager to

appear _____ that she _____ accepted a

third helping of roast beef and mashed potatoes because she thought

_____ meant always saying "yes" to your hostess.

sincere
sincerely
sincerity

7. At the retirement dinner given in his honor, the clergyman arose from his seat

and said with astonished _____ , "I _____

want to thank you for your many generous gifts, and it is my

_____ wish that you welcome your next pastor with the same

warmth with which you're saying good-bye to me."

suitable
unsuitable
suitably

8. Luke thought he was _____ dressed for the Garfield's party until his spouse told him that a tuxedo was completely _____ for watching the Super Bowl and that the clothes he normally wore on Sunday afternoon would be more _____.

persuade
persuasion
persuasive

9. Anthony had such confidence in his _____ abilities that he knew, with just a little _____, he could _____ his friends to invest in his latest business adventure.

unfortunate
unfortunately
fortune
misfortune

10. In spite of her recent _____, Rosella believed she was not nearly so _____ as her neighbor whose entire _____ had mysteriously disappeared from the family safe which, _____, he had forgotten to lock.

Review: Lessons 1-12

1   **Word Review.** Use the words listed below to fill in the blanks.

atom	eternity	peso	scoundrel
bristle	missile	prairie	sluice
circuit	motive	retaliation	verdict
delicatessen	odyssey	savage	volume

_____ 1. a book; a large amount; the loudness of a sound

_____ 2. a circular route or path; the path taken by an electric current

_____ 3. a man-made channel for conducting water with a valve or gate to regulate the flow

_____ 4. a shop that sells cooked or prepared foods ready for serving

_____ 5. a short, coarse, stiff hair

_____ 6. a vast area of flat or rolling grassland, especially the plain of central North America

_____ 7. a villain

_____ 8. a reason or cause that makes a person act

_____ 9. an extended adventurous wandering

_____ 10. an object, especially a weapon, intended to be thrown or shot

_____ 11. the act of doing something to get even for an injury, wrong, etc.

_____ 12. the basic unit of money in Mexico, Cuba, and many South American countries

_____ 13. the decision reached by a jury at the conclusion of a legal proceeding

_____ 14. the smallest unit of an element that is able to take part in chemical reactions

_____ 15. the totality of time without beginning or end

_____ 16. untouched by man and civilization; not cultivated; wild; fierce; vicious or merciless

2 Which Word Does Not Fit? On the line to the right, write the word that doesn't fit with the other words.

1. checkers	chess	Old Maid	poker	solitaire
2. damage	impair	injure	jilt	wound
3. exhausted	tired	weakened	weary	withdrawn
4. Australia	Austria	France	Holland	Switzerland
5. amazement	awe	endearment	respect	wonderment
6. earnest	qualified	serious	sincere	wholehearted
7. alert	cautious	unsafe	wary	watchful
8. bayou	bog	marsh	prairie	swamp
9. annoy	bother	disturb	grieve	irk
10. actress	hostess	stewardess	widow	widower
11. hoe	shears	shovel	spade	trowel
12. diary	journal	log	record	report
13. flourish	increase	prosper	thrive	wield
14. advertise	back	support	uphold	vouch

3 A Review of Sounds. Choose the word in which the sound for the underlined letter or letters is the same as in the first word in each row. Write that word on the line.

1. **ch**orus:	**Ch**inese	**ch**emistry	**ch**iefly	**ch**ute
2. **lowd**own:	t**ow**	t**ow**el	t**ow**er	tr**ow**el
3. **pro**ceed:	**pro**phecy	**pro**verb	**pro**sper	**pro**file
4. **reg**ulate:	avera**g**e	bei**g**e	**g**ourd	**g**ene
5. **sp**ouse:	b**ou**t	d**ou**ble	res**our**ce	s**ou**py
6. **vein**:	conc**ei**ted	perc**ei**ve	sl**ei**gh	s**ei**zure
7. **bear**d:	h**ear**se	p**ear**l	w**ear**	w**ear**y
8. **curtain**:	m**ain**land	barg**ain**	rem**ain**s	str**ain**er
9. **dough**nut:	th**ough**tless	thr**ough**	t**ough**	thor**ough**
10. **argue**:	vag**ue**	iss**ue**	leag**ue**	plag**ue**

4   What Is Often Said When... On the line at the left, write the letter of best answer.

_____   1. ...a friend explains his unwillingness to talk with you: "I just don't want to _____ you with my problems."

     (a) burden   (b) disgust   (c) shame   (d) trust

_____   2. ...a hostess accidentally drops a platter of Swedish meatballs on a guest's lap: "_____ ! "

     (a) Ah   (b) Gee whiz   (c) Whew   (d) Whoops

_____   3. ...a student does not know for sure what the answer to a question might be: "Let me make a(n) _____ guess."

     (a) awkward   (b) educated   (c) scholarly   (d) shrewd

_____   4. ...a student has _no_ idea what the answer to a question is: "It's _____ to me!"

     (a) Greek   (b) Hebrew   (c) Polish   (d) Russian

_____   5. ...a tourist in a big city observes the buses during rush hour: "How can people endure being packed like _____ into these buses day after day?"

     (a) beetles   (b) kangaroos   (c) raccoons   (d) sardines

_____   6. ...a husband and wife are quarreling about the use of the family car: "You _____ scheduled the car for the repair shop at the same time as my bowling tournament."

     (a) deliberately   (b) merely   (c) openly   (d) temporarily

_____   7. ...a candidate is running for public office: "And if elected, I promise you a _____ budget."

     (a) balanced   (b) brand-new   (c) costly   (d) decent

_____   8. ...a grandmother tries to calm her anxious daughter: "You talk as if your son invented trouble. Why, I could write _____ about all the trouble you got into at that age!"

     (a) paragraphs   (b) texts   (c) topics   (d) volumes

_____   9. ...a mother discovers that the leftovers she had planned to serve for supper have all been eaten: "Okay, who's the guilty _____?"

     (a) bruiser   (b) culprit   (c) swindler   (d) traitor

_____   10. ...a salesclerk asks you if you need any assistance: "No, thank you, I'm just _____ . "

     (a) browsing   (b) designing   (c) scanning   (d) shoplifting

5 **A Review of Standard Usage.** Each of the following sentences has four underlined sections. Choose the number of the section that is incorrect. Then circle that number in the answer row. If there is no incorrect section, circle number 5.

1 2 3 4 5   1. When Tom wanted to <u>teach</u> his younger brother how to become a shoplifter, his
                        1
older brother <u>preceded</u> to explain that this <u>sort of</u> behavior was <u>altogether</u> wrong.
                  2   3   4

1 2 3 4 5   2. "The reason I'm early," explained Mr. Washington to his bewildered boss, "<u>is that</u> I
                                                                                              1
had agreed to give my landlady a lift to her job; and, even though I <u>could of</u>
                                                                         2
suggested the bus, I <u>proceeded</u> to offer her a ride to make her feel a little guilty
                          3
about the <u>latest</u> rent increase."
              4

1 2 3 4 5   3. <u>Being that</u> the detective knew there was no sense of loyalty <u>among</u> the three
          1   2
brothers, he also knew that <u>hardly any</u> time would pass before they <u>proceeded</u> to
                                 3   4
blame each other for the robbery.

1 2 3 4 5   4. As the school nurse cleaned the student's bruises, she scolded, "You <u>ought</u> to know
                                                                                    1
better than to jump <u>off</u> the top of the slide. You <u>could have</u> broken your entire body.
                          2   3
But you're very lucky—everything seems to be <u>alright</u>."
                                                    4

1 2 3 4 5   5. "I don't think we <u>should have</u> bothered to go to that movie tonight," said Charles to
                              1
his wife. "<u>Since</u> we had <u>all ready</u> seen it once, we <u>ought</u> to have saved that money
              2   3   4
toward our vacation."

1 2 3 4 5   6. Realizing that her students were not <u>all ready</u> to take the test, Mrs. Peck <u>preceded</u> it
                                                      1   2
with a review of the material. Even so, Steven did poorly on it and <u>proceeded</u> to
                                                                         3
blame Mrs. Peck for his low grade, claiming the test was <u>altogether</u> too hard.
                                                              4

6 **On Fear and Courage.** Study the poems below and then answer the questions.

Do You Fear the Force of the Wind?
by Hamlin Garland

Do you fear the force of the wind,
The slash of the rain?
Go face them and fight them,
Be savage again.
Go hungry and cold like the wolf,
Go wade like the crane:
The palms of your hands will thicken,
The skin of your cheek tan,
You'll grow ragged and weary and swarthy,
But you'll walk like a man!

Courage
by Karle Wilson Baker

Courage is armour
A blind man wears;
The calloused scar
Of outlived despairs:
Courage is Fear
That has said its prayers.

1. In "Do You Fear the Force of the Wind?" Garland advises readers to face and fight whatever they fear. For the three characters below, describe what they fear and how they fight it.

   (a) Odysseus in "Nobody and the Cyclops"

   What he fears: _____

   _____

   How he fights it: _____

   _____

(b) Mrs. Wang in "The Old Demon"

What she fears: _____

_____

How she fights it: _____

_____

(c) the wife in "Who Shall Dwell..."

What she fears: _____

_____

How she fights it: _____

_____

2. The last two lines of Baker's poem define courage as "Fear that has said its prayers." How does this definition relate to each of the characters cited below? Be sure to include details to support your answers.

Odysseus: _____

_____

_____

Mrs. Wang: _____

_____

_____

the wife: _____

_____

_____

3. In their statements about fear and courage, do the two poets seem to agree or disagree? Be sure to include reasons which support your answer.

_____

_____

_____

_____

_____

_____

_____

Unit 4
Brushes with Death

A German writer once wrote, "All interest in disease and death is only another expression of interest in life." This statement helps to explain why the subject of death is such a popular theme among writers. In this unit, you will read about the reactions of people who believe they are about to die and see how those close to them are affected.

The reading for Lesson 13 is taken from the last act of a well-known play entitled *On Golden Pond*. In the scene you will be reading, the elderly husband suffers an attack of severe heart pain, and his wife, for the first time, fears that he is about to die.

"The Execution," the reading for Lesson 14, is based on an actual experience that happened to the famous Russian writer, Fyodor Dostoyevsky. In 1849, Dostoyevsky was sentenced to death for his political activities. The reading describes his thoughts and feelings on the day he is to die in front of a firing squad.

In "A Day's Wait," the story in Lesson 15, a misunderstanding leads a young boy to believe that he is gravely ill. This story shows us that even those closest to us can sometimes be unaware of how we are feeling.

"The Last Leaf," the story for Lesson 16, is taken from an O. Henry story of the same title. Again, the main character—this time a woman—is certain that death is near at hand.

Lesson 13

The Hard and Soft *g*

The hard **g** sounds like the **g** in *gasoline*, *gargle*, and *insignia*. It is usually followed by the vowels *a*, *o*, or *u*.

gal	wag	eagle	spigot	marigold	angle	morgue
galaxy	waggle	beagle	bigot	fungus	triangle	vogue
guidance	haggle			penguin	rectangle	fatigue
gangrene	straggle			jaguar		

The soft **g** sounds like the **g** in *Georgia, clergy,* and *shrinkage*. It is usually followed by the vowels *e* or *i*.

gel	logic	legend	bandage	sewage
gelatin	tragedy	agenda	mileage	hostage
genius	tragically	surgeon	postage	beverage
generator		pigeon	wreckage	outrageous
genuine		margarine		

---

1 Definitions. Match the words listed below with the correct definitions.

agenda
bigot
fatigue
fungus
gelatin
gangrene
generator
genuine
haggle
hostage
legend
logic
outrageous
spigot
tragedy
vogue

_____ 1. a jelly formed by boiling the specially prepared skin, bones, and tissues of animals, and used in foods, drugs, and photographic film

_____ 2. a list of things to be done, especially the program for a meeting

_____ 3. a machine that converts mechanical energy into electrical energy

_____ 4. a person held until certain terms have been fulfilled

_____ 5. a story which hasn't been proven true but is nevertheless handed down from earlier times

_____ 6. a system of reasoning

_____ 7. another word for faucet

_____ 8. a drama or story that has an unhappy ending

_____ 9. any of certain plants which include yeasts, molds, and mushrooms

_____ 10. cruel, rude, or insulting

_____ 11. physical or mental weariness resulting from hard work

_____ 12. real; not counterfeit

_____ 13. a person who does not recognize or respect the rights or opinions of other races, religions, or political groups

_____ 14. the current fashion, style, or practice

_____ 15. the death and decay of tissue in a part of the body, usually a limb, due to failure of blood supply, injury, or disease

_____ 16. to bargain over the price of something

Words for Study

Ethel	humiliated	grimaces	parlor
cottage	exits	angina	Monopoly
energetic	downstage	who'd	iodine
Parcheesi	Wilmington	moron	quaint

On Golden Pond
by Ernest Thompson

The setting is the living room of a summer home on Golden Pond in Maine. It is late morning in the middle of September. Norman and his wife Ethel are closing up the cottage and preparing to go home. Norman is 79. His hair is white. He wears glasses. He walks slowly but upright. Ethel, who is 69, is small but energetic beyond belief. They are best of friends, with a keen understanding of each other after 46 years of marriage.

Norman: Want to play a quick game of Parcheesi before we go? Loser drives.

Ethel: No. Haven't you been humiliated enough? You owe me four million dollars.

Norman: Double or nothing?

Ethel: When we get home, Norman. We've got the whole winter ahead of us.

Norman: Yes.

Ethel: Come on, let's get the other boxes, and be gone. *(She heads into the kitchen. Norman stays where he is, looking about. Ethel calls from offstage.)* Norman! Would you come here?

Norman: *(He crosses to the kitchen door.)* What is it? *(He exits.)*

Ethel: *(Offstage)* Get the last box if it's not too heavy. *(She enters.)*

Norman: *(Offstage)* Of course it's not too heavy. Good God, this is heavy!

Ethel: Tsk. Well, wait and I'll help you with it then.

Norman: *(Offstage)* You're trying to kill me.

Ethel: I've thought about it. *(She carries her box downstage as he comes out with his.)*

Norman: Good God! *(He crosses to the platform. She waits for him at the door. He moves slowly.)* Whatever have you got in here?

Ethel: My mother's china. I've decided to take it to Wilmington and use it there. *(Norman is feeling his way down the steps.)* We hardly ever eat off it here. Are you all right?

Norman: Your mother never liked me.

Ethel: Oh, stop. She loved you.

Norman: Then why did she have such heavy china? Oh, my God.

Ethel: Set it down if it's too much trouble. Norman! *(He is in pain. He leans against the couch, still holding the box.)* Norman! Put the box down!

Norman: *(He groans.)* Unh. I don't want to break your mother's china. Ouch.

Ethel: Norman! *(She drops her box with a tremendous crash. She runs to Norman. He drops his box.)*

Norman: Whoops. *(He sags against the couch, clutching his chest. She tries to hold him.)*

Ethel: Sit down, you fool. *(She helps him to the couch. He slumps.)* Where's your medicine?

Norman: I don't know. You packed.

Ethel: Oh, God! What did I do with it? I'm afraid it's in the car. *(She runs to the door and exits, her speech continuing outside.)* Which suitcase? Which suitcase? *(Norman grimaces and clutches his chest. He glances* *around the room, spots a book on the couch beside him. He reaches for it, opens it, grimaces again. Ethel runs back in with a little jar.)* What are you doing, you nitwit? Give me that book! *(She grabs it and throws it onto the floor.)*

Norman: What are you doing?

Ethel: I'm trying to save your life, damn you. Whoever designed these caps is a madman. There, take this and put it under your tongue.

Norman: What is it?

Ethel: Nitroglycerin. Put it under your tongue.

Norman: You must be mad. I'll blow up.

Ethel: Do it! *(Norman takes the pill. She kneels beside him, watching. He breathes deeply and leans his head back, his eyes closed. Ethel begins to weep.)* Oh, dear God, don't take him now. You don't want him, he's a poop. Norman? Norman!

Norman: *(His eyes closed.)* Maybe you should call a doctor. We can afford it.

Ethel: Oh, yes! *(She jumps up.)* Of course. I should have done that. Dear God. *(She rushes to the phone and dials "0".)* Hello, hello. Dear God. How are you feeling, Norman?

Norman: Oh, pretty good. How are you?

Ethel: Norman, how's the angina?

Norman: The what?

Ethel: The pain, dammit!

Norman: Oh. It's pretty good, as pain goes.

Ethel: Is the medicine doing anything?

Norman: No.

Ethel: Why don't they answer the phone?

Norman: Who'd you call?

Ethel: The stupid operator. *(Into the receiver)* Hello?...Hello? *(getting frantic)* Hello, hello, hello, hello, hello, hello! Whatever is the matter with her?

Norman: She's slow.

Ethel: How do you feel now?

Norman: I don't know.

Ethel: Are you planning to die? Is that what you're up to? Well, while I'm waiting for this moron to answer the phone, let me just say something to you, Norman Thayer, Junior. I would rather you didn't.

Norman: Really?

Ethel: Yes! This stupid, stupid, woman. I'm going to have to call a hospital directly. *(She slams down the phone, and pulls out the phone*

book.) Where do you look for hospitals? Yellow pages. Hospital, hospital. They're not listed. Oh, wait....

Norman: Ethel.

Ethel: *(Fearing the worst)* Yes! What is it!?

Norman: Come here.

Ethel: Oh, God. *(She rushes over and kneels by his side.)* Yes, Norman. My darling.

Norman: Ethel.

Ethel: *(Crying)* Yes. I'm here. Oh, Norman.

Norman: Ethel. I think I feel all right now.

Ethel: Are you serious?

Norman: I think so. My heart's stopped hurting. Maybe I'm dead.

Ethel: It really doesn't hurt?

Norman: Really doesn't. Shall I dance to prove it?

Ethel: *(Falling against him)* Oh, Norman. Oh, thank God. I love you so much. *(A moment passes. She cries. Norman puts his arm around her.)*

Norman: Now my heart's starting to hurt again. *(He holds her close.)* Sorry about your mother's china. *(He pulls himself forward to look at it.)*

Ethel: You're such a poop. Sit still and don't move.

Norman: Are you mad at me?

Ethel: Yes. Why did you strain yourself? You know better.

Norman: I was showing off. Trying to turn you on.

Ethel: Well, you succeeded. There's no need for you to try that sort of thing again.

Norman: Good.

(For a long moment they sit without moving. She stares at him as though she's trying to memorize him. He smiles down at her. The moment passes and she glances away.)

Ethel: *(After a pause)* Norman. This was the first time I've really felt we're going to die.

Norman: I've known it all along.

Ethel: Yes, I know. But when I looked at you across the room, I could really see you dead. I could see you in your blue suit and a white starched shirt, lying in Thomas's Funeral Parlor, your hands folded on your stomach, a little smile on your face.

Norman: How did I look?

Ethel: Not good, Norman.

Norman: Which tie was I wearing?

Ethel: I don't know.

Norman: How about the one with the picture of the man fishing?

Ethel: Shut up, Norman. *(Pause)* You've been talking about dying ever since I met you. It's been your favorite topic of conversation. And I've *had* to think about it. Our parents, my sister and brother, your brother, their wives, our dearest friends, practically everyone from the old days on Golden Pond, all dead. I've seen death, and touched death, and feared it. But today was the first time I've felt it.

Norman: How's it feel?

Ethel: It feels...odd. Cold, I guess. But not that bad, really. Almost comforting, not so frightening, not such a bad place to go. I don't know.

Norman: *(He holds her head for a moment.)* Want to see if you can find my book?

Ethel: Here it is. *(She picks it up from the floor.)* Going to take it?

Norman: Nope. It belongs here. Put it on the shelf. *(She crosses and returns the book to its place.)* I'll read it next year.

Ethel: Yes. Next year. *(She wanders around behind the couch.)* We'll have the whole summer to read and pick berries and play Monopoly, and Billy can come for as long as he likes, and you two can fish, and I'll make cookies, and life will go on, won't it?

Norman: I hope so.

Ethel: I guess I'll go down and say goodbye to the lake. Feel like coming?

Norman: Yes. *(He rises slowly.)*

Ethel: You sure you're strong enough?

Norman: I think so. If I fall over face first in the water you'll know I wasn't.

Ethel: *(Waiting for him)* Well, go easy, for God's sake. I'm only good for one near miss a day.

---

2 Understanding the Play. Answer the following questions in good sentence form.

1. What is the cause of Norman's angina attack?

   _____

2. What does Ethel offer as the reason for having thought about death in the past?

   _____

   _____

3. What action symbolizes Norman and Ethel's hope that they will be returning to Golden Pond next summer?

   _____

   _____

4. Write a brief but complete paragraph in which you describe Norman and Ethel's marriage. Include evidence from the dialogue and their actions to support your point of view.

   _____

   _____

   _____

   _____

   _____

   _____

   _____

3 What Do You Think? According to Ethel, she thinks about death only when she is forced to—when relatives or friends have died. Norman, on the other hand, thinks about death quite often. In a brief but complete paragraph, describe which of these two views you think is a better attitude toward death.

_____

_____

_____

_____

_____

4 **Synonyms and Antonyms.** Choose a synonym to fill in the first blank in each sentence. Choose an antonym to fill in the second blank.

Synonyms		Antonyms	
aimless	eternal	ancestor	outgoing
callous	fatigued	crude	sensible
carefree	outrageous	deliberate	tasteless
counterfeit	swarthy	energetic	temporary
courteous	withdrawn	fair	warmhearted
descendant	zesty	genuine	worried

1. Dark and _____ are antonyms for _____ .

2. Everlasting and _____ are antonyms for _____ .

3. Happy-go-lucky and _____ are antonyms for _____ .

4. Offspring and _____ are antonyms for _____ .

5. Phony and _____ are antonyms for _____ .

6. Spicy and _____ are antonyms for _____ .

7. Purposeless and _____ are antonyms for _____ .

8. Shocking and _____ are antonyms for _____ .

9. Shy and _____ are antonyms for _____ .

10. Polite and _____ are antonyms for _____ .

11. Unfeeling and _____ are antonyms for _____ .

12. Weary and _____ are antonyms for _____ .

5 **Tone of Voice.** In a play, the actors and actresses use their voices to express feeling. In a story, the author must use words to describe how their characters speak. Decide which word best describes the tone of voice the characters would probably use in the following situations. Write the word on the line in each sentence.

1. "What chalk?" asked Lucy _____ when the teacher asked her who had thrown the chalk while he was writing the homework assignment on the blackboard.

   (a) aimlessly   (b) energetically   (c) hopefully   (d) innocently

2. Enjoying the puzzled look on her niece's face, Aunt Rose added _____ , "This discussion will make perfect sense to you when you read the letter that's waiting for you at your apartment."

   (a) automatically   (b) fearfully   (c) mysteriously   (d) impatiently

3. "Come on, baby," the teamster said _____ as he tried again and again to start the engine. "Just one more haul. I know you can do it."

   (a) abruptly   (b) coaxingly   (c) negatively   (d) resentfully

4. As the recruit fought back his tears, the veteran said _____ , "Come on, son, it's not that bad. Before you know it, you'll be an old hand at all of this."

   (a) bossily   (b) encouragingly   (c) jokingly   (d) nastily

5. Mounting his horse, the sheriff _____ told his deputy, "I'll get that scoundrel if it's the last thing I do."

   (a) grimly   (b) indifferently   (c) thoughtfully   (d) wishfully

6. "But why can't I try out for the hockey team?" asked the boy _____ , even though his parents seemed to consider the issue closed.

   (a) persistently   (b) practically   (c) precisely   (d) privately

7. "Good afternoon, gentlemen," said the governor _____ , because he didn't want to give the reporters the impression he was "just one of the boys."

   (a) casually   (b) impolitely   (c) formally   (d) traditionally

8. "All right! All right! You can use my stereo for the party," said Herbert's cousin

_____ . "But don't expect another favor from me for the rest of your life!"

   (a) gleefully   (b) grudgingly   (c) tenderly   (d) treacherously

9. "An ounce of prevention is worth a pound of cure," said Gary's grandmother _____

when the four-year-old demanded to know why she had put iodine on his cut.

   (a) dreamily   (b) foolishly   (c) guiltily   (d) wisely

10. "Yes, sweetheart, I heard every word you said," replied Annabel's spouse _____ , as

he patted her hand and continued reading the account of last night's basketball game in the *Tribune*.

   (a) absent-mindedly   (b) frankly   (c) regretfully   (d) spitefully

6 **Vacations around the World.** Norman and Ethel enjoyed vacationing at Golden
   Pond, Maine. Use the place names listed below to identify where other people want
   to spend their vacations. A good dictionary can help you find most, but not all, of
   the answers.

Amsterdam	Boston	Jamestown
Atlantic City	Dead Sea	Las Vegas
Austria	Greece	Philadelphia
Bethlehem	Hawaii	Utah
Black Sea	Ireland	Washington, D.C.

1. The Joneses planned to visit _____ on the next three-day holiday weekend
   because, although they had lived in Massachusetts all their lives, they had never toured the
   state capital.

2. Mr. Beaumont decided to visit _____ on his way from Missouri to Seattle
   because he was curious to see what a casino was like.

3. Mr. Rogers decided a vacation in _____ , the "City of Brotherly Love," was just
   the thing to lift his spirits and help him forget the strife he felt at work.

4. Grace's fond memories of Monopoly made her want to go to _____ to take a
   walk on the Boardwalk.

5. Adam bought an airline ticket to _____ so he could become better acquainted
   with Holland and enjoy the vast fields of tulips.

6. Dr. Miller made reservations at an inexpensive hotel in _____ so that he could
   do some research at the Library of Congress during winter recess.

7. Mr. Colt arranged a class field trip to _____ , the first permanent English colony in the U.S., so that his students could get a better understanding of it.

8. The _____ is a popular vacation spot for beach-lovers in the Soviet Union.

9. _____ was Phil's favorite place to vacation in the British Isles, mainly because of the quaint and lively pubs found there.

10. When Nancy told her brother that she was going to fly to _____ , he asked her to send him a postcard of the Great Salt Lake.

11. Mrs. Monroe wanted to spend her vacation in _____ , because she longed to ski in the scenic Alps.

12. When Helen won a one-week, all-expenses-paid trip to _____ she could hardly believe that she was, at last, going to visit the home of Aesop and Homer.

13. Having read books about the scrolls found near the _____ which shed light on Jewish customs in the first century A.D., Mr. Isaacs hoped that, by setting aside money from each paycheck, he could actually be there during Passover.

14. "All right! All right! We'll take a cruise to _____ to celebrate my retirement. But, just don't enroll me in any of those silly hula contests!" said Mr. Campbell to his wife at the end of a lengthy argument.

15. Constance and her family were looking forward to joining thousands of other pilgrims to celebrate Christmas in _____ , the town of Jesus's birth.

Lesson 14

The Hard and Soft c

The hard **c** sounds like the **c** in c̲ushion, c̲omparison, and Arc̲tic. It is usually followed by the vowels *a*, *o*, or *u*.

carnival	column	calculate	Jacob	encamp	fabric
canal	columnist	calculator	vacuum	encase	tonic
canary			calculation	zinc	terrific
cavity			mimic		
comedy				majestic	
cuckoo					
casualty					

The soft **c** sounds like the **c** in c̲emetery, c̲ensus, and inc̲ident. It is usually followed by the vowels *e* or *i*.

cement	celery	reception	icily	malice
ceremony	celebration	receptionist	Sicily	jaundice
cedar	celebrity		larceny	noticeable
censor			menace	
censorship				
	citrus	discipline		
	civil	disciple		
	civilian			

1 **Definitions.** Match the words listed below with the correct definitions.

cavity
citrus
civilian
columnist
disciple
fabric
jaundice
larceny
majestic
malice
menace
mimic
Sicily
tonic
vacuum
zinc

_____ 1. a bluish-white chemical element which is used as a protective coating for iron

_____ 2. a condition in which the eyeballs, the skin, and the urine become abnormally yellow as a result of bile pigments in the blood

_____ 3. a hole or hollow place; a hollow place in a tooth, especially when caused by decay

_____ 4. a material made from threads or fibers by weaving, knitting, felting, etc.

_____ 5. anything, as certain medicines, supposed to make a person feel better or more energetic

_____ 6. a space with nothing in it at all

_____ 7. a student or follower of any teacher or school of religion; an early follower of Jesus

_____ 8. a writer of a newspaper column

_____ 9. an island off the southern tip of Italy

_____ 10. any person who is not an active member of the armed forces

_____ 11. any trees or shrubs that bear oranges, lemons, limes, or other such fruit

_____ 12. a threat; a troublesome person

_____ 13. grand; royal; having great dignity

_____ 14. inclined to copy someone else; a person who does this

_____ 15. the unlawful taking of another's goods; theft

_____ 16. the desire to harm others or to see others suffer; ill will; spite

Words for Study

execution	tzar	scaffold	crucifix
Fyodor	absolute	Gospels	tempo
Dostoyevsky	biography	proclaim	charade
condemned	biographer	wart	confrontation

The Execution

The famous Russian writer Fyodor Dostoyevsky confronted death in a way that was quite different from Norman's brush with death in the drama *On Golden Pond*. In 1849, Dostoyevsky was condemned to die for his involvement with a group that was accused of plotting against the tzar. The tzar was the absolute ruler of the Russian people.

In this reading, which is taken from a biography about Fyodor Dostoyevsky, the biographer describes the day appointed for the execution of Dostoyevsky and the other condemned men.

*   *   *

On that day which was the last of his youth, Fyodor was lying on his narrow cot when he heard steps in the corridor, whispers, the clanking of swords, sudden commands followed by the creaking of the key in the rusty lock. It was about half-past five in the morning and still dark. The door opened. In the light of a lantern, Fyodor saw an unknown officer standing there. Suddenly the officer announced that by orders of the Tzar the prisoner had been sentenced to death by shooting. The officer stepped back, the door was closed, and once more there was darkness in the cell.

Afterward, when Fyodor had recovered from the shock, he remembered that nothing had been said about when the sentence would be carried out.

About half an hour later one of the prison guards entered the cell, bringing with him a small package containing the clothes worn by the prisoner when he had entered prison eight months before. There was a thin overcoat, coat, trousers, shirt, tie, socks, heavy-soled boots. Fyodor put them on and was then led out into the courtyard. The first light was coming through the fog.

He shivered in the cold winter air. There was deep snow on the ground.

"What is happening?" he asked one of the guards.

"We are forbidden to tell you," the guard answered, and about this time Fyodor made out the shapes of five carriages. Mounted soldiers in light blue uniforms, with naked swords in their hands, came wheeling across the prison courtyard.

Slowly the courtyard was filling with prisoners. He could make out many with whom he had been arrested. They were not allowed to talk. Someone shouted that the prisoners were to get into the carriages—four to each carriage. A soldier jumped in after them. There was the crack of a whip, and soon all the carriages were rolling out of the courtyard. Fyodor said: "What are they going to do to us?"

"We have been told to tell you nothing," the soldier answered.

The glass in the carriage window was covered with a film of frost, and when Fyodor began to rub the frost away, the soldier stopped him. "Please don't do that," he said. "They'll have me flogged, if you do."

So the prisoners huddled together in silence, gazing straight in front of them or throwing secret glances at the window. It seemed an endless journey, but was in fact only three miles. At last the carriages came to a halt on the square overlooked by the Church of the Holy Virgin with its five golden domes, which could be seen dimly through the floating mist.

When Fyodor stepped out of the carriage, he realized he had come to the place of execution.

Already the crowds had gathered. In the middle of the square a small, sturdy platform had been built during the night. It was covered with black cloth which sparkled with snow. There were steps leading up to the platform. In front, a little to one side, were three thick oak stakes: to these the condemned men would be tied before they were shot.

Because the steps were narrow, the prisoners were led up to the platform in twos. Fyodor wanted to embrace the other prisoners and exchange words of comfort, but there was no time, and besides, as soon as they left the carriages they were marched to the scaffold. A priest ran before them, holding a cross and the Gospels.

The purpose of the Tzar was to instill fear in his prisoners and to torture them in such a way that they would become aware of the vastness of their crimes. Therefore, he prolonged the punishment.

Frozen, their faces turning blue, wearing only the clothes they were wearing on the spring day when they were arrested, they stood on the platform while an official proceeded to proclaim their names, their crimes, and the punishments which the Tzar in his mercy had chosen for them.

Fyodor could not believe he was going to die.. He had the curious feeling that it was all a nightmare, and very soon he would wake up. Just at the moment when he heard the words: "...condemned to death by shooting" after his own name had been pronounced, the sun came out through the mist and lit the beautiful golden domes of the Church of the Holy Virgin. It occurred to him that this was a sign that he would not die, and none of the others would die.

But by the time the official had finished reading the list, Fyodor had lost all hope. In a dazed way he observed a wart on the cheek of one of the soldiers, and then he saw a copper button shining in the sun. The fog was clearing.

The official was replaced by a priest who invited the prisoners to make their confessions.

Only one man confessed, but when the priest offered them the crucifix to kiss, they all knelt and kissed it. The priest went on to deliver a short sermon on the text: "The wages of sin is death." He spoke in a weak voice of the joys of Heaven, and the eternal joy which awaited them in the life to come.

When he had finished, two men climbed onto the platform and broke swords over the heads of all those who were noblemen, thus testifying that they no longer possessed any rights or privileges. This was the last act before the execution. In a sense the breaking of the swords was the worst punishment, removing the men from the world of honor; the actual shooting would be almost less tragic.

For a very long time the prisoners had remained on the platform, numbed and shivering, but the tempo was quickening. The men who had broken the swords left the platform, but the priest remained, muttering prayers. Another general rode up and shouted: "Father, you have done your work! There is no need to stay up there!" The priest walked down the steps.

Some soldiers then mounted the platform with the white robes in which the condemned were always clothed when they were led to their deaths. These robes took the form of white hooded shrouds with long sleeves trailing the ground.

Swords flashed, a trumpet sounded, and there was a roll of drums as three of the men were led down the steps and marched to the stakes where they were bound with ropes. Fifteen soldiers took up position. The command rang out: "Take aim!" and the soldiers lifted their rifles to their shoulders. In a moment the commanding general would shout: "Fire!" and then there would be wet bloodstains on the white shrouds.

Fyodor no longer had any hope that his life would be spared. He believed he had at most five minutes to live. In his agony he tried to imagine himself dead. It astonished him that a man could be full of life and consciousness one moment, the next moment nothing at all.

There was a strange stir on the platform. Everyone was turned and looking in the direction of an officer riding full-tilt across the square, waving a white handkerchief. The rider rode straight up to the general and handed him a sealed letter. The soldiers still had their rifles at their shoulders.

"Lower arms!" the general shouted, and then he began to read the letter he had just received, signed by the Tzar in his own hand.

The letter was very long. Fyodor listened, but he heard very little of it. Just as when he was told for the first time that he was condemned to death by shooting and could not believe it, so now, learning that he was about to be pardoned or at least to suffer a punishment less than death, he could not believe that he would be spared.

Everyone knew that the Tzar had deliberately arranged this charade to punish and torture the prisoners. Fyodor, who was tenth on the list, was sentenced to four years hard labor. Only one of the men, whose name was Palm, received a full pardon. Palm fell to his knees and began praying and exclaiming: "How good the Tzar is! Oh, how grateful I am to the Tzar!" Another of the prisoners shouted bitterly: "It would have been better if they had shot us!" but no one paid any attention to him.

For a few more minutes the prisoners remained on the platform. Some were already suffering from frostbite. All in their different ways were suffering from the fever of joy now that death had been lifted from them. They embraced one another and wept. Only one prisoner seemed indifferent, but he had in fact gone mad while he was being tied to the stake.

At last, some clothes were given to them. Having reduced the prisoners to quivering fear and shown his power over them, it pleased the Tzar to show his mercy and generosity; and he gave them new felt boots, new sheepskin overcoats, and new fur hats. Soon the prisoners were being ordered off the platform to the waiting carriages.

They walked through the snow like men walking through a nightmare. None of the prisoners recovered from the experience; they all bore the scars to the end of their days.

Adapted from *Dostoyevsky: A Human Portrait* by Robert Payne. Copyright © 1958, 1961 by Sheila Lalwani Payne. New York: Alfred A. Knopf, 1961. pp. 86–93.

2   **Understanding the Reading.** Put the letter of the correct answer on the line to the left.

_____ 1. Dostoyevsky was condemned to die because he was accused of _____ .

(a) stealing food to feed his family
(b) staying home to write books rather than going to work
(c) plotting against the Tzar
(d) failing to vote in an election

_____ 2. Which of the following is described as being worse than death?

(a) insanity   (c) prison sentence
(b) loss of noble rights   (d) torture and fear

_____ 3. Dostoyevsky temporarily believed he was not going to be executed _____ .

(a) after he had kissed the crucifx
(b) after the official finished reading the list of crimes
(c) after he observed the sun's rays shining on the church
(d) after he was taken from the prison cell and entered the carriage

_____ 4. Later, having lost all hope that his life would be spared, Dostoyevsky began to _____ .

   (a) curse the day he was born   (c) prepare for confession
   (b) think about the meaning of life   (d) notice unimportant details

_____ 5. When Dostoyevsky learned that he had been pardoned, his first reaction was _____ .

   (a) disbelief   (c) indifference
   (b) anger   (d) joy

_____ 6. One of the prisoners was indifferent to the Tzar's pardon because _____ .

   (a) he considered execution a better fate than a sentence to hard labor
   (b) he had been considering suicide anyway
   (c) he was no longer sane
   (d) he no longer valued life since he had lost the privileges of a nobleman

_____ 7. Ordered off the platform, the prisoners _____ .

   (a) joked about their confrontation with death
   (b) were anxious about what the future held for them
   (c) were grateful to the Tzar for his mercy
   (d) would always remember this experience

_____ 8. Which of the following symbolized the condemned men?

   (a) the white robes   (c) the white handkerchiefs
   (b) the Gospels   (d) the broken swords

_____ 9. Which of the following symbolized the Tzar's mercy?

   (a) the carriages   (c) new clothing the Tzar gave the condemned men
   (b) the crucifix   (d) the Church of the Holy Virgin

_____ 10. The Tzar had prolonged the punishment of the prisoners because _____ .

   (a) he loved charades
   (b) he wanted to heighten their fear and awareness of their wrongdoing
   (c) he wanted to show the public what happened to men who committed crimes
       against the state
   (d) they were noblemen who deserved greater attention than common criminals

3 **Which Word Does Not Fit?** On the line to the right, write the word that does not fit with the others.

1. Aphrodite	Athena	Hermes	Odysseus	Poseidon	_____
2. bellow	howl	roar	scream	whimper	_____
3. bandit	cannibal	hoodlum	mugger	outlaw	_____
4. courteously	earnestly	frankly	honestly	sincerely	_____
5. cube	rectangle	sphere	square	triangle	_____
6. announce	broadcast	proclaim	propose	publish	_____
7. enfold	founder	submerge	swamp	sink	_____
8. almond	chestnut	coconut	pecan	walnut	_____
9. agony	folly	grief	suffering	woe	_____
10. Denmark	Finland	Norway	Sweden	Switzerland	_____
11. cultivate	frustrate	hinder	interrupt	restrain	_____
12. bog	field	grassland	meadow	prairie	_____
13. altar	alter	pew	Psalms	pulpit	_____
14. earthquake	flood	hurricane	plague	typhoon	_____
15. absolute	distinct	pure	total	utter	_____
16. age	century	era	period	vast	_____

4 **Who Might Know Most About...?** Match each person in the first column with what he or she might know most about.

artist   _____   1. appointments and switchboards

chemist

colonist   _____   2. chords and melodies

columnist   _____   3. editors and publishers

humorist

motorist   _____   4. easels and charcoal

pharmacist   _____   5. frontiers and settlements

physicist

pianist   _____   6. gags and punch lines

psychiatrist   _____   7. good places for vacations

naturalist

nutritionist   _____   8. matter and energy

receptionist   _____   9. the cost of gasoline

tourist

typist   _____   10. keyboards and correction fluid

                        _____   11. nervous breakdowns

                        _____   12. plants and animals

                        _____   13. prescriptions and pills

                        _____   14. the composition of matter

                        _____   15. vitamins and diets

Question: Having completed this exercise, what do you think the suffix -*ist* means?

_____

5 Look It Up. To find out more about tzars, use a dictionary or encyclopedia to help you answer the following questions.

1. What are the two other spellings listed in the dictionary for the word *tzar*?

   _____   _____

2. What is a *tzar*? _____

   _____

3. The last tzar of Russia was Nicholas II. What were the dates of his life?

   _____

4. In what year was Nicholas II crowned tzar? _____

5. What were the dates of Nicholas II's reign? _____

6. What was the fate of Nicholas II? _____

   _____

Nicholas II

Courtesy of Hillwood Museum, Washington D.C.

6   **The Mystery Tzar.** The letters of the word in each box can be used to form another word. Use the clues to help you figure out what that other word is. Then, put the number of the clue into the circle. The circled numbers in each row—both across and down—will add up to 34. Write the first letter of each rewritten word on the correct lines at the end of the puzzle and you will discover the name of the tzar who ruled during "The Execution." To get you off to a good start, the first and last clues have been answered for you.

CRATE ⑯ TRACE	ASIDE ◯	THERE ◯	CANOE ◯	=34
BLEAT ◯	ANGLE ◯	STALE ◯	LEAFS ◯	=34
WEEPS ◯	SHORE ◯	CAROB ◯	SLIDE ◯	=34
TONES ① NOTES	CAUSE ◯	FLIER ◯	SHORN ◯	=34
=34	=34	=34	=34	

√1. Reminders to yourself
2. Thoughts or opinions
3. A poisonous snake of Asia and Africa
4. Goats butt you with these if you irk them.
5. The Atlantic or Pacific
6. The opposite of *most*
7. This heavenly being wears a halo.
8. What brooms do

9. This has four legs, but it's not an animal.
10. This has four legs, and it's an animal ridden by cowpunchers.
11. This knocks people out during an operation.
12. These cause a dog to scratch.
13. Wastes time
14. A gun fired from the shoulder
15. Thanksgiving favorite: cranberry _____.
√16. To outline

The Mystery Tzar:

<u>N</u> __ __ __ __ __ __ __   __ __ __   __ __ __ __ <u>T</u>
1   2   3   4   5   6   7   8   9   10   11   12   13   14   15   16

Lesson 15

The Letter y

waylay	balcony	bygone	cymbal	sycamore	cylinder	paralyze
bayonet	surgery	bylaw	Cynthia	synagogue	syringe	paralysis
heyday	sentry	cypress	cynical	sympathy	Syria	analyze
	majesty	hydrogen	hysteria	sympathetic	pyramid	analysis
	pansy	hyena	hysterical	gymnastic	crystal	
	ebony	python	hypocrite·	homonym		
						hypnotize
					Floyd	hypnosis
	pygmy				Lloyd	hypnotist
	Sydney				foyer	
	dynasty					

1 **Definitions.** Match the words listed below with the correct definitions.

analyze
cynical
cypress
ebony
foyer
hydrogen
hypocrite
sentry
Sydney
synagogue
Syria
syringe
waylay

_____ 1. a building used for Jewish worship and religious instruction

_____ 2. a colorless, odorless chemical element and the most plentiful element in the universe; its symbol is H

_____ 3. a country on the eastern Mediterranean covering about 72,000 square miles

_____ 4. a guard, especially a soldier posted at some spot to prevent the passage of unauthorized persons

_____ 5. a medical instrument used to inject fluids into the body or draw them from it

_____ 6. a person who pretends to have certain beliefs, feelings, or moral values that he really doesn't have

_____ 7. an evergreen tree growing in a warm climate; the branches of this tree are a symbol of mourning

_____ 8. a tree of southern Asia having a dark wood; the wood of these trees is used in cabinetwork and for piano keys

_____ 9. sneering; bitterly mocking; scornful of the goals or good qualities of others

_____ 10. the capital of New South Wales, Australia

_____ 11. the lobby or entrance room of a public building

_____ 12. to break something down into its individual parts in order to learn more about the nature of the whole

_____ 13. to lie in wait for and attack from ambush; to delay the progress or movement of

Words for Study

Schatz	influenza	Howard Pyle	covey	commenced
miserable	epidemic	varnished	quail	kilometers
purgative	pneumonia	slithered	springy	absolutely

A Day's Wait

by Ernest Hemingway

He came into the room to shut the windows while we were still in bed and I saw he looked ill. He was shivering, his face was white, and he walked slowly as though it ached to move.

"What's the matter, Schatz?"

"I've got a headache."

"You better go back to bed."

"No. I'm all right."

"You go to bed. I'll see you when I'm dressed."

But when I came downstairs he was dressed, sitting by the fire, looking a very sick and miserable boy of nine years. When I put my hand on his forehead, I knew he had a fever.

"You go up to bed," I said, "you're sick."

"I'm all right," he said.

When the doctor came, he took the boy's temperature.

"What is it?" I asked him.

"One hundred and two."

Downstairs, the doctor left three different medicines in different colored capsules with instructions for giving them. One was to bring down the fever, another a purgative, the third to overcome an acid condition. The germs of influenza can only exist in an acid condition, he explained. He seemed to know all about influenza and said there was nothing to worry about if the fever did not go above one hundred and four degrees. This was a light epidemic of flu, and there was no danger if you avoided pneumonia.

Back in the room I wrote the boy's temperature down and made a note of the times to give the various capsules.

"Do you want me to read to you?"

"All right. If you want to," said the boy. His face was very white, and there were dark areas under his eyes. He lay still in the bed and seemed very detached from what was going on.

I read aloud from Howard Pyle's *Book of Pirates*; but I could see he was not following what I was reading.

"How do you feel, Schatz?" I asked him.

"Just the same, so far," he said.

I sat at the foot of the bed and read to myself while I waited for it to be time to give another capsule. It would have been natural for him to go to sleep, but when I looked up he was looking at the foot of the bed, looking very strangely.

"Why don't you try to go to sleep? I'll wake you up for the medicine."

"I'd rather stay awake."

After a while he said to me, "You don't have to stay in here with me, Papa, if it bothers you."

"It doesn't bother me."

"No, I mean you don't have to stay if it's going to bother you."

I thought perhaps he was a little lightheaded and after giving him the prescribed capsules at eleven o'clock I went out for a while.

It was a bright, cold day, the ground covered with a sleet that had frozen so that it seemed as if all the bare trees, the bushes, the cut brush and all the grass and the bare ground had been varnished with ice. I took the young Irish setter for a little walk up the road and along a frozen creek, but it was difficult to stand or walk on the glassy surface, and the red dog slipped and slithered and I fell twice, hard, once dropping my gun and having it slide away over the ice.

We flushed a covey of quail under a high clay bank with overhanging brush, and I killed two as they went out of sight over the top of the bank. Some of the covey lit in trees, but most of them scattered into brush piles, and it was necessary to jump on the ice-coated mounds of brush several times before they would flush. Coming out while you were poised unsteadily on the icy, springy brush they made difficult shooting and I killed two, missed five, and started back pleased to have found a covey close to the house and happy there were so many left to find on another day.

At the house they said the boy had refused to let anyone come into the room.

"You can't come in," he said. "You mustn't get what I have."

I went up to him and found him in exactly the position I had left him, white-faced, but with the tops of his cheeks flushed by the fever, staring still, as he had stared, at the foot of the bed.

I took his temperature.

"What is it?"

"Something like a hundred," I said. It was one hundred and two and four tenths.

"It was a hundred and two," he said.

"Who said so?"

"The doctor."

"Your temperature is all right," I said. "It's nothing to worry about."

"I don't worry," he said, "but I can't keep from thinking."

"Don't think," I said. "Just take it easy."

"I'm taking it easy," he said and looked straight ahead. He was evidently holding tight onto himself about something.

"Take this with water."

"Do you think it will do any good?"

"Of course it will."

I sat down and opened the pirate book and commenced to read, but I could see he was not following, so I stopped.

"About what time do you think I'm going to die?" he asked.

"What?"

"About how long will it be before I die?"

"You aren't going to die. What's the matter with you?"

"Oh, yes, I am. I heard him say a hundred and two."

"People don't die with a fever of one hundred and two. That's a silly way to talk."

"I know they do. At school in France the boys told me you can't live with forty-four degrees. I've got a hundred and two."

He had been waiting to die all day, ever since nine o'clock in the morning.

"You poor Schatz," I said. "Poor old Schatz. It's like miles and kilometers. You aren't going to die. That's a different thermometer. On that thermometer, thirty-seven is normal. On this kind, it's ninety-eight."

"Are you sure?"

"Absolutely," I said. "It's like miles and kilometers. You know, like how many kilometers we make when we do seventy miles in the car?"

"Oh," he said.

But his gaze at the foot of the bed relaxed slowly. The hold over himself relaxed too, finally, and the next day it was very slack and he cried very easily at little things that were of no importance.

2   **Understanding the Story.** You may need to use a dictionary to help you answer some of the questions below.

1. *Fahrenheit* is the name of the temperature scale Americans use. What is the boiling point on a

   Fahrenheit temperature scale? _____

2. Which two characters in "A Day's Wait" think in terms of the Fahrenheit temperature scale? _____

   _____

3. *Centigrade* is the name of the temperature scale most Europeans use. What is the boiling point

   on a *centigrade* temperature scale? _____

4. Which character in "A Day's Wait" thinks in terms of the centigrade temperature scale? _____

5. Which character is waiting in "A Day's Wait" and what is he waiting for? _____

   _____

6. Why does Schatz think he is going to die? _____

   _____

   _____

7. Why do you think the father goes out hunting instead of staying with his son?

   _____

   _____

   _____

8. How does Schatz come to realize that he is not going to die?

   _____

   _____

   _____

9. How do you know that Schatz was feeling a great deal of tension during "A Day's Wait"?

   _____

   _____

   _____

3   **Word Relationships.** Choose the answer which best completes each statement and write it on the line.

1. Beverage is to dessert as _____ .
   - (a) cider is to pudding
   - (b) glass is to plate
   - (c) hot is to cold
   - (d) shortcake is to lemonade

2. Microphone is to newscaster as _____ .
   - (a) auction is to auctioneer
   - (b) gossip is to columnist
   - (c) nightstick is to patrolman
   - (d) tourniquet is to surgeon

3. Cobra is to slither as _____ .
   - (a) bulldozer is to swerve
   - (b) hostage is to kidnap
   - (c) prowler is to lurk
   - (d) stowaway is to stalk

4. Severe is to serious as _____ .
   - (a) fragment is to piece
   - (b) resident is to citizen
   - (c) condemn is to die
   - (d) almond is to nut

5. Unite is to divorce as _____ .
   - (a) adapt is to conform
   - (b) advise is to listen
   - (c) adore is to yearn
   - (d) alternate is to vary

6. Stalk is to celery as _____ .
   - (a) batch is to fudge
   - (b) wheat is to grain
   - (c) clove is to garlic
   - (d) quart is to milk

7. Little Rock is to Arkansas as _____ .
   - (a) Chicago is to Illinois
   - (b) Denver is to Colorado
   - (c) Detroit is to Michigan
   - (d) Wilmington is to Delaware

8. Shabby is to threadbare as _____ .
   - (a) permanent is to repaired
   - (b) photographic is to glamorous
   - (c) respectable is to famous
   - (d) traditional is to customary

9. Draggle is to straggle as _____ .
   - (a) juggle is to clown
   - (b) gaggle is to geese
   - (c) haggle is to gyp
   - (d) waggle is to waddle

10. Cowardly is to chicken as _____ .
   - (a) bald is to eagle
   - (b) friendly is to robin
   - (c) graceful is to peacock
   - (d) nutty is to cuckoo

4 **Multiple Meanings.** As you know, a word can have many meanings. In this exercise, only one dictionary definition has been given for each word. This is followed by four sentences in which the underlined word is used correctly. Find the sentence in each set in which the underlined word means the same as the given dictionary definition. Write the letter of that sentence in the blank on the left.

_____ 1. **flush:** to glow, especially with a reddish color

    (a) At first, the burglar did not see the iron safe, which was <u>flush</u> against the wall.

    (b) "..but with the tops of his cheeks <u>flushed</u> by fever..."

    (c) Each time you <u>flush</u> a toilet, five to seven gallons of water are used.

    (d) "We <u>flushed</u> a covey of quail under a high clay bank..."

_____ 2. **angle:** a scheme

    (a) Gail wanted to belong to the most popular clique in school so badly that she <u>angled</u> for their approval by treating them to sodas at the local ice cream parlor.

    (b) It was apparent from the way the shortstop <u>angled</u> his bat that he intended to bunt.

    (c) Terry would have had a perfect score on the math test if only he had recalled the number of degrees in a right <u>angle</u>.

    (d) When Phyllis told Walt that they could be rolling in money by the end of the week, he eyed her warily and said, "Okay, what's the <u>angle</u>?"

_____ 3. **credit:** a source of honor or praise

    (a) Angry that the family schedule seemed to revolve around her brother's sports activities, Joyce shouted, "You may be a <u>credit</u> to the high school wrestling team, but as far as I'm concerned, you're just a big nuisance!"

    (b) Steven realized that if he flunked chemistry, he would be one <u>credit</u> short of graduating.

    (c) When Mrs. Hunter asked her boss who had told him that they could leave work early, he confidently replied, "One of no less <u>credit</u> than the general manager."

    (d) When Gary saw the blazers displayed in Franklin's Men's Clothing Shop, he wished he hadn't lost his <u>credit</u> rating.

_____ 4. **blunt:** extremely frank and outspoken

    (a) "Don't use my good sewing scissors to clip your coupons, or they'll be too <u>blunt</u> for me to use," warned Elizabeth.

    (b) Mr. Martin had never thought of his intelligence as <u>blunt</u>, but he truly couldn't make heads nor tails out of what the radio announcer was saying.

    (c) So <u>blunt</u> were the professor's judgments that Brady was frightened to ask her opinion of a poem he had just written.

    (d) The many arguments about strategy <u>blunted</u> the commanders' spirits at the weekly staff meeting.

_____ 5. **provision:** a measure of preparation

    (a) After making <u>provisions</u> for the care of his pets, Floyd drove to the bank to purchase traveler's checks for his trip.

    (b) Because there was no <u>provision</u> in the rental agreement for the upkeep of the furnace and water heater, Mrs. Scott had to pay for the repairs herself.

    (c) Mr. Van Buck told his son that he would give him a Rolls-Royce as a graduation present on the <u>provision</u> that he never smoke again.

    (d) The pioneers waited anxiously for the supply wagon to arrive, for their <u>provisions</u> were running very low.

_____ 6. **labor:** a group of workers

    (a) After four hours in <u>labor</u>, Polly gave birth to a healthy, ten-pound, four-ounce boy.

    (b) Disheartened, Karen was convinced that even if she <u>labored</u> at the gym for two hours each evening, she still wouldn't be able to shed those extra five pounds.

    (c) During his press conference, the governor proudly pointed out that the <u>labor</u> force in his state enjoyed more benefits than ever before.

    (d) Noting that the foreman had talked about his grievance for at least twenty minutes, the worker finally said, "Uh, I think you're <u>laboring</u> the point, sir."

---

5   **Working with Measurements.** Use a dictionary to help you answer the questions below.

1. If you drove 50 miles to visit a friend, how many kilometers would you have traveled?

    _____

2. How many meters are in one kilometer? _____

3. If a parking meter were a meter high, how many inches high would it be? _____

4. What is the freezing point on a centigrade temperature scale? _____

5. What is the freezing point on a Fahrenheit temperature scale? _____

6. What is the full name of the person for whom the Fahrenheit temperature scale is named? _____

_____

7. In what country did this man live? _____

8. What were the dates of his life? _____

6 **Homonyms.** *Homonyms* are words that sound alike but are different in both spelling and meaning. Complete the following sentences with the correct homonyms.

ad
add

1. "I might _____," said Mrs. Ford icily to her spendthrift husband, "that _____ is merely a come-on; and if you fall for it, you'll just be spending more money than we already don't have."

lessen
lesson

2. "If you scholars could _____ the horseplay a bit, we might be able to get through today's _____," growled the exasperated professor.

chute
shoot

3. "_____ me if I'm wrong," said Harry to his outraged wife, "but I didn't throw your favorite velvet gown down the laundry _____."

aid
aide

4. "How do you expect me to _____ you with this project when you refuse to show me what you want?" said the _____ helplessly.

hoarse
horse

5. "If you kids continue to _____ around," said Bob in a _____ voice, "I'm going to be minus my vocal cords, and your mother's going to be minus a babysitter."

foul
fowl

6. "I thought that _____ smelled _____," shrugged the cook as she watched her employer being carried out of the mansion on a stretcher.

but
butt

7. "I don't mind being the _____ of your cynical remarks, _____ don't expect any sympathy from me when the shoe's on the other foot," Troy told his girlfriend.

vary
very

8. "If you can't _____ the menu," complained the _____ disagreeable diner, "could you at least try using a few spices to disguise the taste of this lousy stuff you call gourmet food."

ball
bawl

9. "You can't stand there and _____ your eyes out every time you hit a foul _____," the manager explained to the rookie third baseman.

weakly
weekly

10. "Well, you won't have me to kick around any more at our _____ meetings," said the principal _____, "because I've just been fired."

fir
fur

11. "How can you accuse me of not conserving our natural resources just because I bought a _____ tree? You want an outrageously expensive _____ coat under it on Christmas morning," fumed Mr. Carpenter.

shear
sheer

12. "It's _____ madness to go out to _____ sheep when you're just

beginning to recover from pneumonia," fretted the rancher's wife.

plum
plumb

13. "The reason I'm home early," Daniel explained to his mother, "is that the teacher wanted

us to learn a silly verse about a little boy who stuck in his thumb and pulled out a

_____ and when I told her she must be _____ crazy, they expelled

me from kindergarten."

cents
scents
sense

14. "It doesn't make any _____ to consider buying perfume when we have only

fifty _____ between us, so why don't we just spray the _____ on

us and then we'll be ready for our dates," reasoned Jill.

cite
sight
site

15. "I don't have to _____ all the reasons you shouldn't be hanging around our

peace-loving town," the sheriff grimly told the gang. "But if you're not out of my

_____ by sunset, this _____ will mark your last stop before the

morgue."

Lesson 16

The Sound for *ph*

phooey	graphite	Adolphe	sophomore	lymph
pheasant	graphic	Randolph	dolphin	nymph
Philippines	autograph	Rudolph	asphalt	triumph
philosophy	biographical	Joseph	pamphlet	triumphant
philosopher	autobiography	Josephine	prophecy	triumphantly
phosphorus	autobiographical	Humphrey	amphibian	
phobia		Sophie	cipher	
Phoenix		Sophia	decipher	
orphan	hyphen	saxophone		
orphanage	hyphenate	xylophone		
		symphony		

1 **Definitions.** Match the words listed below with the correct definitions.

amphibian
asphalt
autobiography
decipher
dolphin
graphic
lymph
pamphlet
pheasant
philosophy
phobia
phosphorus
prophecy
saxophone
triumph

_____ 1. a watery, yellowish liquid that contains white blood cells and removes bacteria from the tissues

_____ 2. a highly poisonous element used in safety matches, fertilizers, glass, steel, etc.

_____ 3. a mixture used in paving, roofing, and waterproofing

_____ 4. a persistent, abnormal, or illogical fear of a particular thing or situation; any strong fear or dislike

_____ 5. a prediction; the inspired speech of a prophet, viewed as a statement of divine will

_____ 6. a wind instrument having a single-reed mouthpiece, finger keys, and made in a variety of sizes (invented in 1846 by Adolphe Sax)

_____ 7. an unbound printed work, usually with a paper cover

_____ 8. any of various cold-blooded, smooth-skinned animals, such as a frog, toad, or salamander; an aircraft that can take off and land either on land or on water

_____ 9. a long-tailed bird noted for the brilliant feathers of the male, often hunted for sport

_____ 10. a sea mammal related to whales but generally smaller and having a beaklike snout

_____ 11. described in colorful detail; clearly outlined

_____ 12. a system of thought that concerns itself with truth and wisdom

_____ 13. the story of a person's life written by himself

_____ 14. to convert from a code to plain text; to decode

_____ 15. victory; success; to win

Greenwich	similar	procession	model
studio	trod	ragtime	professional
Joanna	mercury	Idaho	mingled
cafeteria	Naples	Behrman	janitor

The Last Leaf

by O. Henry

In a little district west of Washington Square, the streets have run crazy. They make strange angles and curves. One street crosses itself a time or two. An artist once discovered an excellent possibility in this street. Suppose a collector with a bill for paints, paper, and canvas should, in traveling this route, suddenly meet himself coming back, without a cent having been paid on account!

So, to quaint old Greenwich Village the art people soon came prowling, hunting for north windows and Dutch attics and low rents.

At the top of a squat, three-story brick building, Sue and Johnsy had their studio. "Johnsy" was the nickname for Joanna. One was from Maine; the other from California. They had met at an Eighth Street cafeteria and found their tastes in art so similar that they decided to share a studio.

That was in May. In November a cold, unseen stranger whom the doctors called Pneumonia stalked about the city touching one here and there with his icy finger. Over on the East Side, he walked boldly, striking his victims by scores. But, in the Village, his feet trod slowly through the maze of narrow streets.

Mr. Pneumonia was not what you would call a kindly old gentleman. He struck Johnsy; and she lay, scarcely moving, on her painted iron bedstead, looking through the small Dutch window-panes at the blank side of the next brick house.

One morning the busy doctor invited Sue into the hallway with a shaggy, gray eyebrow.

"She has one chance in—let us say, ten," he said, as he shook down the mercury in his thermometer. "And that chance is for her to want to live. This way people have of lining up on the side of the undertaker makes the entire medical profession look silly. Your little lady has made up her mind that she's not going to get well. Has she anything on her mind?"

"She—she wanted to paint the Bay of Naples some day," said Sue.

"Paint? Bosh! Has she anything on her mind worth thinking about twice—a man, for instance?"

"A man?" said Sue sharply. "Is a man worth—but, no, doctor; there is nothing of the kind."

"Well, it's the illness, then," said the doctor. "I will do all that I can do. But whenever my patient begins to count the carriages in her funeral procession, I subtract 50 per cent from the healing power of medicine. If you will get her to ask one question about the new winter styles in cloak sleeves, I will promise you a one-in-five chance for her, instead of one in ten."

After the doctor had gone, Sue went into the workroom and cried a Japanese napkin to a pulp. Then she swaggered into Johnsy's room with her drawing board, whistling ragtime.

Johnsy lay with her face toward the window. Sue stopped whistling, thinking she was asleep.

She arranged her board and began a pen-and-ink drawing for a magazine story. As she was sketching the figure of the hero, an Idaho cowboy, she heard a low sound, several times repeated. She went quickly to the bedside.

Johnsy's eyes were open wide. She was looking out the window and counting—counting backward.

"Twelve," she said, and a little later "eleven;" and then "ten," and "nine;" and then "eight" and "seven" almost together.

Concerned, Sue looked out the window. What was there to count? There was only a bare, dreary yard to be seen, and the blank side of the brick house forty feet away. An old, old ivy vine, twisted and decayed at the roots, climbed halfway up the brick wall. The cold breath of autumn had stricken its leaves from the vine until its skeleton branches clung, almost bare, to the crumbling bricks.

"What is it, Johnsy?" asked Sue.

"Six," said Johnsy, in almost a whisper. "They're falling faster now. Three days ago there were almost a hundred. It made my head ache to count them. But now it's easy. There goes another one. There are only five left now."

"Five what, Johnsy? Tell me."

"Leaves. When the last one falls, I must go, too. I've known that for three days. Didn't the doctor tell you?"

"Oh, that's nonsense!" scorned Sue. "What have old ivy leaves to do with your getting well? Try to take some broth now, and let me get back to my drawing, so I can sell it, and buy port wine for you and pork chops for my greedy self."

"You needn't get any wine for me," said Johnsy, keeping her eyes fixed out the window. "There goes another. No, I don't want any broth. That leaves just four. I want to see the last one fall before it gets dark. Then I'll go, too."

"Johnsy, dear," said Sue, bending over her, "will you promise me to keep your eyes closed, and not look out the window until I am done working? I must hand those drawings in by tomorrow. I need the light, or I would pull the shade down."

"I'm tired of waiting. I'm tired of thinking. I want to turn loose my hold on everything and go sailing down, down, just like one of those poor leaves."

"Try to sleep," said Sue. "I must call Behrman up to be my model for the old hermit miner. I'll not be gone a minute. Don't try to move until I come back."

Old Behrman was a painter who lived on the ground floor beneath them. He was past sixty and a failure at art. He had been always about to paint a masterpiece, but had never yet begun it. He earned a little by serving as a model to those young artists who could not pay the price of a professional. He drank a great deal of gin and still talked of his coming masterpiece. For the rest he was a fierce little old man, who scorned softness in anyone, and who regarded himself as the protector of the two young artists in the studio above.

Sue found Behrman smelling strongly of gin in his dimly lighted den below. In one corner was a blank canvas on an easel that had been waiting there for twenty-five years to receive the first line of the masterpiece. She told him about Johnsy, and how she feared she would, indeed, float away when her slight hold upon the world grew weaker.

Old Behrman, with his red eyes plainly streaming, cried, "Vass! Is dere people in de world mit der foolishness to die because leafs dey drop off from a stupid vine? Gott! Some day I vill baint a masterpiece, and ve shall all go away. Gott! yes."

Johnsy was sleeping when they went upstairs. Sue pulled the shade down to the window sill and motioned Behrman into the other room. In there they peered out the window fearfully at the ivy vine. Then they looked at each other for a moment without speaking. A persistent, cold rain was falling, mingled with snow. Behrman, in his old blue shirt, took his seat as the hermit-miner on an upturned kettle for a rock.

When Sue awoke from an hour's sleep the next morning, she found Johnsy with dull, wide-open eyes staring at the drawn green shade.

"Pull it up," she ordered, in a whisper. "I want to see."

Wearily, Sue obeyed.

After the beating rain and fierce gusts of wind throughout the night, there yet stood out against the brick wall one ivy leaf. It was the last on the vine. Still dark green near its stem, it hung bravely from a branch some twenty feet above the ground.

"It's the last one," said Johnsy. "I thought it would surely fall during the night. I heard the wind. It will fall today, and I shall die at the same time."

"No, no!" cried Sue. "Think of me, if you won't think of yourself. What would I do?"

But Johnsy did not answer. The most lonesome thing in all the world is a soul when it is making ready to go on its mysterious far journey. One by one the ties that bound her to friendship and to earth were loosed.

The day wore away, and even through the twilight they could see the lone ivy leaf clinging to its stem against the wall. And then, with the coming of the night the north wind was again loosed, while the rain still beat against the windows and pattered down from the low Dutch roofs.

When it was light enough Johnsy, the merciless, commanded that the shade be raised.

The ivy leaf was still there.

Johnsy lay for a long time looking at it. And then she called to Sue, who was stirring her chicken broth over the gas stove.

"I've been a bad girl, Sue," said Johnsy. "Something has made the last leaf stay there to show me how wicked I was. It is a sin to want to die. Bring me a little broth now and then pack some pillows about me. I will sit up and watch you cook."

An hour later she said, "Some day I hope to paint the Bay of Naples."

The doctor came in the afternoon, and Sue had an excuse to go into the hallway as he left.

"Even chances," said the doctor. "With good nursing, you'll win. And now I must see another case I have downstairs. Behrman, his name is— some kind of artist. Pneumonia, too. He is an old, weak man, and the attack is severe. There is no hope for him."

The next afternoon Sue came to the bed where Johnsy lay. "I have something to tell you," she said. "Mr. Behrman died of pneumonia today in the hospital. He was ill only two days. The janitor found him on the morning of the first day in his room downstairs, helpless with pain. His shoes and clothing were wet through and icy cold. They couldn't imagine where he had been on such a dreadful night. And then they found a lantern, still lighted, and a ladder that had been dragged from its place and some scattered brushes. Look out the window, Johnsy, at the last ivy leaf on the wall. Didn't you wonder why it never moved or fell when the wind blew? Ah, it's Behrman's masterpiece—he painted it there the night the last leaf fell."

Adapted from "The Last Leaf" by O. Henry. Reprinted from *Collected Stories of O. Henry*. Edited by Paul J. Horowitz. Copyright © 1977 by Crown Publishers, Inc. Used by permission of Crown Publishers, Inc.

2   **Understanding the Story.** Put the letter of the correct answer on the line to the left.

_____ 1. Johnsy is seriously ill with _____ .

     (a) a digestive disorder   (c) pneumonia

     (b) gangrene   (d) smallpox

_____ 2. The doctor's attitude toward women artists is _____ .

     (a) encouraging   (c) respectful

     (b) realistic   (d) scornful

_____ 3. At first, the doctor predicts Johnsy will not get better because _____ .

     (a) her symptoms are so alarming

     (b) she has lost her will to live

     (c) she has waited too long to seek professional care

     (d) the epidemic has resulted in so many deaths

_____ 4. Mr. Behrman is probably from _____ .

     (a) eastern Europe   (c) northern Africa

     (b) India   (d) southern Italy

_____ 5. Mr. Behrman's major source of income is _____ .

     (a) painting   (c) modeling

     (b) begging   (d) keeping the apartment building clean

_____ 6. Which of the following symbolizes Johnsy's desire to live?

     (a) port wine   (c) the last leaf

     (b) the Bay of Naples   (d) the raised shade

_____ 7. Which of the following symbolizes Johnsy's desire to live—according to the doctor?

     (a) a lower temperature   (c) sipping chicken broth

     (b) an interest in fashions   (d) Sue's tender care

_____ 8. At the end of the story, Johnsy _____ her earlier behavior.

     (a) condemns   (c) excuses

     (b) defends   (d) ignores

_____ 9. Which of the following indicates that "The Last Leaf" was not written recently?

     (a) the artists' studios   (c) the ivy vine

     (b) the doctor's house calls   (d) the narrow streets

3 **What Do You Think?** Answer these questions in good sentence form. Be sure to include details which support your point of view.

1. If "The Last Leaf" had continued for another sentence or two, how do you think Johnsy would have reacted upon learning that Behrman had given his life for her?

_____

_____

2. Describe the difference between Schatz in "A Day's Wait" and Johnsy in "The Last Leaf" regarding their attitude toward approaching death.

_____

_____

_____

_____

3. Describe the difference between Schatz's and Johnsy's reactions when they realize they are not going to die.

_____

_____

_____

_____

4 **Hyphenated Words.** Fill in each blank with the best answer. Don't forget the hyphens!

1. The _____ technical training Ted had received in his night school course resulted in his finding a job almost immediately.

   (a) all-out   (b) all-round   (c) all-star   (d) all-time

2. The doctor was such a(n) _____ fellow that he could explain the most complicated symptoms in a way his patients could understand.

   (a) down-to-earth   (c) happy-go-lucky
   (b) good-for-nothing   (d) out-and-out

3. Daily exercises helped Jack become a _____ he-man.

   (a) well-balanced   (c) well-fed
   (b) well-built   (d) well-mannered

4. A coward is not usually described as _____ .

   (a) chicken-hearted   (c) thick-skinned
   (b) lily-livered   (d) yellow-bellied

5. Mr. Garfield had a _____ view of the accident because he happened to be raising the shades in the livingroom of his thirtieth-floor apartment when the two cars collided.

    (a) bird's-eye   (b) cold-eyed   (c) dry-eyed   (d) starry-eyed

6. Mrs. McDonald was so _____ that she seemed to spend as much time poking about her desk and looking in the drawers for her glasses as she did working.

    (a) open-minded   (c) absent-minded
    (b) high-minded   (d) single-minded

7. During the interview, the interviewer's gaze made Linda feel so _____ that she wished she could crawl into a hole and disappear.

    (a) self-conscious   (c) self-interested
    (b) self-important   (d) self-taught

8. By the time Adolphe became a _____ lawyer, he was so tired of reading small print that he began to wish he had chosen another profession.

    (a) full-bodied   (c) full-fashioned
    (b) full-dress   (d) full-fledged

9. You are speaking _____ when you say something in a serious tone of voice but mean it as a humorous remark.

    (a) hand-to-mouth   (c) off-the-record
    (b) matter-of-fact   (d) tongue-in-cheek

10. Being very _____ , Josephine didn't know how to accept compliments on her fine performance graciously.

    (a) self-addressed   (c) self-evident
    (b) self-critical   (d) self-seeking

11. A nervous person might be described as _____ .

    (a) high-pitched   (c) high-sounding
    (b) high-priced   (d) high-strung

12. "How can you plead 'not guilty' when the police caught you _____?" the judge asked the defendant.

    (a) cold-blooded   (b) head-on   (c) red-handed   (d) thin-skinned

13. The behavior of a hypocrite is best described as _____ .

    (a) mealy-mouthed   (c) up-and-down
    (b) two-faced   (d) wishy-washy

14. "We're all just fine. Everything is _____ now," Sophie replied when her mother asked if she and the children had recovered from their colds.

    (a) hanky-panky   (c) hunky-dory
    (b) helter-skelter   (d) hurdy-gurdy

15. As he read a biography of Thomas Edison, Lloyd wondered if the inventor ever fully realized that his creations would have such _____ consequences.

    (a) far-off   (b) far-out   (c) far-reaching   (d) far-sighted

5 **The $24 Swindle.** "The Last Leaf" is set in Greenwich Village, which is a section of Manhattan. To learn more about how the Indians sold Manhattan to the Dutch in 1626, fill in the blanks with the words listed below.

absolutely	colonies	outright	rival
betrayed	colony	particularly	settled
chuckling	intelligent	purchase	situation
claim	official	quibble	unsettling

Peter Minuit with the Indians

By now it is probably too late to do anything about it, but the _____ fact remains that the so-called sale of Manhattan Island to the Dutch in 1626 was a totally illegal deal. This is how it happened.

On May 4, 1626, Peter Minuit was sent by the Dutch West India Company to be the _____ director-general of what is now known as Manhattan. Now the Dutch knew that the British, who had established _____ at Plymouth and Jamestown, would not be _____ pleased at the establishment of a Dutch _____ . Neither would the French.

So, the Dutch decided to make their _____ of Manhattan as legal as possible, hoping that if the Indians backed up their _____ , the British or French would not attack.

Minuit did what seemed like the _____ thing: he asked the first Indians he saw if he could see their chief. Now the chief wasn't sure what it meant to sell land. The land was, after all, Mother Earth to the Indians, and they felt you could no more sell it _____ than you could sell the sky.

What the chief did know was that a _____ tribe controlled the upper three quarters of Manhattan, but the chief wasn't one to _____ over small points. He took the sixty guilders' worth of knives, axes, clothing, and beads and went _____ back to Brooklyn.

Everybody _____ down and was happy except the rival tribe who could do _____ nothing. Even if they had wanted to fight, the Dutch had guns and they didn't. The only thing the _____ tribe could do was try to make the best of an impossible _____ .

Adapted from "The $24 Swindle" by Nathaniel Benchley by permission of Marjorie Benchley. "The $24 Swindle" first appeared in *American Heritage,* December 1959

Review: Lessons 1-16

1   **Word Review.** Put the letter of the best answer on the line to the left.

_____   1. _____ is known for its fragrant odor.

     (a) Cedar   (b) Ebony   (c) Maple   (d) Walnut

_____   2. Which "ship" is frequently engaged in business transactions?

     (a) censorship   (b) courtship   (c) dealership   (d) leadership

_____   3. A _____ is an example of a fungus.

     (a) crystal   (b) gel   (c) narcotic   (d) mushroom

_____   4. A person might take a double dose of tonic to relieve his or her _____ .

     (a) casualness   (b) drowsiness   (c) madness   (d) meanness

_____   5. A mallet is part of the equipment used in _____ .

     (a) badminton   (b) polo   (c) soccer   (d) tennis

_____   6. A slang description for an intellectual person is _____ .

     (a) bookmark   (b) brainstorm   (c) egghead   (d) smart aleck

_____   7. A _____ is an example of an artificial waterway.

     (a) bay   (b) canal   (c) channel   (d) cove

_____   8. A synonym for *foyer* is _____ .

     (a) basement   (b) parlor   (c) pantry   (d) lobby

_____   9. A synonym for *humiliate* is _____ .

     (a) debate   (b) degrade   (c) deprive   (d) derive

_____   10. In the North, a _____ is a warmly welcomed prelude to spring.

     (a) cardinal   (b) pheasant   (c) robin   (d) woodpecker

_____   11. _____ is the largest island in the Mediterranean Sea.

     (a) Sicily   (b) Sydney   (c) Syracuse   (d) Syria

_____   12. To the gossip columnist, a _____ person is usually someone of consequence.

     (a) noteworthy   (b) praiseworthy   (c) seaworthy   (d) trustworthy

_____   13. Taxpayers are a basic source of _____ for the government.

     (a) civilization   (b) legends   (c) mourning   (d) revenue

_____   14. If you _____ another person, you confuse or bewilder him.

     (a) buffalo   (b) jaguar   (c) hyena   (d) pigeon

_____   15. A grimace is often a sign of _____ .

     (a) contempt   (b) genius   (c) hysteria   (d) triumph

_____   16. A _____ would most likely attempt to hide his or her malice toward others.

     (a) bigot   (b) disciple   (c) hypocrite   (d) prude

2 **Word Review.** Fill in the blanks with the set of words that makes the best sense in each sentence.

1. A _____ is an example of a _____ .
   (a) geyser - vacuum   (c) sergeant - civilian
   (b) penguin - bird   (d) stereo - generator

2. The _____ _____ the audience with his prejudiced statements.
   (a) bigot - enraged   (c) hostage - paralyzed
   (b) genius - hynotized   (d) humorist - flustered

3. A generator converts _____ energy into _____ energy.
   (a) electrical - mechanical   (c) manmade - mechanical
   (b) manmade - electrical   (d) mechanical - electrical

4. A(n) _____ is an example of a _____ .
   (a) agenda - meeting   (c) bayonet - sword
   (b) beagle - hound   (d) saxophone - stringed instrument

5. The Congresswoman's _____ throughout the television interview

   _____ not only her campaign manager, but also her loyal supporters.

   (a) abruptness - unified   (c) dignity - blemished
   (b) coarseness - embarrassed   (d) malice - endeared

6. The gypsy fortuneteller gazed into her crystal ball and advised Floyd not to be so

   _____ about his career because in time it would be marked with

   _____ .

   (a) burdened - misery   (c) jaundiced - brilliance
   (b) cynical - execution   (d) shortsighted - hysteria

7. Many citizens consider the widespread abuse of _____ to be a(n)

   _____ to the well-being of our society.

   (a) computers - embarrassment   (c) narcotics - menace
   (b) hypnosis - humiliation   (d) plastic - encouragement

8. As she prepared her husband's breakfast, Mrs. Olson observed, "I cannot _____

   a more _____ way to begin such a beautiful day than by reading that dreadful

   newspaper."

   (a) analyze - instructive   (c) conceive - unpleasant
   (b) assume - logical   (d) identify - embarrassing

9. The traffic commission discussed _____ measures that could be taken to avoid

the possibility of future _____ occurring at the treacherous intersection.

(a) airtight - brawls   (c) protective - tragedies
(b) guaranteed - failures   (d) temporary - breakdowns

10. Marching proudly in the Labor Day _____ , the high school band looked

_____ in their royal blue uniforms.

(a) auditorium - confined   (c) procession - outrageous
(b) parade - majestic   (d) stadium - noticeable

11. "My niece is so _____ that you'd think her brains were made out of

_____ ," sighed Uncle Edward sadly.

(a) awkward - overshoes   (c) intelligent - gelatin
(b) hardheaded - cement   (d) understandable - galaxies

12. After the plumber's helpful _____ of the problem with his disposal, Frank

realized that his attitude toward repairmen was much too _____ .

(a) analysis - cynical   (c) guidance - traditional
(b) discipline - hysterical   (d) logic - probable

3   **Word Sound Review.** Choose the word in each line that has the same sound as
the underlined letter or letters in the first word and write your choice on the line.

1. **dignity:**	gel	godliness	legend	magician	_____
2. **alternate:**	alcohol	calendar	halter	palace	_____
3. **voltage:**	golf	jolly	polish	Polish	_____
4. **chow:**	billow	elbow	powder	tow	_____
5. **theft:**	thaw	thereafter	thine	thou	_____
6. **hydrogen:**	hyena	hymnbook	hypnosis	hysteria	_____
7. **terrific:**	ceremony	disciple	larceny	vocal	_____
8. **beagle:**	agenda	jaguar	tragedy	genius	_____
9. **balance:**	balcony	cavity	reception	vacuum	_____
10. **subdue:**	league	residue	morgue	vogue	_____
11. **obey:**	eyelid	geyser	heyday	volley	_____
12. **mystery:**	analyze	python	rhyme	symbol	_____

4 **Find the Homonym.** Next to each word listed below write its homonym. Then, match each homonym you have written with the correct description. Study the example before you begin.

aisle ___isle___   cord _____   sore _____

banns _____   dough _____   tense _____

beat _____   genes _____   weed _____

coax _____   seen _____   yoke _____

_____ 1. a combination of musical notes

_____ 2. a common contraction

_____ 3. a female deer

_____ 4. a section of a play

_____ 5. a red vegetable

___isle___ 6. a small island

_____ 7. forbids

_____ 8. pants made from a strong cotton

_____ 9. popular soft drinks

_____ 10. teepees

_____ 11. the most nutritious part of the egg

_____ 12. to rise high in the air

5 **A Poet's View of Dying.** Read the following excerpt from a poem by Edna St. Vincent Millay (1892–1950) and then answer the questions which follow.

Excerpt from **Moriturus**
by Edna St. Vincent Millay

Withstanding Death
  Till Life be gone,
I shall treasure my breath,
  I shall linger on.

I shall bolt my door
  With a bolt and a cable;
I shall block my door
  With a bureau and a table;

With all my might
  My door shall be barred.
I shall put up a fight,
  I shall take it hard.

With his hand on my mouth
  He shall drag me forth,
Shrieking to the south
  And clutching at the north.

1. What is the speaker's view of dying in this poem? Be sure to include evidence from the poem to support your point of view.

_____

_____

_____

_____

2. How do you think each of the following people would react to the view of dying presented in this poem? Be sure to support your answer with evidence from the stories.

   a. Norman in *On Golden Pond*: _____

_____

_____

_____

b. Dostoyevsky in "The Execution": _____

_____

_____

_____

c. Schatz in "A Day's Wait": _____

_____

_____

_____

d. Johnsy in "The Last Leaf": _____

_____

_____

_____

Unit 5
Giving

The last unit in this book deals with the theme of giving. Sometimes the best way to begin exploring a topic is to take a look at a situation in which just the opposite is described. This unit begins just this way.

The reading for Lesson 17 is two folktales about greed and selfishness. The characters are not at all generous but spend their time dreaming and scheming about ways to improve their personal happiness.

"To Have or to Be," the reading for Lesson 18, is from the writings of Erich Fromm, a German-born philosopher who came to the United States in 1934 and has taught at various universities in addition to writing many books. As the title suggests, Dr. Fromm believes that *having* and *being* represent two very different approaches to life—one that is selfish and one that is giving.

The reading for Lessons 19 and 20 is a play called "The Woman Who Willed a Miracle." The title character in this play is a woman who is very unlike the characters in the two folktales in Lesson 17. Based on actual events, the play describes the activities of a couple whose main concern is the happiness of someone other than themselves.

Lesson 17

Silent Letters

hedge	nestle	know-it-all	rhinestone	wriggle	ghostly
wedge	trestle	Knoxville	Rhode Island	Wright	ghastly
fidget	jostle	knoll	rhinoceros	playwright	ghetto
midget	bustle	knighthood	rhythm	wrangle	ghoul
cartridge	rustle	knave	rhythmical	wreath	gherkin
porridge	rustler		rhapsody	wretched	
abridge	hustler				lasagna
badger				salve	yacht
				salmon	khaki

1 **Definitions.** Match the words listed below with the correct definitions.

abridge
bustle
ghastly
gherkin
ghoul
jostle
khaki
knoll
porridge
rhinestone
rustle
salve
wrangle
wreath
wretched
Wright

_____ 1. a color ranging from light olive brown to light yellowish brown; a sturdy wool or cotton cloth of this color

_____ 2. a colorless, manmade gem that often sparkles like a diamond

_____ 3. a ring of flowers or leaves worn on the head, placed on a grave, or used as a decoration

_____ 4. a small cucumber, especially one used for pickling

_____ 5. a small rounded hill or mound

_____ 6. an evil spirit or demon in Moslem folklore which is said to rob graves and feed on corpses; one who delights in anything that is disgusting or revolting

_____ 7. an ointment

_____ 8. boiled oatmeal, usually eaten with milk at breakfast

_____ 9. miserable; sad; very unpleasant

_____ 10. terrifying; dreadful; having a deathlike color; extremely unpleasant or bad

_____ 11. the last name of the brothers who invented and flew the first heavier-than-air craft in 1903

_____ 12. to hurry about busily and with energy; excited activity; commotion

_____ 13. to knock or push together; collide

_____ 14. to quarrel or bicker noisily or angrily

_____ 15. to reduce the length of a short story, book, etc.; to condense

_____ 16. to steal cattle; to move with soft whispering sounds

Words for Study

mortal	sovereign	violently	ancient
Jupiter	bundle	empire	Armenia
ridiculous	thereupon	appreciated	appropriate
cowered	prudently	peasant	bade

Two Tales of Mortal Foolishness

In these two folktales, the main characters are given the chance to change their lives. In the first tale, Jupiter, the Roman god who ruled over all the other gods and human beings, gives a woodcutter three wishes. In the second folktale, God gives a poor Armenian the Gift of Luck.

* * *

The Ridiculous Wishes

Once there was a poor woodcutter who, growing weary of a life of toil, wished that he could be at rest. Never, he declared, since the day he was born, had cruel heaven granted a single one of his desires.

One day when he was in the woods, complaining of his miserable lot, Jupiter appeared to him, thunderbolt in hand. The poor man cowered before him in terror. "I ask for nothing," he cried. "I'll drop my wishes, master, if you drop your thunder. Surely that's a fair bargain."

"There is no need to be afraid," replied Jupiter. "I have heard your complaints and have come to show you how wrongly you judge me. I, the sovereign master of the world, promise to grant the first three wishes you make, whatever they may be. Now think carefully before you make them, for your whole happiness depends on them."

So saying, Jupiter went back to heaven, while the woodcutter gaily shouldered his bundle of wood and made off for home.

"Yes," he said to himself. "I must decide nothing lightly. I must ask my wife what she thinks."

"Hey, Fanny," he cried, as he entered the cottage, "let's have a big fire and a good meal.

We are rich for life. We have only to make three wishes."

Thereupon he told his wife all that had happened. The good woman began to form vast schemes in her mind, but, remembering the importance of acting prudently, she said:

"My dear, we must spoil nothing by impatience. We must talk this over very carefully. We had better sleep on it and leave our first wish for tomorrow."

"That is just what I think," said her husband. "But now, go and draw some of that special wine from the cellar."

When she came back, he drank deeply and, leaning back in his chair before the fire, said: "To go with such a fine blaze, we could do very well with a few feet of black pudding."

He had no sooner spoken than, to his wife's amazement, a very long sausage issued from a corner of the fireplace and came snaking towards her.

She gave a cry. Then realizing that this was the answer to the wish which her husband had so stupidly uttered, she began to abuse him violently. "When you could have an empire, with gold, pearls, rubies, diamonds, splendid clothes, all you can wish for is black pudding!"

"Well," he said. "I was wrong. I have done an extremely silly thing. I will do better next time."

"Yes, yes," she cried. "That is what you say. But only a donkey would make such a wish."

Purple with rage, the husband almost wished his wife to the devil, and perhaps he might have done worse.

"Man," he said, "is born to suffering. A plague on this sausage! I wish to heaven that it would stick to your nose!"

The wish was immediately granted, for no sooner had he spoken than four feet of black pudding fastened themselves to the end of his wife's nose. The effect was not pretty, although by hanging over her mouth the sausage prevented Fanny from talking—an advantage which the husband appreciated for a few peaceful moments.

"With the last remaining wish," he said to himself, "I could still become a king at a single throw. But we must consider the queen's appearance and whether she would like to sit on the throne with a nose over a yard long. She must decide whether she will become a princess and keep that horrible nose, or remain a woodcutter's wife and have a face like other people."

Fanny well knew the power of royalty—when one wears a crown, one's nose is always perfect. Yet, since the desire to look pleasant is stronger still, she decided after all to keep her peasant's bonnet.

So, the woodcutter was still a woodcutter. He never became a mighty king. His purse was not filled with gold. He was only too glad to use his last wish to restore his wife to her former state.

* * *

The Foolish Man

Once there was and was not in ancient Armenia a poor man who worked and toiled hard from morn till night, but nevertheless remained poor.

Finally one day he became so discouraged that he decided to go in search of God in order to ask Him how long he must endure such poverty and to beg of Him a favor.

On his way, the man met a wolf.

"Good day, brother man," said the wolf. "Where are you bound in such a hurry?"

"I go in search of God," replied the man. "I have a complaint to lodge with Him."

"Well," said the wolf, "would you do me a kindness? When you find God, will you complain to Him for me, too? Tell Him you met a half-starved wolf who searches the woods and fields for food from morning till night—and though he works hard and long, still finds nothing to eat.

Ask God why He does not provide for wolves since He created them."

"I will tell Him of your complaint," agreed the poor man, and continued on his way.

As he hurried over the hills and through the valleys, he chanced to meet a beautiful maid.

"Where do you go in such a hurry, my brother?" asked the maid.

"I go in search of God," replied the man.

"Oh, kind friend, when you find God, would you ask Him something for me? Tell Him you met a maid on your way. Tell Him she is young and fair and very rich—but very unhappy. Ask God why she cannot know happiness."

"I will tell Him of your trouble," promised the poor man, and continued on his way.

Soon he met a tree which seemed all dried up and dying even though it grew by the side of a river.

"Where do you go in such a hurry, O traveler?" called the dry tree.

"I go in search of God," answered the man. "I have a complaint to lodge with Him."

"Wait a moment, O traveler," begged the tree, "I, too, have a question for God. Please ask Him why I am dry both in summer and winter. Though I live by this wet river, my leaves do not turn green. Ask God how long I must suffer. Ask Him that for me, good friend."

The man listened to the tree's complaint, promised to tell God, and continued once again upon his way.

Finally, the poor man reached the end of his journey. He found God seated beneath the ledge of a cliff.

"Good day," said the man as he approached God.

"Welcome, traveler," God returned his greeting. "Why have you journeyed so far? What is your trouble?"

"Well, I want to know why there is injustice in the world. Is it fair that I toil and labor from morn till night and yet never seem to earn enough for a full stomach, while many who do not work half as hard as I live and eat as rich men do?"

"Go then," replied God. "I present you the Gift of Luck. Go find it and enjoy it to the end of your days."

"I have yet another complaint, my Lord," continued the man, and he proceeded to list the complaints and requests of the starved wolf, the beautiful maid, and the parched tree.

God gave appropriate answers to each of the three complaints, whereupon the poor man thanked Him and started on his way homeward.

Soon he came upon the dry, parched tree.

"What message did God have for me?" asked the tree.

"He said that beneath your trunk there lies a pot of gold which prevents the water from seeping up your trunk to your leaves. God said your branches will never turn green until the pot of gold is removed."

"Well, what are you waiting for, foolish man!" exclaimed the tree. "Dig up that pot of gold. It will make you rich—and permit me to turn green and live again!"

"Oh, no," protested the man. "I have no time to dig up a pot of gold. God has given me the Gift of Luck. I must hurry and search for it." And he hurried on his way.

Presently, he met the beautiful maid who was waiting for him. "Oh, kind friend, what message did God have for me?"

"God said that you will soon meet a kind man who will prove to be a good life's companion to you. No longer will you be lonely. Happiness and contentment will come to you," reported the poor man.

"In that case, what are you waiting for, foolish man?" exclaimed the maid. "Why don't you stay here and be my life's companion."

"Oh, no! I have no time to stay with you. God has given me the Gift of Luck. I must hurry and search for it." And the man hurried on his way.

Some distance away, the starving wolf impatiently awaited the man's coming, and hailed him with a shout.

"Well, what did God say? What message did He send to me?"

"Brother wolf, so many things have happened since I saw you last," said the man. "I hardly know where to begin. On my way to seek God, I met a beautiful maid who begged me to ask God the reason for her unhappiness. And I met a parched tree who wanted God to explain the dryness of its branches even though it stood by a wet river.

"I told God about these matters. He bade me tell the maid to seek a life's companion in order to find happiness. He made me warn the tree about a pot of gold buried near its trunk which must be removed before the branches can receive nourishment from the earth.

"On my return, I brought God's answers to the maid and to the tree. The maid asked me to stay and be her life's companion, while the tree asked me to dig up the pot of gold.

"Of course, I had to refuse both since God gave me the Gift of Luck—and I must hurry along to search for it!"

"Ah-h-h, brother man, and what was God's reply to me?" asked the starving wolf.

"As for you," replied the man, "God said that you would remain hungry until you met a silly and foolish man whom you could eat up. Only then, said God, would your hunger be satisfied."

"Hmmmmmm," mused the wolf, "where in the world will I find a man more silly and stupid than you?"

And he ate up the foolish man.

Adaptation of "The Ridiculous Wishes" from *The Fairy Tales of Charles Perrault* translated by Geoffrey Brereton. Reprinted by permission of Anne Brereton. Adaptation of "The Foolish Man" from *Once There Was and Was Not* by Virginia Tashjian. Copyright © 1966 by Virginia A. Tashjian. Reprinted by permission of Virginia A. Tashjian.

2 **Understanding the Folktales.** Answer these questions in good sentence form.

1. In the first folktale, when the woodcutter learns from Jupiter that his first three wishes will be granted, how does he think his life will be changed?

_____

_____

2. Why don't events turn out quite as the woodcutter imagined?

_____

_____

3. In the second folktale, how does the foolish man act foolishly?

_____

_____

_____

4. How are the woodcutter's and the foolish man's actions alike?

_____

_____

_____

5. What, if anything, do the woodcutter and the foolish man learn from their experiences?

_____

_____

_____

_____

What do you think? It has been said that "misfortune begins in the failure to take advantage of opportunity." How does this saying apply to the main characters in the two folktales you have just read?

_____

_____

_____

_____

_____

3 **Character Descriptions.** Decide which word from the list at the left a storyteller might use to describe each of the characters below. Write the word in the blank. Use each word only once.

bewitched
boastful
bustling
courageous
ghastly
God-fearing
heartbroken
humble
innocent
moronic
prudent
sly
sovereign
weary
wrangling

_____ 1. a bickering husband and wife

_____ 2. a cautious hero

_____ 3. a daring knight

_____ 4. a very foolish man

_____ 5. a ghoulish witch

_____ 6. a pooped peasant

_____ 7. a jilted lover

_____ 8. a lowly woodcutter

_____ 9. a busy housewife

_____ 10. a powerful ruler

_____ 11. a pure young maiden

_____ 12. a religious pilgrim

_____ 13. a scheming fox

_____ 14. a smug know-it-all

_____ 15. an enchanted princess

4 **Occupations.** Listed below are four occupations in which people write for a living. For instance, a person who writes a play is called a *playwright*. Match the words on the left with the occupations. Use each word only once.

acts
casts
chapters
dates
dialogue
diaries
headlines
personal letters
play-offs
rhyme
rhythm
scenery
scores
stanzas
trades
verse

Playwrights

1. _____

2. _____

3. _____

4. _____

Poets

1. _____

2. _____

3. _____

4. _____

Biographers

1. _____

2. _____

3. _____

4. _____

Sportswriters

1. _____

2. _____

3. _____

4. _____

5 **More about Armenia.** Use the words listed below to complete these sentences about Armenia.

control	instruments	region	square
distinct	invaded	religion	translated
farm	manufactured	remainder	university
fled	murdered	Soviet	World War I

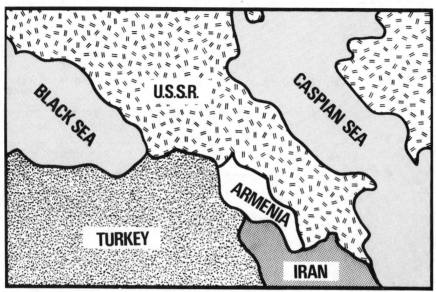

The white area shows the Armenian Soviet Socialist Republic. It is one of the 15 republics in the Soviet Union.

More than two thousand years ago, the Armenian Empire stretched from the Caspian Sea to the Mediterranean Sea. Since that time, Armenia has been _____ many times and ruled by other nations, but a _____ Armenian culture has continued to exist. In 55 B.C., the Romans invaded Armenia and Armenia became part of the Roman Empire. About A.D. 300, Armenia became the first nation to accept Christianity as a state _____ . During the 400s, the Armenians invented an alphabet, _____ the Bible, and established their first

_____ .

About six hundred years later, a group of Turks invaded Armenia and took _____ . By 1514 another group of Turks had invaded Armenia and was ruling it.

In 1894 the Turks began a campaign to wipe out the Armenians. The campaign reached a peak during _____ . By 1918, about 1,800,000 Armenians had been _____ and thousands more had _____ to other countries. The remaining Armenians finally defeated the invading Turks and established an independent country.

In 1920 the _____ Union and Turkey both invaded Armenia. The Soviet Union took control over eastern Armenia. Turkey took control over the _____ of Armenia.

The eastern part of what was Armenia is now one of the 15 republics in the Soviet Union. It is a mountainous _____ that covers about 11,500 _____ miles in the southwestern part of that country.

Today many Armenians work in industry, although some _____ or herd for a living. Among the main _____ goods are chemicals, machinery, and precision _____ . Armenians also make important contributions in the fields of science and technology.

6 **More about Black Pudding.** Just in case you, too, want a black pudding, here is a special recipe so you can make it yourself. See if you can put the recipe steps in the correct order. The first step is numbered to get you started.

Fried Black Pudding with Apples

_____ Serve this tasty dish with mashed potatoes and red cabbage.

_____ After you have strained the blood, mix it thoroughly with flour, the scalded fat, salt, pepper, cloves, and herbs.

_____ Cut cooked black pudding into ⅜-inch-thick slices, flour them, and fry them.

__1__ Dice finely 1 pound, 2 ounces pork fat and scald.

_____ Fill the pig's intestines, which have been thoroughly cleaned, with the mixture, but do not pack the mixture tightly.

_____ Fry apple slices in butter and place them on top of slices of black pudding.

_____ Poach the black pudding mixture for 2 hours.

_____ While pudding is frying, cut apples into slices of the same thickness.

_____ While scalding the pork fat, strain 1¾ pint pig's blood.

Lesson 18

Double Consonants

To sound out a word with double consonants, divide the word between the two consonants. The first vowel is usually, but not always, short.

challenge	pebble	ripple	blossom	nugget
ballad	meddle	jitters	possum	rummage
asset	Cheddar	jimmy	posse	rubbish
dazzle	pennant	shimmy	pollute	hubbub
raffle	leggings	shimmer	fodder	shuffle
waffle	eddy	minnow	motto	summit
narrate	essay	hiccups	horrid	Brussels
Sabbath	essence	giddy	collapse	burro
rabbi	session	Skivvies	commerce	burrow

1 **Definitions.** Match the words listed below with the correct definitions.

asset
burrow
commerce
eddy
essay
essence
fodder
giddy
jimmy
motto
nugget
pollute
rubbish
Sabbath
shimmer
summit

_____ 1. a brief sentence, phrase, or single word used to express a goal or ideal, such as "In God we trust"

_____ 2. a current, as of water or air, moving against the direction of the main current, especially in a circular motion

_____ 3. a hole or tunnel dug in the ground by a small animal, such as a rabbit or mole, for a place of safety or a home

_____ 4. a short composition on a single subject, usually presenting the personal views of the author

_____ 5. a short crowbar with curved ends, often regarded as a burglar's tool; to pry open with this tool

_____ 6. a small lump, especially one of natural gold

_____ 7. a useful or valuable quality or thing; a valuable item that is owned

_____ 8. dizzy; having a reeling, lightheaded sensation

_____ 9. feed for livestock, often consisting of coarsely chopped stalks and leaves of corn mixed with hay, straw and other plants

_____ 10. garbage; litter; worthless material

_____ 11. the buying and selling of goods, especially on a large scale, as between cities or nations; business; trade

_____ 12. the highest point or part; the top, especially of a mountain

_____ 13. the most important element; the quality or qualities of a thing that give it its identity

_____ 14. the seventh day of the week, Saturday, observed as the day of worship and rest by Jews and some Christian sects; the first day of the week, Sunday, observed as the day of worship and rest by most Christian churches

_____ 15. to dirty; to make impure

_____ 16. to shine with a flickering light; a glimmer

versus	crave	opponent	adolescent
contrary	mode	ego	sacrifice
Latin	acceptable	species	superior
development	stimulate	infant	conquer

To Have or to Be

The choice of *having* versus *being* does not appeal to common sense. *To have*, so it would seem, is a normal function of our life: in order to live we must have things. Moreover, we must have things in order to enjoy them. In a culture in which the highest goal is to have—and to have more and more—and in which one can speak of someone as "being worth a million dollars," how can there be a choice between having and being? On the contrary, it would seem that the very essence of being is having; that if one *has* nothing, one *is* nothing.

Having as a way of existence comes from the nature of private property. To acquire, to own, and to make a profit become the basic rights of the individual living in the *having* society. What the sources of property are does not matter; nor does possession impose any obligations on the property owners.

This kind of property may be called *private* property (from Latin *privare*, "to deprive of"), because the person or persons who own it are its sole masters, with full power to deprive others of its use or enjoyment.

This desire for private property can be seen in our relationships also. People express it in speaking of "*my* doctor," "*my* dentist," "*my* workers," and so on. Also, people experience an unending number of objects, even feelings, as property. Take health and illness, for example. People who discuss their health do so with a feeling of ownership, referring to *their* sicknesses, *their* operations, *their* treatments, *their* diets, *their* medicines.

Ideas and beliefs can also become property, as can even habits. For instance, anyone who eats the same breakfast at the same time each morning can be disturbed by even a slight change in that routine, because his habit has become a property whose loss endangers his security.

Yet the great Masters of Living have made the choice between having and being a central issue of their teachings. Buddhism, for example, teaches that in order to arrive at the highest stage of human development, we must not crave possessions. Jesus teaches: "For whosoever will save his life shall lose it; but whosoever will lose his life for my sake, the same shall save it. For what is a man advantaged, if he gain the whole world, and lose himself, or be cast away?" (Luke 9:24-25).

"To have" seems to be a simple expression. Every human being *has* something: a body, clothes, shelter—on up to the modern man or woman who has a car, a television set, a washing machine, etc. Living without having something is practically impossible. Why, then, should having be a problem?

Because the society we live in is devoted to acquiring possessions and making a profit, we rarely see any evidence of the being mode of existence. Most people see the having mode as the most natural mode of existence, even the only acceptable way of life. This makes it especially difficult for people to understand that having is only one possible approach to life. The following simple examples of how having and being are demonstrated in everyday life may help you to understand these two different modes of existence.

Students in the having mode of existence will listen to a teacher's lecture, understand it as best they can, and take notes in their notebooks so that, later on, they can memorize their notes and

Approximately 1500 words passim (abridged and adapted) from *To Have or to Be?* by Erich Fromm. Volume Fifty in the World Perspective Series planned and edited by Ruth Nanda Anshen, Copyright © 1976 by Erich Fromm. Reprinted by permission of Harper & Row, Publishers, Inc.

thus pass an examination. But the content of the teacher's lecture does not become part of their own individual thought, enriching and widening it. The students and the content of the lectures remain strangers to each other.

Students in the having mode have but one aim: to hold onto what they "learned," either by entrusting it firmly to their memories or by carefully guarding their notes. They do not have to produce or create something new. In fact, the *having*-type individuals feel somewhat disturbed by new thoughts or ideas.

The process of learning has an entirely different quality for students in the being mode. What they listen to at a teacher's lecture stimulates their own thinking processes. New questions, new ideas, new ways of looking at situations arise in their minds. Their listening is an alive process. Of course, this type of learning can occur only if the lecture offers stimulation in the first place. Empty talk cannot be responded to.

Another example of the difference between having and being can be easily observed in conversations. Let us consider a typical conversation between two people in which A *has* opinion X and B *has* opinion Y. Each identifies with his own opinion. What matters to each is to find better arguments to defend his opinion. Neither expects to change his own opinion, or that his opponent's opinion will change. Each is afraid of changing his own opinion, precisely because it is one of his possessions and its loss would be too painful.

The situation is somewhat different in a conversation that is not meant to be a debate. In this type of conversation, the people forget about themselves, about their own knowledge and the positions they have. Their egos do not stand in the way. For this reason, they can fully respond to the other person and his ideas. They give birth to new ideas because they are not holding onto anything. Thus the conversation ceases to be an exchange of information or knowledge and becomes a dialogue in which it does not matter any more who is right.

The basic characteristic of the being mode is activity—not in the sense of outward activity, of busyness, but of inner activity. To be active means to give expression to our talents, to the wealth of human gifts which—though in varying degrees—every human being has. It means to

grow, to flow out, to love, to rise above the prison of one's own ego, to be interested, to give.

Only to the extent that we decrease the having mode—that is, stop finding security and identity by clinging to what we have, by "sitting on it," by holding onto our ego and our possessions—can the being mode come forth. *To be* requires giving up selfishness and self-centeredness.

In our society the having mode of existing is thought to be rooted in human nature and, thus, unchangeable. The same idea is expressed in the belief that people are basically lazy and that they do not want to work or do anything else unless there is something in it for them. Hardly anyone doubts this negative concept. Yet, it is not true. In fact, to the members of many different societies of both past and present, the concept of natural human selfishness and laziness would seem as strange as their concepts seem to us.

The truth is that both the having and the being modes of existence are possibilities in human nature. Our desire to survive tends to further the having mode, but selfishness and laziness are not the only traits we have.

We human beings have an inner and deeply rooted desire to be: to express talents, to be active, to be related to others, to escape the prison cell of our selfishness. The truth of this statement is proven by so much evidence that a whole volume could easily be filled with it:

1. The data on animal behavior: experiments and direct observation show that many species undertake difficult tasks with pleasure, even when no material rewards are offered.

2. The data on infant behavior: recent studies show the ability and need of small infants to respond actively to complex stimulation.

3. The data on learning behavior: many studies show that the child and adolescent are lazy because learning material is presented to them in a dry and dead way that cannot arouse their genuine interest. If the pressure and boredom are removed and the material is presented in an alive way, remarkable activity and learning take place.

4. The data on work behavior: experiments have shown that if workers are allowed to

be truly active, responsible, and knowledgeable in their work role, they find even the most boring work interesting and challenging.

5. The data on social and political life: history is filled with examples of how human beings have been willing to sacrifice "blood, sweat, and tears" for a meaningful cause.

Perhaps the goal of helping and sacrificing is given only lip service by many; yet the activity of a goodly number of people matches their stated values—values which are based on being rather than having.

The *having* mode of existence, an attitude which is centered on property and profit, produces the desire—indeed the need—for power. To control other living human beings we need to use power to break their resistance. To maintain control over private property we need to use power to protect it from those who would take it from us because they, like us, can never have enough. In the having mode, one's happiness lies in one's feeling superior to others, in one's power, and in the last analysis, in one's ability to conquer, rob, and kill. In the *being* mode, it lies in loving, sharing, and giving.

Having is based on something that weakens through use. For, indeed, whatever one has can be lost. On the contrary, in *being*, what is spent is not lost. The powers of the being mode grow through the process of being expressed—the power of reason, the power of intellectual and artistic creation, the power of love.

2   **Understanding the Reading.** Put the letter of the best answer on the line to the left.

_____ 1. According to Erich Fromm, many other societies _____ .

(a) are unsuccessful in attempting to perfect the *having* mode of existence
(b) have expressed envy toward our material wealth
(c) do not share our values and beliefs
(d) should strive to model themselves after our values

_____ 2. Fromm maintains that most of us have difficulty understanding the *being* mode of existence because _____ .

(a) our society is not geared to this concept
(b) it is a complex concept
(c) we have no time to consider its value
(d) it is such a common function that we don't bother to give *being* much thought

_____ 3. According to Fromm, most of us find the *having* mode of existence _____ .

(a) challenging   (b) irksome   (c) natural   (d) stimulating

_____ 4. Fromm suggests that the original meaning of the word *private* is _____ .

(a) incorrect   (b) negative   (c) neutral   (d) positive

_____ 5. Fromm uses the example *my doctor* to show that most of us _____ .

(a) enjoy a close, personal relationship with our physicians
(b) feel more accepted if we use the same expressions as everyone else
(c) tend to think of our doctors as property
(d) want to believe our doctor is superior to our friends' doctors

_____ 6. Which activity would Fromm probably identify as most related to the *being* mode of existence?

(a) going to class
(b) completing a homework assignment
(c) studying for an examination
(d) thinking about the subject matter

_____ 7. Fromm cites data in order to support his claim that _____ .

(a) human beings are more interested in having than in being
(b) modern research is on his side
(c) private property is the foundation of our civilization
(d) the essence of human beings is the soul

_____ 8. Fromm contends that the "Masters of Living" _____ .

(a) taught the *being* mode of existence
(b) taught the *having* mode of existence
(c) were unconcerned with either *being* or *having*
(d) were widely appreciated by the people of their time

_____ 9. This reading is best described as a(n) _____ .

(a) story   (b) autobiography   (c) biography   (d) essay

3   **What Do You Think?** Answer these questions in good sentence form.

1. Would Erich Fromm see the characters in the two tales you read in Lesson 17 as pursuing the *having* or *being* mode of existence? Be sure to use examples from the folktales to support your viewpoint.

_____

_____

_____

_____

2. Do you think Fromm is correct in describing *being* as a better way of life than *having*? Briefly develop reasons based on your experiences to support your viewpoint.

_____

_____

_____

_____

3. Fromm describes our society as a *having* society. Assuming that he is correct, do you think we should or ever will become a *being* society? Again, develop reasons to support your point of view.

_____

_____

_____

_____

4   **Word Relationships.** Complete each statement with the best answer.

1. Paragraph is to essay as _____.
   - (a) graph is to textbook
   - (c) postage is to envelope
   - (b) map is to geography
   - (d) stanza is to ballad

2. Rhinoceros is to Africa as _____.
   - (a) tiger is to Asia
   - (c) reindeer is to Central America
   - (b) penguin is to North Pole
   - (d) kangaroo is to South America

3. Squishy is to squashy as _____.
   - (a) determined is to impatient
   - (c) glassy is to glittery
   - (b) entangled is to entwined
   - (d) mortal is to immortal

4. Knoxville is to Tennessee as _____.
   - (a) Cincinnati is to West Virginia
   - (b) Phoenix is to New Mexico
   - (c) Syracuse is to South Carolina
   - (d) Wilmington is to Delaware

5. Wealth is to poverty as _____.
   - (a) mansion is to shack
   - (c) injustice is to prejudice
   - (b) shack is to mansion
   - (d) prejudice is to injustice

6. Confuse is to bewilder as _____.
   - (a) erupt is to smolder
   - (c) badger is to pester
   - (b) censor is to enslave
   - (d) jostle is to shimmy

7. Lecture hall is to professor as _____.
   - (a) Christianity is to Christian
   - (c) infant is to playroom
   - (b) student is to classroom
   - (d) synagogue is to rabbi

8. Coward is to yellow as _____.
   - (a) brute is to black
   - (c) rookie is to green
   - (b) maiden is to golden
   - (d) bigot is to red

9. Wreath is to decoration as _____.
   - (a) Cheddar is to sandwich
   - (c) milk is to porridge
   - (b) hiccups are to illness
   - (d) salve is to medicine

10. Ghoul is to ghoulish as _____.
   - (a) busybody is to meddlesome
   - (c) demonstrator is to lawless
   - (b) companion is to lifelong
   - (d) hustler is to courageous

5 **On Latin and Language.** Use the word sets at the left to complete the following sentences correctly. For each sentence, you will have *one* word left over.

calculated
consists
influence
persists
roots

1. Although Latin is no longer spoken, its _____

_____ ; for it has been _____ that

half the words in our dictionary have, either directly or indirectly, Latin

_____ .

ancient
derived
old-fashioned
Romance
tongue

2. The languages spoken by the people living in Italy, Spain, France, Portugal,

and Romania are called _____ languages because they

were _____ from Latin, the mother

_____ of _____ Rome.

Hemisphere
independent
political
two
three

3. Latin America, a vast region in the Western _____ south

of the United States, is divided into thirty-three _____

countries and twelve other _____ units; it gets its name

from the fact that its _____ major languages are Spanish,

French, and Portuguese.

A.D.
B.C.
buckle
century
inscription

4. The earliest Latin _____ we have found is on a belt

_____ which was discovered near Rome and which experts

believe dates back to the seventh _____

_____ .

established
grammar
pore
pour
scholars

5. By 100 B.C., a group of Roman _____ had

_____ the _____ rules that have been

passed on to the students who _____ over their Latin

textbooks in high schools and universities today.

along
language
large
peak
throughout

6. Latin, at its _____ , was the _____

spoken _____ North Africa, half of Europe, and

_____ parts of Western Asia.

conquer
conquerable
conquered
conquerors
unconquered

7. Even when Rome was _____ , Latin remained

_____—an unusual occurrence in history; for usually, the

_____ impose their own language upon those whom they

_____ .

despite
presence
presents
testify
traditional

8. Our own history is an example of the more _____ pattern;

for, _____ the fact that 26 states, hundreds of towns, lakes,

rivers, and streams _____ to the strength of the Native

Americans' _____ , we have borrowed only a few hundred

words from them for use in everyday speech.

exceedingly
however
translator
translate
translation

9. It is thought, _____ , that the main reason we did not

borrow more words from Native Americans was that their languages were

_____ difficult to _____ and

pronounce. For example, the _____ of the word

nummatchekodtantamoonganunnonoas in one Indian language means

our loves.

circumstances
importance
objects
phases
phrases

10. Recognizing the _____ of language in the growth and

development of a culture, Thomas Jefferson wrote in 1813, "The new

_____ under which we are placed call for new words, new

_____ , and for the transfer of old words to new

_____ ."

Adapted from *The World Book Encyclopedia.* © 1987 World Book, Inc.

6 **State Search.** It was mentioned in the previous exercise that 26 states owe their names to North American Indian tribes. Can you find them all in the diagram? The words are formed in the diagram forwards, backwards, up, down, and diagonally, but they are always in a straight line and they are never formed by skipping over any letters. Letters may be used more than once and the words often overlap. You will not need to use all the letters. To get you off to a good start, the first one has been done for you.

√Alabama
Alaska
Arizona
Arkansas
Connecticut
Idaho
Illinois
Iowa
Kansas
Kentucky
Massachusetts
Michigan
Minnesota
Mississippi
Missouri
Nebraska
North Dakota
Ohio
Oklahoma
Oregon
South Dakota
Tennessee
Texas
Utah
Wisconsin
Wyoming

```
N A G I H C I M Y K C U T N E K W
E O P W U O I U A R I Z O N A A I
B A R O H L A K O B D G X W S N O
R R Q T C O B H R Y E E I Y I S W
A U T A H R A M E R L E P O O A A
S O U T H D A K O T A S P M N I T
K A N S I S A S I U W S I I I R O
A U T N E K B K H C A E S N L U S
S T L O S O H R O I R N S G L O E
S H E A M E A A S T O N I U I S N
I K L X V M P E A C A E S S R S N
M A S S A C H U S E T T S A T I I
A L A B A S M I N N E I I N I M M
I O A W A S W Y A N M W M O N T A
N L A M O H A L K O H A D A K O T
A R K A N S A S E C O N N E C T I
```

210 Lesson 18

Lesson 19

More Work with Two Consonants in the Middle of Words

magnet	stencil	pistol	goblin	jumble
mascot	textile	piston	bombard	musket
capsize	gremlin	tidbit	flounder	butler
campus	escort	tinsel	chowder	utmost
atlas	elder	tinder	ordeal	plunder
album	festive	blister	morbid	surpass
pamper	kernel	crimson	porpoise	hurdle
drastic	verbal	Lisbon	corsage	nurture

1 **Definitions.** Match the words listed below with the correct definitions.

bombard
crimson
drastic
festive
flounder
goblin
kernel
mascot
nurture
ordeal
plunder
surpass
textile
verbal

_____ 1. any of several deep or bright reds or purplish reds

_____ 2. a grain or seed, as of a cereal grass, enclosed in a hard husk; a nucleus; essence; core

_____ 3. a haunting ghost; an ugly, elfin creature of folklore, thought to work evil or mischief

_____ 4. a person, animal, or object believed to bring good luck; especially, one kept as the symbol of an athletic team or other organization

_____ 5. a severely difficult or painful experience that tests character or endurance; a trying experience

_____ 6. fabric, especially one that is woven or knitted

_____ 7. especially severe; extreme; violently effective

_____ 8. associated with words

_____ 9. merry; joyous; relating to a feast or festival

_____ 10. to attack persistently; to attack with bombs, explosive shells, or missiles

_____ 11. to go beyond the limit or extent of; to exceed

_____ 12. to move clumsily, as to regain balance; a fish

_____ 13. to nourish; to educate or train; the act of promoting development or growth

_____ 14. to rob of goods by force, especially in time of war

Words for Study

narrator	premature	crooning	deny
visible	cerebral palsy	diapers	considerable
unaccustomed	retarded	formula	dangling
uncomfortable	vitality	Gladys	overwhelmed

The Woman Who Willed a Miracle: Part I

by Arthur Heinemann

Scene One

Narrator: Joe Lemke opens the porch door to admit a young nurse's aide. Joe is a quiet but caring man who peers curiously at the baby Jenny carries. With a blanket wrapped carefully around the infant's head, however, no face is visible.

Joe: Come in, Miss, we're ready.

Jenny: I'm Jenny Matthews, from the hospital. I have his things in this bag. Could you help me with him?

Narrator: Unaccustomed to holding babies, Joe grips the baby awkwardly. Then, as he pulls back the baby's blanket, Joe stops in shock.

Jenny: Didn't the hospital tell you?

Joe: Well, yes. But I didn't think—

Jenny: *(uncomfortable)* He was premature, you know. He has cerebral palsy and they say he's retarded—though how can they tell at six months?

May: *(shouting from another room)* What's keeping you, Joe?

Joe: Coming!

Jenny: Mrs. Lemke knows, doesn't she?

Joe: *(nodding)* Yes. The bedroom's this way.

Jenny: I was just wondering why the hospital chose her.

Joe: May's been nurse to a lot of babies. She's had training, both here and in England. She's British, you know.

Narrator: Just at that moment, May darts in from the bedroom. She's a tiny woman, but her energy and vitality make up for her size. She's about Joe's age—close to 50—and her speech is nonstop.

May: Good day to you, miss. I'll have a pot of tea up in a minute—soon's I look to the little one. Let's have him, Joe. *(crooning over the infant)* He doesn't weigh more than a feather! But we'll change that. We'll put flesh on him and roses in his cheeks. *(gently pushing the blanket from the child's face)* You've got him so bundled it's a wonder he can breathe. There, lad, Leslie—isn't that the name the hospital gave you? Let's have a look—

Narrator: May sees the baby's features and turns to Jenny in shock and fury.

May: What did they do to his eyes?

Jenny: *(stammering)* They had to operate.

May: They took them <u>out</u>???

Jenny: There was something wrong with them. I don't know what.

May: Ah, the poor little creature. As if there wasn't enough he suffered! And his mum— what did she say about it?

Jenny: She wasn't there. She left the hospital right after he was born and she never came back.

May: *(protectively)* Never mind, Leslie. We'll make you comfy now and see to your feeding. *(Cradling the baby in her arms, she goes into the bedroom.)* Come, baby, give us a smile. Just a little one. Don't you want to? You don't have to then. Would you rather cry a bit? *(to Jenny)* Not a move out of him. Is he always like that?

Jenny: Seems to be.

May: There's no strength in him, that's why. And no spirit. No wonder—the way they treated him.

Jenny: The hospital did all they could.

May: I'm not blaming you, miss. Are his things in that bag?

Narrator: Jenny nods, and May opens the bag.

Its contents are few—a couple of bottles, some diapers, and a few undershirts.

May: Is that all they could spare?

Jenny: *(hesitating)* They said he wouldn't need much.

May: What kind of thinking is that?

Jenny: *(softly)* They didn't expect him to live long.

May: *(outraged)* Well, you go back and tell them I said they're wrong!

Narrator: After Jenny leaves, May attempts to feed the baby. She tries one formula and gets no response. Then she patiently returns to the sink to prepare a second formula.

May: *(testing the formula on her wrist)* Still a bit hot. *(settling into a rocking chair)* Ah, look at him lying so still—you'd think he was dead already. He holds himself so stiff, Joe—it's like he was frightened. *(kissing the baby's cheek)* Maybe you can't see me, but you can feel my lips. Feel that? That's what you have to do. Come now, drink.

Narrator: The baby does not respond.

Joe: Do you suppose he's deaf, too?

May: The hospital said no. Dear God, tell me what I have to do!

Scene Two

Narrator: Gladys, the Lemke's neighbor, stops by to see the new baby.

Gladys: He'll be dead before the week's out. You know it as well as I.

May: Nobody comes to my house to die. Ask Mr. Perry. *(She points to a crooked, stunted evergreen tree growing outside.)* Remember when the man was going to throw that tree away? I told him I'd feed it and put it in good soil and talk to it. Now if I could do that for a tree, I can do it for a babe.

Gladys: That baby is as weak as a newborn—and hardly any bigger. His heartbeat's just a flutter.

May: I'm not denying it. I told God about it, and He said—give it a try. And that's what I'm doing.

Gladys: I say, you and God have the strangest conversations!

Narrator: After Gladys leaves, May tries to feed the baby again. Joe watches with concern, fearing failure as much as May.

May: *(to the baby)* Don't pay attention to them

that say you're going to die. I never let anyone die that wasn't ready for it. And you're not ready—or God wouldn't have sent you to me.

Joe: She knows what she's talking about, Leslie.

May: I've looked death in the face before and sent it packing!

Joe: It's a miracle you lived, May.

May: That was a long time ago. Not even fourteen and working in a factory. One day it just blew up and hundreds of people were blown to bits. They said I'd die—but I fooled them. And you, Leslie—you'll fool them too!

Scene Three

Narrator: Ten years have passed. May and Joe—nearing sixty now—still care for Leslie. In the bedroom, they watch closely as Dr. Edwards gives the boy an examination. Though Leslie is ten years old, his body is the size of a four-year-old's. He is slight, his muscles twitch from time to time, and he still wears diapers. His body is limp, and his face is forever expressionless.

May: What's the word, Doctor?

Dr. Edwards: The same. His lungs are clear, his heart sound.

May: Don't you think the palsy's not as bad?

Dr. Edwards: *(gently)* I think you're seeing what you want to see.

May: But when I exercise him—moving his arms and legs—the twitching's let up considerable.

Joe: She works over him morning and night.

Dr. Edwards: I've got to be blunt with you, May. He's no better than he was when you first brought him to me. He can't sit or stand. You have to feed him, diaper him, bathe him, dress him, carry him...

May: So?

Dr. Edwards: It's a miracle you've kept him alive this long. It's an even greater miracle that at your age, you can do so much. You're sixty years old, May—

May: Fifty-nine! I've managed so far—and Joe's a big help.

Joe: I'll be retiring soon and be able to do even more.

Dr. Edwards: You've both done all you can. *(pausing for a moment)* I've done some investigating, and I've got the name of a place that looks after children like Leslie.

The staff is good, and they know how to handle such cases—

May: He's not a case! He's a child! Why do you think I've kept him all these years? Institutions don't care for children like Leslie—or love them. And loving is what Leslie needs!

Dr. Edwards: Does he respond to your loving?

May: He does indeed!

Dr. Edwards: Does he smile? Does he even cry? He doesn't utter a sound, does he?

May: He knows when we're with him.

Joe: That's right. I can feel it.

Dr. Edwards: All I'm asking is that you be fair to yourselves.

May: We do what we want.

Dr. Edwards: All right, I won't argue with you. I've never seen anyone like you, May, for stubbornness!

Narrator: After the doctor leaves, May sits on the bed next to Leslie.

May: We'll manage, won't we, Leslie? Just like always. Maybe you are too much for me to carry about now, but we'll find a way. *(raising her eyes)* God, you'll tell me, won't you? And is it asking too much to let Leslie show me a little something? A wee sign that he hears me, and knows how I love him?

Narrator: Later that week, Joe sits at his worktable finishing up a leather belt. The belt is extra-wide, with two straps fastened in the back, made to hold a child's wrists.

Joe: Finished!

May: *(trying it on)* You could have been a leather worker, Joe. It's beautiful.

Joe: Does it fit?

May: Let's give it a try.

Narrator: Joe cinches the belt around May's waist, leaving the straps dangling in the back. Then he picks Leslie up and puts the boy's hands into the straps, tightening them about his wrists.

May: Not too tight, now. We don't want to hurt his little wrists. All right, let him go, Joe.

Narrator: Joe releases Leslie. His body sags, but he is held upright against May by the straps.

May: Do you think it'll support him? *(twisting around to see)* It doesn't upset him, does it?

Joe: I can't tell.

May: Does it feel strange, Leslie? It never dawned on me you couldn't know what it was to stand or walk—not seeing a thing. But now you'll feel my legs move, and maybe soon you'll move yours the same.

Joe: He's not too heavy for you?

May: No. Is he moving at all?

Joe: He just drags behind you.

May: Then I'll keep on walking till he moves. I'm walking, Leslie, just the way I want you to—and you <u>will</u>, someday. You'll stand, and then you'll take one step and another.

Narrator: During the next few weeks, May takes Leslie outdoors repeatedly. She props him up against the fence, clasping his fingers to the fence. Each time she releases the boy, his body sags to the ground as if there were no bones or muscles in it. But May doesn't give up—nor does Joe. During the summer months May and Joe even take Leslie swimming. And one day, to May's astonishment, she notices something new.

May: Joe! He moved in the water! He moved his arms and his legs!

Joe: I didn't see anything.

May: He moved, sure as I'm standing! Let's run back to the house, Joe, and try to stand him up. He'll feel more sure of himself there.

Narrator: They rush home with Leslie, hurriedly adjusting Leslie's hands so that they grip the fence wire. Fearfully, May releases her hold on Leslie. For a moment he seems about to sag as always, his hands slipping and his knees buckling. Then Leslie's hands tighten on the fence and he <u>stands</u>—supporting himself. It lasts only a moment before he collapses as always. But May is overwhelmed by joy.

May: God bless you, love. You did it! Oh, thank you, God—for helping us and especially him.

Continued in the next lesson...

Adapted from Arthur Heinemann's screenplay, *The Woman Who Willed a Miracle.*
Reprinted with permission of the dick clark company, inc.

2   **Understanding the Play.** Answer the following questions in good sentence form.

1. Cite evidence that indicates the hospital did not expect Leslie to live very long.

   _____

   _____

2. What connection does May Lemke see between the stunted evergreen tree and Leslie?

   _____

   _____

3. What does Dr. Edwards refer to as "a miracle"?

   _____

   _____

4. Why does Dr. Edwards call May "stubborn"?

   _____

   _____

5. For what reason does May offer a prayer of thanksgiving in the last scene?

   _____

   _____

3 **Word Review.** Fill in the blanks with the set of words that makes the best sense in each sentence.

1. _____ is the _____ state in the United States.
   - (a) Missouri - most independent
   - (b) Rhode Island - smallest
   - (c) New York - most densely populated
   - (d) Texas - largest

2. Eddie was pleasantly surprised to find the _____ he had to read for English class had been _____ because he couldn't endure reading lengthy accounts of other people's lives.
   - (a) autobiography - published
   - (b) autobiography - continued
   - (c) biography - abridged
   - (d) biography - expanded

3. At the meeting held in the high school auditorium, the guidance counselor was _____ with angry cries of protest when he announced that scholarship programs would be _____ cut.
   - (a) bombarded - drastically
   - (b) bombed - actively
   - (c) escorted - severe
   - (d) hustled - outrageously

4. In order to _____ the false impression given to the jury by the truck driver, the lawyer decided to use all the _____ to the accident.
   - (a) analyze - data
   - (b) appreciate - tests
   - (c) correct - eyewitnesses
   - (d) explain - information

5. An example of a beast of _____ is a _____ .
   - (a) burden - burro
   - (b) mischief - lap dog
   - (c) South America - camel
   - (d) the jungle - timber wolf

6. Bill's _____ was so big that he was completely _____ in everything but himself.
   - (a) salary - absorbed
   - (b) heart - determined
   - (c) physique - destructive
   - (d) ego - disinterested

7. Often, we _____ our way through difficult situations in an effort to hide the fact that, inwardly, we are _____ .
   - (a) badger - selfish
   - (b) bluster - cowering
   - (c) discover - courageous
   - (d) fidget - restless

8. When the drum majorette _____ under the pressure of drilling constantly for

the state finals, she prayed she would never again have to confront such a(n)

_____ .

(a) capsized - tragedy   (c) collided - collision
(b) collapsed - ordeal   (d) competed - embarrassment

4   **Synonyms and Antonyms.** Choose a synonym to fill in the first blank in each sentence. Choose an antonym to fill in the second blank.

Synonyms		Antonyms	
awesome	immortal	composed	ignore
blossom	meddle	deny	joyous
comfortable	noble	dishonest	purposeful
confess	random	distressful	resist
divine	wretched	fade	temporary
fidgety	yield	humdrum	worldly

1. Admit and _____ are antonyms for _____ .

2. Amazing and _____ are antonyms for _____ .

3. Interfere and _____ are antonyms for _____ .

4. Bloom and _____ are antonyms for _____ .

5. Buckle under and _____ are antonyms for _____ .

6. Everlasting and _____ are antonyms for _____ .

7. Heavenly and _____ are antonyms for _____ .

8. High-minded and _____ are antonyms for _____ .

9. Hit-or-miss and _____ are antonyms for _____ .

10. Jittery and _____ are antonyms for _____ .

11. Pleasant and _____ are antonyms for _____ .

12. Sorrowful and _____ are antonyms for _____ .

5 **Word Families.** Choose the correct word from each set to complete these sentences correctly.

comfortable
comfortably
uncomfortably

1. Nestled _____ in her mother's arms, the baby slept peacefully, unaware of the commotion going on around her.

appreciated
appreciation
appreciative

2. The sportswriter was _____ of the fact that his editor did not overwhelm him with extra assignments during the World Series.

prudent
prudently
imprudent

3. Even though his boss's invitation to attend the fall harvest festival was hardly Tom's idea of a stimulating afternoon, he thought it would be _____ to refuse the offer.

mortal
immortal
immortality

4. Hoping to make him feel better after he spilled a glass of milk, Molly reminded her young son that he was a mere _____ and that occasional accidents were to be expected.

moral
immoral
immorality

5. Conscious of his responsibilities as a father, Rudolph tried to set a good example of _____ behavior.

wretch
wretched
wretchedly

6. The candidate knew he was a _____ for giving the reporter misleading information about his opponent, but he was desperate in his desire to win the election.

immense
immensely
immensity

7. Unlike May and Joe, many people would have been discouraged by the _____ of the task of raising Leslie Lemke.

mischief
mischievous
mischievously

8. Mrs. Trenton's nine-year-old nephew had acted so _____ in the barbershop that the barber could have sworn he was bewitched.

develop
development
undeveloped

9. Bucky turned crimson upon hearing his sister's announcement that her best friend wanted to _____ a closer relationship with him.

athletic
athletics
athlete

10. As the policewoman snapped the handcuffs on the breathless shoplifter, she remarked cynically, "You're not only a bad crook, but you're a lousy _____ as well. I think a crippled turtle could have given me more of a chase."

6 **Using the Dictionary.** Even though many of our words come from Latin, we have borrowed words from other languages as well. Use a dictionary to help you match the words listed below with the languages from which we have borrowed them. Algonquian is a family of North American Indian languages spoken in an area from southern Canada to the Carolinas and from the Atlantic Coast to the Rocky Mountains.

bureau	chipmunk	peso	solitaire
burro	gourmet	possum	strudel
chauffeur	hamburger	raccoon	tomahawk
chili	kindergarten	sauerkraut	tornado

Algonquian

1. _____

2. _____

3. _____

4. _____

French

1. _____

2. _____

3. _____

4. _____

German

1. _____

2. _____

3. _____

4. _____

Spanish

1. _____

2. _____

3. _____

4. _____

Lesson 20

Four-Letter Words

alto	helm	liar	dote	dupe
ably	memo	lima	dole	dual
alas	sewn	Lima	posy	lure
arid	rely	Iran	gory	burr
lava	defy	Iraq	Oslo	null
Xmas	anew	idol	oboe	mull
carp	epic	bias	oral	suet
taco	Zeus	vial	onyx	cult
Bach	ne'er	tier	Noel	lulu

1 **Definitions.** Match the words listed below with the correct definitions.

arid
dole
dote
dupe
gory
helm
lure
mull
ne'er
null
oral
suet
tier
vial

———————————— 1. a gift or share of money, food, or clothing given as charity; grief; sorrow

———————————— 2. a person who is easily deceived or used; to deceive

———————————— 3. a small container, usually glass, for liquids

———————————— 4. anything that tempts or attracts with the promise of gaining pleasure or reward

———————————— 5. bloody; characterized by bloodshed or acts of violence

———————————— 6. having no legal force; of no consequence or value

———————————— 7. lacking moisture; parched by heat; dry

———————————— 8. one of a series of rows placed one above another

———————————— 9. spoken rather than written

———————————— 10. the poetic contraction of *never*

———————————— 11. the hard fatty tissues around the kidneys of cattle and sheep, used in cooking and making tallow

———————————— 12. the wheel, tiller, or whole steering gear of a ship; a position of leadership or control

———————————— 13. to consider or go over mentally; to heat and spice a beverage, such as wine or ale

———————————— 14. to express extreme love or fondness, used with *on* or *upon*; to be foolish or feeble-minded

Words for Study

haltingly	musicians	repetition	devotion
Tchaikovsky	sequence	*idiot savant*	guttural
concerto	specialist	serial	enthusiastic
attentively	Chopin	specific	solitary

The Woman Who Willed a Miracle: Part II

by Arthur Heinemann

Scene Four

Narrator: Six years later, a 16-year-old Leslie moves with a good deal of effort. Sometimes he shuffles along behind Joe, adjusting his steps to his father's. More often, Leslie walks along the fence, gripping its links for support, placing one foot haltingly in front of the other. One day, Joe and May lead Leslie out to the garden for some fresh air and sunlight. Although the boy's face shows no expression, he tilts his head so that the sun falls fully on his face.

May: That's the sun shining on your face. Doesn't it feel good? Warm and gentle as an angel's kiss.

Narrator: Joe walks slowly with Leslie, holding him from behind. Although Leslie's face shows no sign of understanding, May's talk never stops.

May: Now we're on the grass, passing our favorite tree. Would you like to touch it, Leslie?

Narrator: May takes one of Leslie's hands and holds it out to touch the needles.

May: The needles stick, don't they? *(As they arrive at the fence, May puts Leslie's gloves on.)* Now for your gloves, right hand first, then the left, so you don't tear your hands on the wires. Now both hands on the fence, and off we go!

Narrator: Neighbors often pass Leslie as he beats an unsteady path up and down the grass alongside the fence. Usually they greet Leslie warmly, never expecting an answer. One day, however, a new boy approaches Leslie.

Stranger: Hey, you! What's your name?

Narrator: Leslie stops walking. He still grips the fence, but his body stiffens in reaction to the strange voice.

Stranger: I asked you, what's your name? What's the matter? Are you some kind of retard?

Narrator: Suddenly May becomes aware of the conversation. She looks up just in time to see the boy clumsily mimicking Leslie's walk.

May: Get away from him! Leave him alone! You ought to be ashamed! *(Putting her arms around Leslie, she urges him inside.)* There, Leslie, it's all right. No need to be frightened. He was a stupid stranger who didn't know you. Let's go in and we'll turn on the radio and listen to some pretty music.

Narrator: Then May raises her eyes up to heaven in still another prayer.

May: Dear God, you've got to do something for this lad! It's not fair, letting him be the butt of teasing like that!

Narrator: Inside, May turns on a radio program that features a Tchaikovsky piano concerto. She knits while Leslie and Joe sit nearby listening to the classical music. Suddenly Leslie reaches for a bit of May's knitting wool. Tugging the wool taut, he plucks a sound from it.

May: *(whispering)* What do you make of that, Joe?

Joe: I've seen him do it before.

Narrator: Both May and Joe continue to watch Leslie in silence—as though speaking might break the spell.

May: He likes music, that's for sure. Look how attentively he listens. Do you suppose we could get a piano? I could play for him—and sing.

Joe: He does seem to like music. Maybe a piano would be a good idea.

Scene Five

Narrator: Several days later, a pair of piano movers arrive with a secondhand piano. May ushers them into Leslie's room, where the movers squeeze the piano between the boy's bed and the wall. After the movers leave, May sits at the worn piano bench.

May: Do you know what this is, Leslie? It's a piano—what the musicians on the radio play.

Narrator: Joe helps Leslie up onto the piano bench alongside May. May holds Leslie's hands, striking each note, singing as she does.

May: Come, Leslie, shall we sing?

Narrator: May sings a few folk songs she learned many years earlier in England. As she sings, she guides Leslie's hands over the notes. Then she puts her lips to his cheek to let him know where the singing comes from. In spite of all May's help, Leslie does not respond.

May: *(sadly)* We'll try tomorrow.

Narrator: During the next several days, May and Leslie sit at the piano daily. At each session, May guides Leslie's hands. Though the boy remains expressionless, May never loses hope. Then one night, as moonlight shines through their bedroom windows, Joe and May are awakened by music.

May: Did you leave the TV on, Joe?

Joe: I don't think so.

May: But I hear music. I'll go look.

Narrator: First May checks the television—but it's turned off. Still the music persists. It's the Tchaikovsky concerto, and it's coming from Leslie's room. Not knowing what to think, May hurries to the open doorway of Leslie's room, flicks on the light, and gasps.

May: Joe! Oh, dear God! Come quick!

Narrator: Joe comes sleepily out of the bedroom and stares at Leslie with astonishment. There, sitting in his pajamas, is Leslie—playing a sequence from Tchaikovsky! He sits rather insecurely, and palsy shakes him from time to time—interrupting his playing. But the more he plays, the surer his playing becomes, until he finishes the entire passage.

May: *(weeping)* Oh, dear God. You've shown us a miracle!

Narrator: May and Joe, tears streaming down their cheeks, hug Leslie. In the weeks that follow, Leslie learns song after song, sometimes classical, sometimes popular. Leslie's fame spreads throughout the state. Reporters interview the Lemkes, and scientists also show great interest. One day a brain specialist named Dr. Vince comes. He plays a recording of a Chopin piece on the stereo—a song that Leslie has never played before. After Leslie listens...

Dr. Vince: Would you ask Leslie if he would mind trying that?

May: He's heard you, Doctor. Up with you, Leslie. The doctor wants to hear you play.

Narrator: Once Dr. Vince and May have helped Leslie to the piano, the boy begins an almost perfect repetition of the dazzling showpiece played on the record.

Dr. Vince: You're sure he's never played that before?

May: Quite sure.

Dr. Vince: How long has he been doing this?

May: Let's see. It was late in May, I believe.

Dr. Vince: Less than seven months! Amazing! I've read of instances like this. But in all my years as a doctor, this is the first case I've seen. The scientific term for it is idiot savant.

May: You mean this has happened to others?

Dr. Vince: Yes. There was one man who would watch a train of freight cars go by. As the last car passed, he could give the total of all the serial numbers on all the cars, instantly.

May: But could any of these people play like Leslie?

Dr. Vince: I don't know of any. May, tell me a bit

more about Leslie. He never shows any emotion, does he?

May: Never. Never a smile, or a cry—even when he hurts himself.

Dr. Vince: And he doesn't speak?

May: No, but I'm working on that. Singing to him. Talking to him with my lips up to his cheek. And doctor—he'll speak someday.

Dr. Vince: You're an amazing person, Mrs. Lemke, do you realize that?

May: My Joe is too. I couldn't have done a thing without him.

Dr. Vince: *(overcome by emotion for a moment)* As I was about to say—we really can't explain people like Leslie. It's as if the brain were a bundle of wires—hopelessly jumbled—and somehow two of those wires cross by accident and produce a genius in one specific area. But without doubt, your devotion to Leslie has made this possible.

Scene Six

Narrator: Later that week, Gladys and May sit in the kitchen with Leslie, who is finishing a piece of cake.

May: There, Leslie. You've finished the last crumb. Now would you mind playing something for us?

Narrator: Gladys watches as Leslie rises from his chair. Feeling with his hands, he moves along the wall to the door of his room and sits at the piano.

May: *(bursting with pride)* He's been doing that for a week now. And dressing himself as well.

Narrator: From the next room, May hears Leslie play the first English ballad she ever taught him. Suddenly she hears a voice singing as well.

May: Joe, is that you? *(to Gladys)* He was working outside.

Narrator: Then—knocking over a chair, not daring to believe what she's heard—May races to Leslie's room.

Leslie: *(singing in a guttural voice, but on key)* She wheeled her wheelbarrow, Through streets broad and narrow...

May: That's just lovely, Leslie. You've got a beautiful voice. Hasn't he, Gladys? And he was hiding it from us all these years!

Narrator: During the weeks to come, Leslie sings and plays constantly. His voice grows stronger, and the neighbors love to sit and listen to him. One night some young neighbors sit on the porch where Joe and May have moved the piano. Joe sits near Leslie while May and Gladys listen from the kitchen. As Leslie finishes a spirited version of Glen Campbell's "Gentle on My Mind," the young people burst into enthusiastic applause. But when the applause dies down, an eerie silence is left.

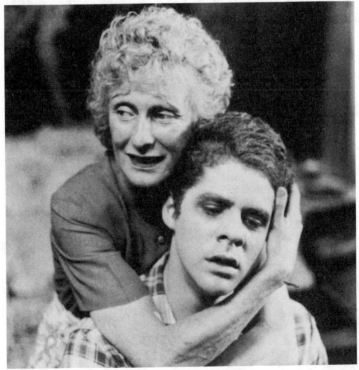

May Lemke and Leslie as portrayed by Cloris Leachman and Leif Green in the TV movie, "The Woman Who Willed a Miracle"

dick clark productions, inc.

Leslie sits motionless, his hands in his lap, his head bowed.

Joe: *(alarmed)* May, come!

May: *(frightened)* What is it? *(She goes up to Leslie and puts her arms around the boy.)* What is it, Leslie?

Narrator: Leslie turns toward May. He is weeping, his face streaked with tears. In wonder he raises his hands to his cheeks and feels the tears.

Leslie: I'm crying!

May: Yes, you are, love. Let it out. You've held it back for a lifetime.

Gladys: He's never cried before?

May: No.

Gladys: Why now?

May: It was the music—and giving it to the rest of us so we could feel it too. Wasn't that it, Leslie? And your finally being a person like everyone else?

Narrator: Leslie's body language seems to say yes. He reaches up and touches one solitary note. May brushes the tears from the boy's face as Gladys approaches him.

Joe: What does the music mean to you, Leslie?

Leslie: <u>Love.</u>

Gladys: What does love mean?

Narrator: Leslie hesitates—as though he's thinking. Then suddenly his body straightens, his hands shoot forward to the keyboard—and he begins to play, singing out boldly with each note.

Leslie: Amazing Grace,
How sweet the sound
That saved a wretch like me.
I once was lost,
But now I'm found,
Was blind but now can see...

Note: This play, adapted from a made-for-TV movie, is based on a real person. Yes, Leslie Lemke does exist.

Adapted from Arthur Heinemann's screenplay, *The Woman Who Willed a Miracle.*
Reprinted with permission of the dick clark company, inc.

2   **Understanding the Play.** Answer the following questions in good sentence form.

1. At the beginning of Scene Four, how many years have passed since Jenny first brought Leslie to May and Joe Lemke?

   _____

2. How do the actions of the stranger prompt May to offer another prayer?

   _____

   _____

   _____

3. Describe how May's prayer is answered.

   _____

   _____

   _____

   _____

4. What is an *idiot savant*?

   _____

   _____

   _____

5. Why does Dr. Vince call May "amazing"?

   _____

   _____

   _____

What do you think? What is the "amazing grace" that Leslie sings of at the end of the play?

   _____

   _____

   _____

3 Which Word Does Not Fit?

Choose the word that does not fit with the rest and write it on the line.

1. oral   spoken   verbal   written   word-of-mouth   _____

2. Erie   Hudson   Huron   Michigan   Superior   _____

3. craving   desire   devotion   passion   urge   _____

4. lasagna   macaroni   pizza   spaghetti   taco   _____

5. Bach   Chopin   Dickens   Mozart   Tchaikovsky   _____

6. foolish   joyous   laughable   moronic   ridiculous   _____

7. abridge   analyze   condense   limit   reduce   _____

8. essence   interest   kernel   root   soul   _____

9. Armenia   Brussels   Lima   Oslo   Warsaw   _____

10. awaken   enliven   entertain   kindle   stimulate   _____

11. cautious   prudent   sensible   wise   intellectual   _____

12. curb   decrease   lessen   retard   stop   _____

13. energy   jitters   liveliness   spirit   vitality   _____

14. morbid   unhealthy   poisonous   realistic   unwholesome   _____

15. sole   solitary   unaccompanied   unescorted   unpopular   _____

16. amethyst   bloodstone onyx   rhinestone   turquoise   _____

4 **Problems.** Although most people are not handicapped in the same way Leslie Lemke is, we all have, or feel we have, our own problems to deal with. Match the words or phrases in the left column with those who most likely think of them as problems. Use each word only once.

ailments
calories
dandelions
deadlines
dishonesty
disobedience
inflation
injuries
jitters
peer pressure
posse
preservatives
reality
sharks
spies

_____ 1. adolescents

_____ 2. athletes

_____ 3. consumers

_____ 4. dieters

_____ 5. dreamers

_____ 6. editors

_____ 7. gardeners

_____ 8. IRS

_____ 9. nutritionists

_____ 10. performers

_____ 11. patients

_____ 12. rustlers

_____ 13. schoolteachers

_____ 14. sentries

_____ 15. swimmers

5 **A Little Latin.** Because many of our words come from Latin, by knowing a little
Latin, we can increase our understanding of the English language. For example,
here are three common Latin prefixes:

uni- which means one
bi- which means two
tri- which means three

Use these prefixes to complete the following exercise. Each prefix is used *four*
times. Study the example carefully before you begin.

_____tri___angle

_____ceps

_____corn

_____cycle

_____focals

_____form

_____mester

_____monthly

_____ped

_____pod

_____sect

_____verse

_____ 1. a fabled creature with a single horn

_____ 2. a vehicle with a single wheel

_____ 3. all existing things

_____ 4. always the same

_____ 5. an animal with two feet

_____ 6. eyeglasses used for both near and
distant vision

_____ 7. happening every two months

_____ 8. to cut or divide into two equal parts

_____ 9. a period of three months

_____ 10. a three-legged stool, stand, etc.

_____triangle_____ 11. a three-sided figure

_____ 12. a three-headed muscle running along
the back of the upper arm

6 **On Living and Loving: A Poet's Point of View.** Read these two poems by Georgia Douglas Johnson (1886-1966) and then answer the questions which follow.

Your World

Your world is as big as you make it.
I know, for I used to abide
In the narrowest nest in a corner,
My wings pressing close to my side.

But I sighted the distant horizon
Where the sky line encircled the sea
And I throbbed with a burning desire
To travel this immensity.

I battered the cordons around me
And cradled my wings on the breeze
Then soared to the uttermost reaches
With rapture, with power, with ease!

The Poet Speaks

How much living have you done?
From it the patterns that you weave
Are imaged:
Your own life is your totem pole,
Your yard of cloth,
Your living.

How much loving have you done?
How full and free your giving?
For living is but loving
And loving only giving.

_____ 1. In "Your World" Johnson compares herself to a(n) _____ .

    (a) bird   (b) infant   (c) pilot   (d) prisoner

_____ 2. *Rapture* in the last line of "Your World" means _____ .

    (a) detachment   (b) joy   (c) security   (d) speed

_____ 3. Which proverb best expresses the theme of "Your World"?

    (a) A bird in the hand is worth two in the bush.
    (b) Haste makes waste.
    (c) Hitch your wagon to a star.
    (d) Look before you leap.

_____ 4. In "The Poet Speaks," Johnson probably asks questions because _____ .

    (a) she considers this to be the polite way to address her readers
    (b) she doesn't have any ready answers
    (c) she is curious about our lives
    (d) she is challenging us to think about our lives

_____ 5. In "The Poet Speaks," the speaker defines *living* as _____ .

    (a) woven patterns
    (b) a totem pole
    (c) full and free
    (d) loving

_____ 6. If the Lemke family read these poems, they would probably _____ Johnson.

    (a) agree with
    (b) argue against
    (c) not understand
    (d) question

Review: Lessons 1 - 20

1 **Word Review.** Match the words listed below with the correct definitions.

abide	campus	ego	mode
adolescence	concerto	elfin	sect
appropriate	devotion	folklore	trestle
ballad	diagonal	guttural	wretch

_____ 1. a composition for an orchestra and one or more solo instruments, usually in three movements

_____ 2. an open, braced framework consisting of vertical, slanted supports and horizontal crosspieces used to support a road or railroad tracks

_____ 3. heartfelt attachment or affection to a person or cause; loyalty

_____ 4. to wait patiently for; to withstand; to accept the consequences of

_____ 5. relating to sounds produced in or near the throat

_____ 6. a poem which tells a story, often of folk origin and intended to be sung, consisting of simple stanzas and usually having a constant refrain

_____ 7. crossing in a slanting direction from corner to corner or side to side.

_____ 8. a group of people that shares the same beliefs or that follows the same leader or teacher, especially in religious matters

_____ 9. a miserable, unfortunate, or unhappy person; a mean person

_____ 10. small and sprightly; mischievous; fairylike

_____ 11. suitable for a particular person, condition, situation, or place; proper; fitting

_____ 12. the grounds of a school, college, or university

_____ 13. the period of physical, mental, and emotional development from the onset of puberty to maturity

_____ 14. the self; the part of the personality that is conscious, most immediately controls behavior, and is most in touch with outer reality

_____ 15. the traditional beliefs, practices, legends, and tales preserved among a people or tribe

_____ 16. a manner or method of doing or acting; the current fashion or style

2 **Who or What Would You Expect to Be...** Match the words in the left column with whom or what they best describe. Use each word only once.

abridged

ancient

arid

dwindling

enthusiastic

festive

intellectual

invisible

mischievous

rhythmical

shimmering

sovereign

treacherous

unwholesome

verbal

wee

_____ 1. a cheerleader

_____ 2. a desert

_____ 3. a king

_____ 4. the Dead Sea scrolls

_____ 5. a philosopher

_____ 6. a pocket dictionary

_____ 7. jazz

_____ 8. a tidbit

_____ 9. a tornado

_____ 10. a wedding

_____ 11. a speech

_____ 12. hydrogen

_____ 13. an endangered species

_____ 14. an imp

_____ 15. junk food

_____ 16. tinsel

3 **A Little More Latin.** A *root* is a basic word part to which prefixes and suffixes can be added. *Cred* is one of the many roots that comes to us from Latin. The root *cred* means *belief* or *trust*. The words in the column at the left are formed from this root. Use these words to complete the sentences.

credentials
credenza
credible
credit
creditor
creed
incredible
incredibly

1. The little town of Tango was buzzing with excitement as the most

   _____ murder trial in its history was about to begin.

2. Reporters who had journeyed from far and wide to cover the trial were required

   to show their _____ in order to be admitted to the section

   reserved for the press.

3. The defendant was the most unpopular Nick Nichols, who liked to think of

   himself as a fair-minded _____ . But to those who had had

   dealings with him, he was nothing but a cutthroat loan shark.

4. From the moment of his arrest, Nichols had protested loudly that he was an

   innocent victim of circumstance—that his fingerprints had gotten on the knife

   when he had put it on the _____ hours before his right-hand

   man was stabbed.

5. To their _____ , the folks of Tango were not so biased that they

   automatically assumed Nichols was indeed guilty.

6. Even his worst enemies found his story _____ ; for it was a well-

   known fact that Nichols was so squeamish that had he intended to murder

   anybody, he certainly would have devised a less gory method.

7. If the townspeople could be said to live by any _____ , it was

   this: every person is entitled to a fair chance—even a scoundrel like Nichols.

8. Nevertheless, everyone hoped the trial would be an _____ long

   one; for nothing this stimulating had ever happened in Tango before and

   probably never would again.

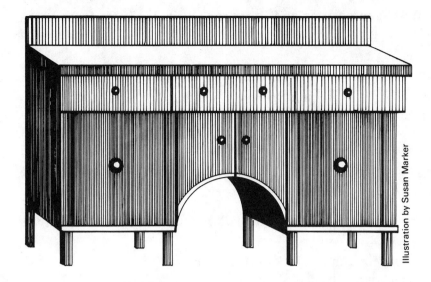

Illustration by Susan Marker

Note: A *credenza* is a piece of dining-room furniture from which food is served. How does this relate to the Latin root *cred* ? In the days of old, one or two servants normally tasted the food first in order to detect the presence of poison. If these servants survived the taste test, the family and guests could then trust the food. As you see, life wasn't necessarily safer in "the good old days."

4 **More Work with Expressions and Proverbs.** Write the letter of the best answer on the line to the left.

_____ 1. The proverb "Spare the rod and spoil the child" cautions us to avoid _____ children.

(a) abusing   (c) nurturing
(b) disciplining   (d) pampering

_____ 2. "Do a good deed daily" is the Boy Scout _____ .

(a) legend   (c) proverb
(b) motto   (d) promise

_____ 3. When you read about a "summit" talk in the newspapers, you're reading about a discussion _____ .

(a) among people at the peak of their careers
(b) in which world leaders are involved
(c) that is the most important event that has ever happened
(d) that takes place on a mountain

_____ 4. When a person "hedges his bets," he _____ .

(a) is addicted to gambling
(b) tells no one of his schemes
(c) protects himself against severe losses
(d) trims his expenses

_____ 5. The proverb "Experience keeps a dear school, but a fool will learn in no other" is addressed to those who are easily _____ .

(a) conquered   (c) duped
(b) educated   (d) satisfied

_____ 6. "Mum's the word" advises us _____ .

(a) to be silent   (c) to know the password
(b) to honor our mothers   (d) to plant flowers

_____ 7. A person who has a "holier-than-thou" attitude is _____ .

(a) humble   (c) religious
(b) generous   (d) judgmental

_____ 8. A person might be called an "iceberg" because _____ .

(a) one never knows what to expect from him
(b) our knowledge of him is so limited
(c) the dangers he presents frighten us
(d) we experience so much coldness from him

_____ 9. The proverb "If you would not be forgotten, as soon as you are dead and rotten, either write things worth reading, or do things worth the writing" advises those who crave _____ .

(a) immorality   (c) morality
(b) immortality   (d) mortality

5 **World Capitals.** Refer to the dictionary or other reference book to help you match the world capitals listed in the left column with their countries.

Baghdad
Beijing   _____ 1. Belgium
Bern
Brussels   _____ 2. Canada
Damascus   _____ 3. China
Lisbon
Madrid   _____ 4. Iran
Oslo
Ottawa   _____ 5. Iraq
Stockholm   _____ 6. Japan
Teheran
Tokyo   _____ 7. Norway

                         _____ 8. Portugal

                         _____ 9. Spain

                         _____ 10. Sweden

                         _____ 11. Switzerland

                         _____ 12. Syria

6 **Find the Quote.** Can you decipher this formula for happiness, which May Lemke in *The Woman Who Willed a Miracle* would have probably agreed with? Refer to the directions in Lesson 8 if necessary.

$\overline{66}$ $\overline{15}$ $\overline{32}$ $\overline{88}$ $\overline{24}$ $\overline{52}$ $\overline{6}$

$\overline{11}$ $\overline{3}$ $\overline{72}$ $\overline{67}$ $\overline{27}$ $\overline{36}$ $\overline{47}$ $\overline{13}$ $\overline{49}$ $\overline{78}$

$\overline{18}$ $\overline{83}$ $\overline{60}$ $\overline{75}$

$\overline{40}$ $\overline{16}$ $\overline{39}$ $\overline{4}$ $\overline{70}$ $\overline{50}$ $\overline{14}$ $\overline{20}$ $\overline{64}$ $\overline{50}$ $\overline{28}$ $\overline{69}$

$\overline{17}$ $\overline{85}$ $\overline{46}$ $\overline{61}$ $\overline{10}$ $\overline{76}$

$\overline{89}$ $\overline{45}$ $\overline{54}$ $\overline{8}$ $\overline{57}$ $\overline{53}$ $\overline{87}$ $\overline{17}$

$\overline{21}$ $\overline{58}$ $\overline{44}$ $\overline{31}$ $\overline{77}$ $\overline{68}$ $\overline{34}$

$\overline{26}$ $\overline{43}$ $\overline{33}$ $\overline{49}$ $\overline{5}$

$\overline{74}$ $\overline{23}$ $\overline{35}$ $\overline{51}$ $\overline{42}$ $\overline{73}$

$\overline{12}$ $\overline{56}$ $\overline{84}$ $\overline{63}$ $\overline{25}$ $\overline{1}$ $\overline{59}$

$\overline{55}$ $\overline{13}$ $\overline{82}$

$\overline{80}$ $\overline{19}$ $\overline{86}$ $\overline{37}$ $\overline{14}$

$\overline{41}$ $\overline{24}$ $\overline{71}$ $\overline{81}$ $\overline{50}$ $\overline{8}$

$\overline{29}$ $\overline{9}$ $\overline{59}$ $\overline{30}$ $\overline{2}$ $\overline{38}$

$\overline{62}$ $\overline{48}$ $\overline{7}$ $\overline{40}$ $\overline{68}$ $\overline{65}$ $\overline{79}$ $\overline{22}$

1. the planet closest to the sun

2. the flavor of Christmas candy canes

3. a garment sometimes worn by men in Scotland

4. the first day of Lent (2 words)

5. a homonym for cereal

6. funny or amusing

7. a side view of an object, especially the human head

8. a mammal of Asia and Africa known for its "laugh"

9. a popular hot beverage

10. an antonym for wealth

11. a headpiece of artificial hair

12. a citrus fruit

13. a formal outfit for men

14. the pattern of sounds in music, dance, poetry, etc.

15. energy that is characteristic of life; spirit

A formula for happiness: $\overline{}_{1} \overline{}_{2} \overline{}_{3} \quad \overline{}_{4} \overline{}_{5} \overline{}_{6} \quad \overline{}_{7} \overline{}_{8} \quad \overline{}_{9} \overline{}_{10} \overline{}_{11} \overline{}_{12} \overline{}_{13} \overline{}_{14} \overline{}_{15} \overline{}_{16} \overline{}_{17}$:

$\overline{}_{18} \overline{}_{19} \overline{}_{20} \overline{}_{21} \quad \overline{}_{22} \overline{}_{23} \overline{}_{24} \overline{}_{25} \quad \overline{}_{26} \overline{}_{27} \overline{}_{28} \overline{}_{29} \overline{}_{30} \quad \overline{}_{31} \overline{}_{32} \overline{}_{33} \overline{}_{34} \quad \overline{}_{35} \overline{}_{36} \overline{}_{37} \overline{}_{38} \quad \overline{}_{39} \overline{}_{40} \overline{}_{41} \overline{}_{42}$,

$\overline{}_{43} \overline{}_{44} \overline{}_{45} \overline{}_{46} \quad \overline{}_{47} \overline{}_{48} \overline{}_{49} \overline{}_{50} \quad \overline{}_{51} \overline{}_{52} \overline{}_{53} \overline{}_{54} \quad \overline{}_{55} \overline{}_{56} \overline{}_{57} \overline{}_{58} \overline{}_{59}$. $\overline{}_{60} \overline{}_{61} \overline{}_{62} \overline{}_{63}$

$\overline{}_{64} \overline{}_{65} \overline{}_{66} \overline{}_{67} \overline{}_{68} \overline{}_{69}$. $\overline{}_{70} \overline{}_{71} \overline{}_{72} \overline{}_{73} \overline{}_{74} \overline{}_{75} \quad \overline{}_{76} \overline{}_{77} \overline{}_{78} \overline{}_{79} \overline{}_{80} \overline{}_{81}$, $\overline{}_{82} \overline{}_{83} \overline{}_{84} \overline{}_{85} \quad \overline{}_{86} \overline{}_{87} \overline{}_{88} \overline{}_{89}$.

Quotation for this puzzle is from the Penny Press puzzle magazine and is used by kind permission of the publisher.